"Tamalyn Dallal has brought us a highly personal account of her encounter with daily life in five Muslim countries. A far cry from the warmongering and sensationalism of the press, this is a tale of everyday women and men, of everyday problems and joys . . . a tale that sheds light not only on five completely different cultures but illuminates our own as well. A wonderful gift to our understanding of the rich diversity of the cultures on our planet, particularly in the lesser known corners of the Muslim world. Mabruk!"

—Helene Eriksen
dance ethnologist

"I cannot think of a better way to escape from the pressures many of us face every day than to read a book like *40 Days & 1001 Nights.* You will taste, see, and feel a different world. Five different worlds, in fact, each filled with exotic foods, captivating dances and warm new friends."

—Bev Harris
author of *Black Box Voting*

"Descriptive, insightful and witty, Tamalyn Dallal's *40 Days & 1001 Nights* is like reading a historian's private travel journal. Full of interesting observations and life experiences while living in each of these exotic and faraway lands, she brings the reader closer to knowing what it's actually like. This is a book for all ages—and an eye-opener. A must-read indeed."

—Bozenka
world renowned "Bellydance Superstar"

"Tamalyn Dallal has captured intimate pictures of everyday life in five corners of the Islamic world. This book, with so many insights into foods, faiths, and covered (or not) clothing for women, may be best when read slowly. Like a big box of chocolates, its nuggets should be savored a bite at a time."

—Carl Harris
The Writers Circle

"Astonishing and captivating adventure! Every word takes you through this inspiring journey as if you are living Tamalyn's experience yourself."

—Amar Gamal
internationally acclaimed Middle Eastern dancer

40 Days & 1001 Nights

One Woman's Dance Through Life in the Islamic World

To Jessica ·
Enjoy!,
Tamalyn Dallal

Tamalyn Dallal

MELATI PRESS

SEATTLE, WASHINGTON

40 Days & 1001 Nights

Melati Press
PO Box 2444
Lynnwood, WA 98073
Tel: 206-226-3882
www.tamalyndallal.com
www.40daysand1001nights.com

ISBN: 978-0-9795155-0-7

Library of Congress Control Number: 2007931401

Editors: Vanessa Shaughnessy and Richard Harris
Cover designer: Paige Clark
Front cover and author photos: Denise Marino
(www.denisemarinophotos.com)
Interior design and typography: Richard Harris
Logo: Silvana Ariza

Printed in the United States of America

CONTENTS

ACKNOWLEDGMENTS

40 Days & 1001 Nights was a labor of love and passion. It became a life-changing experience, usurping many of the notions I had about myself and the world. For people in the countries I visited, many of whom have also made sacrifices to make this book become a reality.

First and foremost, I want to thank my parents, Carl and Ruth Harris, for their unwavering support and belief that I could actually do this. They raised me to realize that any humble human being can and should follow their dream, no matter how seemingly impossible it may be.

I would like to thank my dear friend, the extraordinary photographer Denise Marino, who encouraged me every step of the way, and made sure I took lots of photos. Because of her insistence that I buy a new camera and videotape, I was inspired to make the musical documentary film *40 Days & 1001 Nights: Seeing the Islamic World through the Eyes of a Dancer.*

I also want to thank Helen Nicolaisen for her support and for being a second mother to my cat, Maneki Neko, during the many long months that I was away (and to Maneki Neko for his unconditional love when I came home).

Many thanks to Arief Indrawan for his open hospitality and introductions to people in many parts of Indonesia, to Bambang Praganno for his knowledge, encouragement, and open-mindedness, and to the late Martin Savage, may he rest in peace, for his insights into life in the Siwa Oasis. In Zanzibar, I want to thank Helen Peeks for her help and friendship and the young man whom I call Taariq for opening many heavy and spiked doors I would have never looked behind.

Also, I would like to thank Dr. Mohammed Rawani, Luna, and Angelique Ferat for keeping me busy searching for music, dance, and culture in Jordan. Finally, I wish to thank Melissa Michalak for making it possible to communicate in Xinjiang and Pasha Umer and her family for opening my eyes to the beauty of Uyghur culture.

FOREWORD
by Morocco
(Carolina Varga Dinicu)

Many people consider Morocco one of the most famous and accomplished Middle Eastern dance researchers, teachers and performers in the Western world.

Since 1964, Morocco has written regularly for several publications in her field, and her articles have been reprinted in dance, medical, and feminist publications in the U.S., Germany, Austria, the UK, Australia, Sweden, Finland, and Norway.

She continues her extensive career, performing as a soloist and with her dance company, including notable performances at Lincoln Center and the U.N. General Assembly and many international festivals and venues, and as a lecturer and performer for the NYC Department of Cultural Affairs, Asia Society and Museum of Natural History, First Women's Festival of the Performing Arts, and numerous TV shows and films.

REAL LIFE IS OFTEN WHAT HAPPENS while we're busy making other plans. I never started out to be a dancer, let alone a researcher and teacher of oriental and other folk dances of the Middle East, North Africa, and other lands for over forty-seven years and counting. God has a weird sense of humor.

As a child, whenever adults tired of my continual questions about other places and other cultures, I was told, "Enough! Curiosity killed the cat, you know!" However, I saw plenty of familiar live cats and I was still breathing. So I kept asking. In self defense, mom got me a library card, showed me how to find books about mysterious and exotic countries, and turned me loose on unsuspecting librarians. I realized that there were as many widely varying "answers" to every question as there were tale-tellers. *Who*–and *what*–to believe? How to find the truth?

Being there in-person was the most direct way I could think of. Though it was not feasible at first, I was unbelievably lucky that my early exposure to oriental dance and the many other beautiful folk dances from those areas offered constant in-person glimpses of life in those lands via their own substantial diaspora communities in New York and other U.S. cities. Differing stories by grannies, aunties, and uncles from the various countries made me want to go there myself— to see what was true and real. Fortunately, I didn't need written permission from the male head of my family to travel anywhere I wanted. So I did. I found that everyone had told me his or her truth. There is no one answer.

Extremists exist in all faiths—Christian, Muslim, Jewish or whatever. They were certainly not in the Muslim world I knew from friends here and travel in so many countries over so many years. Nor were they in the world Tamalyn Dallal encountered when she, a like-minded curious and intrepid kitty, set out to find the truth herself and to be with the real people observing their attitudes and lifestyles while spending forty days among each of five very diverse Muslim peoples—in Indonesia, the Siwa Oasis, Zanzibar, Jordan and China.

At first Tamalyn was greeted with caution or suspicion, then welcomed. No—they do not hate all Americans. They recognize the differences between people and governments. Friendly vibes, an open mind, and sharing music and dance are international languages. Willingness to eat the local food helps too.

Tamalyn's accounts of her experiences are interesting, warmly human, and accurate. I've been to Jordan and the Siwa Oasis, but in the 1960s—a very different time. From what she tells us, both places have changed in many ways. I haven't yet been to Indonesia, Zanzibar, or China and never really planned to go. But I am now eager to experience all three, thanks to Tamalyn's descriptions of her adventures.

She tells how the unbelievable devastation of the recent tsunami actually forced the ending of a long-standing war in Banda Aceh! The understanding and goodness of an Indonesian Islamic preacher she consults illustrate the positive elements of a true Muslim and ideal character traits for a religious leader. But my favorite part of the Indonesian section is the touching reason a young girl gives for not yet adopting Muslim dress.

A song, accidentally heard in Siwa, sets Tamalyn off on the road to Zanzibar, a place she'd never even considered in her itinerary. It was not an easy place to get to, but she manages, with the aid of a sweet, sad young man, to find the very musicians and singers whose music called to her. Almost miraculously, she succeeds in arranging for, and actually producing, a recording that will bring the music of those unique, underappreciated *taraab* artists to people all over the world.

Changed political and economic climates made it possible for Tamalyn to get, not only into China, but all the way to its Xinjiang Autonomous Region (albeit without one of her suitcases—a story in itself), an area formerly closed to foreigners and one which has remained Muslim even in the face of Mao, the Cultural Revolution, and the "open market" onslaught of tourism.

Everywhere she went Tamalyn sought and found dance, done by amateurs and professionals, some publicly acceptable and some forbidden outside the immediate family. She even found some dancers performing to her *Bellydance Superstars* music on bootlegged DVDs in China. What a weird feeling that must have been!

I'm truly glad she thought about such a journey and wrote about it so we can all go along. Chalk up another one for curious cats!

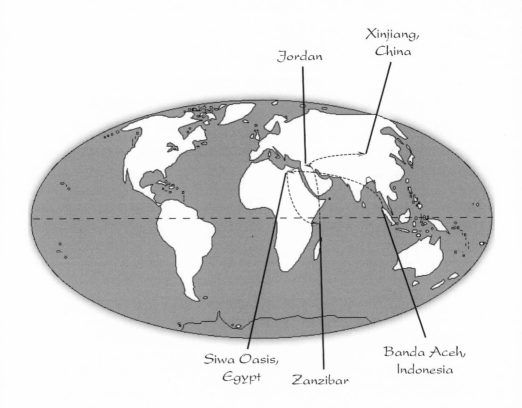

Jordan

Xinjiang,
China

Siwa Oasis,
Egypt

Zanzibar

Banda Aceh,
Indonesia

INTRODUCTION

THE IDEA FOR THIS BOOK WAS BORN IN THE SUMMER OF 2004. As I rode through the mountains of Washington State with my brother, the newspaper in my lap screamed in bold capital letters "AMERICAN BEHEADED." Many people begged me to cancel my upcoming trip to Egypt.

"I can't," I'd protest, "it's going to be the biggest belly-dance convention in the world and my students have already bought their plane tickets. Anyway, the beheading took place in Iraq. I'm going to Egypt." To many people in the U.S., any Muslim country seemed frightening.

I silently watched the mountainous scenery pass by. With my brother, Richard Harris, a successful travel writer, books are always a topic of our conversations. Suddenly, an idea hit. I said, "*40 Days & 1001 Nights*. That's going to be the name of my new book."

Richard pointed out some wildflowers and commented on the warm weather. I continued, "They wouldn't have an international belly-dance convention if it were so dangerous . . . if I go there and everything is normal, I'm going to write a book . . . forty days is how long they say it takes to get below the surface, and I'm sure I'll have lots of stories to tell . . . like Scheherazade in 1001 Nights."

He said, "Maybe you should finish the book you're working on first." We were headed to Berkeley to meet the publisher of another book in the making, *Belly Dancing for Fitness*.

In August 2005 I took the plunge: gave up my apartment, changed my life completely around, and dove in. My budget and timeline would allow me to travel to five countries, with some time off in between to teach dance workshops and earn money for the next destination.

Since most of my life has been spent teaching women (and men) a dance celebrating sensuality, people might think it odd that I would want to explore the Islamic world. How would I find common ground with societies that encourage women to cover from head to toe?

As an American, I wanted to know the truth. There are many conflicting truths: we hear a lot about covered women and terrorism, but there must be more. Countries that are predominately Muslim reach from West Africa to Southeast Asia and include 20 percent of the earth's population. Who are these people? Could they be, as we are led to imagine, masses of American-haters who pose a threat to our way of life? Are there really millions of women cowering in submission beneath black shrouds? I felt an obligation to get to know these people, to see how our actions and attitudes affect their lives, and to get a deeper understanding of their realities.

As a belly dancer, I'd always been fascinated by the ancient pre-Islamic roots: how the dance survives and continues to flourish in countries where Islam is the predominant faith. Although belly dancing has nothing to do with Islam as a religion, it is a much-loved and important part of social interactions between women in many Islamic countries. In the Arab world, when the men are not around and women celebrate—be it an engagement, wedding party or just getting together to prepare a meal—scarves come off the heads and go onto the hips, and the belly dancing begins.

I had no plan or projection of what I expected to find, but given my love of music, dance, food, and colorful clothing, these simple pleasures of life were not to be neglected.

I spent my first forty days in Indonesia. With much help from a stranger, I strayed from the tourist trail into the tsunami devastated area of Banda Aceh, an intensely religious state where *sharia* (Islamic law) is a way of life. I fasted for Ramadhan in Java and visited one of the world's last matriarchal cultures, the Minangkabau of West Sumatra.

2

Deep in the Sahara, my next stop was the Siwa Oasis of Egypt. Winter in the desert was really cold. I spent forty days among the only Berber culture in Egypt. Siwans have an ancient tradition of date and olive farming, and I met a curious cast of characters, some of whom made me realize that not all the behaviors in these parts of the world come from the teachings of the Qur'an.

I followed a song all the way to Zanzibar, where beautiful *taarab* music played in the background as my young neighbor helped me gain access to aspects of Zanzibari life that a tourist rarely sees. Old stone mansions crumbled away and African magic melded with Islamic beliefs.

In Jordan, with the help of a French reporter, a French belly dancer, and a renowned music professor, I was able to delve beneath the modern exterior and get to know a fascinating blend of Bedouins, Palestinian and Iraqi refugees, Circassians, Gypsies, and nomadic Turkmen tribes.

In China's predominately Muslim Xinjiang Autonomous Region, I found tour bus loads of newly affluent Chinese tourists from Beijing and Shanghai and a construction boom trying to polish up this last outpost of the ancient Silk Road and make it shine like Disney World. Beneath the glitter live thirteen ethnic groups including the Uyghurs, who possess many of mankind's cultural treasures, ancient medical practices, and culinary delights.

Through this project I learned that most of what we associate with Islam has nothing to do with the religion and that there is as much variation between countries that embrace Islam as in cultures of the Western world. Equating Osama Bin Laden with Iraq, Indonesia, or Zanzibar, is like comparing Paris Hilton with a survivalist enclave in Idaho, Patagonia, or Moscow.

When I finished traveling in Muslim countries and started traveling through the United States to teach dance workshops in late 2006, the tides were changing. Many people felt deceived by the government and realized they'd been misinformed and told half-truths. They wanted a window into reality.

Throughout the year I spent living *40 Days & 1001 Nights*, I made a documentary film with a tiny hand-held video camera I carried in my purse. When people saw the film, common comments were "I didn't know" and "It was nothing like I expected."

As I shared sushi with a journalist who had heard about my book, he commented, "My assignment in Iran was to seek out a school that teaches women to be suicide bombers." I realized the difference between current world news and *40 Days & 1001 Nights*. He had an assignment: something that sells newspapers. I wasn't looking for anything specific.

If I'd gone searching for the worst and most sordid details on the fringe of society, I might have flirted with danger and made scary headlines. Instead, I had my own set of adventures, living among real people, sharing unexpected moments and unusual stories. I lived life, experiencing the celebrations as well as the sorrows. So *40 Days & 1001 Nights* is about human stories, not news flashes.

Please note that many names have been changed throughout this book in order to protect people's privacy when appropriate.

INDONESIA

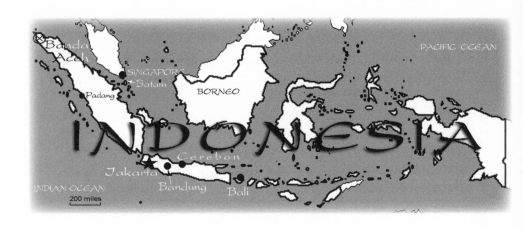

A THOUSAND FACES APPEARED FROM THE DARKNESS, like effervescent bubbles, screaming and singing words that everyone (but me) knew. The sound was Middle Eastern, jungle abandon, and rock'n'roll all mixed together. No one could sit still.

"Who is this?" I wondered as I sat on the stage, lucky to be there instead of among the throngs of fans sitting on one another's shoulders, struggling to get a peek. I poked the woman next to me, "What's his name again?"

"Rafly," she mouthed and returned to her transfixed state.

If music reflects a people, these were some fierce, passionate, and deeply spiritual folks. The wailing horns (called *surunee kale*), driving beats of hand-carved wooden-frame drums (called *rapa-ii*), and electric guitars could not drown out the intensity of Rafly's raw vocals. He seemed to fill the stage and beyond with his charisma. He sang his own lyrics with multiple layers of meaning, from love to social commentary, all the while paying tribute to beloved Allah.

I looked around. Beyond the people, there was a vast wasteland—utter destruction. A magnificent pink and purple sky blanketed splinters of wood and pieces of broken cement.

All of these people had been through more devastation than we could ever imagine. But now, having come on every possible mode of transport (bicycles, motorbikes, and packed in old pickup trucks), they lost themselves in Rafly's music. This was Banda Aceh, Indonesia, one of the world's most fervently religious Islamic cultures, which had been closed to outsiders for decades. A thirty-year civil war had ended three weeks before I arrived, and one of the worst natural disasters in modern history had leveled the place ten months earlier.

How did I end up in Banda Aceh? Let's rewind to my naïve beginnings: responding to common Western attitudes toward the Islamic world, I thought, "There must be more than terrorists and suffering women." As a professional belly dancer I have been listening to Arabic, Turkish, and Persian songs most of my life. I have danced for hundreds of Middle Eastern weddings and dated my share of men from those parts of the world. Something didn't compute. The words I heard and the people I met didn't match the commonly portrayed public images. Had something changed? Could a wave of extremism have enveloped one-fifth of the world's population and made the world a place of danger and fear, worthy of an ever-updated, color-coded alert system?

With a vow to write about whoever and whatever appeared with no predetermined point of view, I began my journey as a rather clueless, bumbling woman in a far-too-revealing top, rolling a massive, unbalanced duffle bag up an escalator in a Singaporean shopping mall. I was looking for the ferry to Indonesia, the most populous Islamic country on earth. The nearest entry point was Batam, an island I knew nothing about.

"Where can I get *teh tarek* around here?"

I thought everyone in Singapore knew this tasty mixture of tea and condensed and evaporated milks, tossed through the air to make it frothy.

"I don't know what that is," the man answered.

"Are you Indonesian?" (Thinking he was and that they probably didn't have teh tarek in his country.)

I handed him a *40 Days & 1001 Nights* business card and he introduced himself as Arief. He was Muslim and instantly became interested in my project.

He said, "I'll help you meet people so you can learn about our culture."

"Why not?" I thought, accepting his offer.

Along came his friend, Alencar. I thought he was Indonesian too, but when he spoke, it was with a Brazilian accent.

"Porque voce vai ate Batam?" I asked him why he was going to Batam in broken Portuguese, and he answered, "Para trabalhar" (that he was going to work).

I had exactly forty days before teaching a belly-dance workshop back in Singapore and then performing in shows in other parts of Asia. If I didn't start immediately, I'd get busy with other things and never start this book.

My ticket read "September 11, 2005, departing from the World Trade Center." I asked, "World Trade Center?"

Alencar said, "That's the name of the mall. Didn't you take an escalator past shops to get here?"

"Oh yeah," I recalled.

Both men looked at me quizzically, asking, "Why Batam?"

"Why not?" I replied.

I was giddy with anticipation. There was magic in the air as we passed pretty buildings and bobbing boats in Singapore Harbor, floated into the open sea, and spotted land in the distance.

☾ ☆ ⁎ ⁎ ₒ

A fancy town car waited at the other end in Batam. Arief asked, "Where are you staying?" I shrugged. We sloshed through muddy streets, past scarred earth and piles of garbage. At Alencar's apartment building, three guards checked the car's trunk and searched the underside with a round mirror on a long stick.

I stayed where the car dropped me off—a fancy business hotel that wasn't in my budget or in keeping with my goal of mingling with locals. It would have to do for the moment.

An hour after I got there, Arief was sitting in the lobby, unfolding an oversized map of Indonesia. "Our country has over 17,000 islands, and I believe you have chosen the ugliest one." He added, "If you're writing a book about the Islamic world, you must begin in Banda Aceh."

"I vowed to stay out of war zones and disaster areas," I protested. Banda Aceh was both.

"The war has been over for three weeks," Arief countered.

A war had been raging for thirty years, and foreigners were strongly urged to stay away. The first time I, and most of the world, had heard of Banda Aceh was December 26, 2004, when it was decimated by the tsunami.

I didn't go on to Banda Aceh as Arief had suggested—not immediately. Instead, I took another ferry to Bintan, an island whose northern coast had been leased to Singapore and developed as a resort area. In a *becak,* a motorbike-powered rickshaw, I toured royal tombs and ruins of the island's old palace. Graveyards full of tiny headstones were decorated with yellow turban-like cloths as a sign of respect for the personages buried within. Everything was yellow, from structures that housed tombs to paint on humble plaster-and-stucco palaces. Even the old vice-royal mosque, called Mesjid Raya, was painted yellow. In the mosque, male worshippers donned small boat-shaped hats, and women wore frilly white headscarves adorned with eyelets and embroidery.

As the sun set, the glistening water looked iridescent and enchanted. I hired a boat all to myself to savor the beauty. The marvelous colors turned out to be an oil slick and garbage floated by with disturbing regularity.

The homestay I found in Tanjung Pinang (Bintan's main town) was called Bong's. I took a simple room upstairs, which was reached by climbing a wooden ladder. My room contained a fan, a saggy bed, graffiti on the walls, and a hanging florescent light. The bathroom downstairs had a toilet designed to build thigh muscles. Squat toilets have two grooved places to put your feet, with ridges to help prevent slipping. You squat and pee, aiming into a hole. It takes some practice in order not to wet one's feet. Mrs. Bong, who spoke a little English, advised me that the bath was "Indonesian style," explaining that I mustn't get into the tub. Instead, a plastic bowl was provided with which to scoop water from the tub and toss it over the body. After lathering up, the bather tosses some more water to rinse off.

In a small alley outside the homestay, neighbors lingered around several tables. Two women prepared staple Indonesian dishes, *mee goreng* (fried noodles with chili) and *nasi goreng* (fried rice with chili), in an outdoor kitchen.

Mrs. Bong was a sixty-something-year-old elegant Chinese woman with full makeup and a flowered frock. Her younger-looking husband was tousled and a bit grumpy, but I sensed trustworthiness in both of them. As I set off to explore the island, she told me, "You should take off those gold chains. Someone will snatch them off your neck . . . do you have a camera? Leave it with me." I left everything with her—passport, dollars, credit cards, cameras, and gold chains. If my instincts had proved deceptive and Mrs. Bong had turned out to be a thief, I would have been in a major pickle.

On my way to the seaside, I sat behind a guide named Adam on his motorbike. We traveled through an idyllic land of coconut palms, leaning wooden huts, little bays with beaches, and old fishing boats that were cast ashore looking like they hadn't been seaworthy for years.

Suddenly, the clouds burst open in a torrential downpour. We pulled over and dashed into a small shop filled with grizzled, beer-drinking men. Adam said, "I love to drink." I mused to myself, "I thought Muslims didn't drink." Lucky for me, he didn't have any money and depended on tourists to buy his beer. I bought him water and tea. As the rain poured on, I cajoled him for a lesson in *Bahasa Indonesia*, a Malay dialect that was officially declared the national language when Indonesia won its independence from the Dutch in 1945. Most Indonesians speak Bahasa as a second language, while using regional languages in their local communities.

"How do you say puppy?"

"Dog is *anjing*, and baby is *ana*, so puppy is *anjing ana*."

I held up my fingers to learn how to count: one is *satu*, two is *duo*, three is *tiga*, four is *empat*, and five is *lima*.

Rain is *ujan*.

Finally, the black clouds cleared and we were on the road again. Our destination was an appealing bay surrounded by a village full of shacks that served day-trippers on weekends, selling food, liquor, and coconuts fresh from the trees. Village men brought flat baskets of tiny fish and set a huge wok-shaped pan to boil over a fire. Before the soup was done, we had to leave to catch the last ferry back from Bintan to Batam.

I returned to the homestay with little time to spare. My bag emerged, everything intact. Mrs. Bong told me, "Watch out for pickpockets at the dock," and made Adam promise to see that I boarded the boat safely.

On the ferry, I met another man. He was a mole-like creature with beady eyes and a dough-boy body. He vied for my attention in competition with a couple of laborers from an eastern island who tried in earnest to speak English with me. They were nice, but I couldn't understand anything they said. I tried to be sociable and tactful with all three. Mr. Mole was one of those self-important, third-world, middle-management types. He worked for a milk company in the next province over. His company's driver was waiting at the dock, and they offered me a ride. We were both staying at the Harmony Hotel, so I accepted (with some trepidation). When the driver exited in an outlying neighborhood, I thought "Oh no," and made it clear that I wanted to go directly to the hotel. Sitting coolly on the edge of my seat, I questioned every turn until we arrived. Mr. Mole had assumed that we had a dinner date, but I told him I was busy.

I really did have plans with Arief, who wanted me to try a popular Indonesian specialty. I followed him, tiptoeing over craters of broken sidewalks, noticing how the buildings that had sprung up in the 70s and 80s already looked forlorn.

Arief led me to a simple restaurant that served Padang food. He said, "Padang is in West Sumatra. You should go there one day." A dozen dishes were piled precariously on the arm of a waiter, who placed them on the table, served us a heap of stuck-together rice, and set down bowls of water to dip our fingers in. Arief explained that patrons only pay for the dishes they eat—those that remain untouched go to another table—and that people only eat with the right hand. The left hand is considered unclean. Eating included tearing apart thick chunks of stringy meat, deboning fish, and wrapping rice in a mysterious boiled leaf. I tried to be dainty, but the hot spices made my nose and eyes run. Soon, I had a mound of filthy, soaking-wet tissues. I tried in vain to clean the chili pepper sauce from under my long fingernails by swishing them in an ever-murkier dish of water.

On my way into the Harmony Hotel, Mr. Mole passed by with a

young prostitute on his arm. He asked if I was going to the hotel's disco, and the girl giggled, "Come, join us!"

Yeah, right!

A beeping text message woke me up the next morning. From Arief, it read "Your ticket to Banda Aceh is ready." He'd sent instructions on where and when to pick it up, and the contact number for a woman named Octa in Banda Aceh. According to Arief's big map, Banda Aceh wasn't far. To me, it seemed worlds away.

I remembered how ten months earlier I'd been waiting for a flight from Seattle to Hong Kong. News reports announced, in a matter-of-fact tone, that a giant wave had barreled across the Indian Ocean and had just hit Indonesia, killing 5,000 people. Soon after, the radio told of 10,000 casualties.

On the layover, I sat in the Tokyo airport. People were glued to a TV showing images of the tsunami with English subtitles—90,000 dead. It said something about Banda Aceh, and I wondered where that was. Soon the death count was over 100,000. The entire world was in shock. With each day the toll mounted, until the number of dead and missing reached nearly 250,000.

New Year's Eve of 2005 was fast approaching. In Hong Kong, the mood was somber. Revelers went through the superficial motions of celebration in a stunned daze. Champagne tops popped at midnight. Obligatory confetti was thrown. But everybody just wanted to get the parties over with. The world was in mourning. Every day headlines screamed more horror stories. Only able to donate money and pray, we felt helpless.

Arief said to go to Banda Aceh, I would have to dress conservatively. "No bare arms. Make sure your tops are loose and reach mid-thigh. And you might have to cover your head to respect local tradition."

According to some interpretations of Islam "a woman covering herself becomes equal to all other women, without regard for beauty, expensive clothes, or body type." Not ready to fully embrace the idea, I searched for my own personal style of conservative dress for Banda Aceh.

As I dug through my duffel bag, a fashion inspiration hit. Requesting a pair of scissors from the front desk, I cut a caftan that I'd been using as a belly-dance costume cover-up, making a diagonal hem and fashioning a headscarf out of the leftover fabric. I wore this over jeans, with a scarf tied at the hips, and my pointy, sparkly cowboy boot–inspired shoes. A bandana secured the matching headgear.

Newspapers showed horrific photos of a jet that had crashed just after takeoff in Medan (my first stop on the way to Banda Aceh) and killed 147 people. The plane I boarded resembled a rundown public bus. The bathroom's dented metal plumbing and its door that didn't lock added to my feeling of insecurity.

Always ready to be a tourist, I wanted to sample the sights of Medan. Continuing my adventures in the wrong shoes, I tripped along broken sidewalks that had wood precariously perched over gaping holes with dirty water stagnating beneath. Halfway across a busy street that had a broken walk light, I noticed an ornately latticed flyover that would have been a better choice of thoroughfare.

I stumbled four more blocks to the Maimoon Palace, which is still inhabited by the regional sultan. Groups of tiny children, the girls in headscarves and the boys in hats, sat on a patch of grass outside. A guard informed me that the palace was closed, but music wafted from inside and I was determined to enter. Finally, a woman ushered me forward into a room where a mock court, with king, queen, and attendants, sat in full golden brocade and jeweled attire. Four dancers with expressive hand movements were accompanied by accordion and percussion instruments, flitting gracefully and changing formations from lines to circles to a diamond shape. Most of the palace was off-limits because the local royal family lived there. Since Indonesia is made of many former kingdoms and sultanates, many sultans still live in their palaces, although they are figureheads with little power.

On my way back, I made sure to use the pretty flyover instead of braving another busy street crossing. While maneuvering unstable and rotting wooden stairs on top of corroded metal, I thought about how looks can deceive. Where I thought would be safe, the situation worsened. Slats of wood were missing, and I stepped around sleeping bodies, taking care not to fall through the exposed holes to the traffic below.

When I arrived in Banda Aceh, my first impression was that it looked a whole lot better than Batam! A gleaming taxi took me past lush greenery and small wooden houses. The taxi dropped me at the headquarters of Islamic Relief, a nonprofit aid agency.

When Octa appeared on the stairway, I was taken aback. She was petite, with a round face and clear, moist, cinnamon-colored skin. Beneath an opaque white headscarf, carefully pinned so as not to show any neck, was a tiny body swathed in a long-sleeved dress with a long skirt underneath. Gauntlets made of thick cotton covered any possibility of exposed flesh, and she wore a jacket on top of all that. Thick white socks covered her sandaled feet. The austere color scheme of black, white, and gray seemed unusual for an Indonesian woman. The heat must have been in the nineties with high humidity. I didn't feel any air conditioning, but she appeared curiously cool and comfortable and didn't sweat a drop.

Octa acted reserved, as if she didn't quite know what to do with me. I wondered if we could find any common ground. She instructed two men to take me to the Sulthan Hotel in a big, shiny red truck emblazoned with the Islamic Relief logo, then stiffly mentioned an exhibition that afternoon. It was some sort of NGO (nongovernmental organization) tradeshow. She said, "Call me and we can go together."

On our way to the hotel, we passed buildings and homes that were hopelessly destroyed right next to others that looked unscathed. The driver pointed to a large modern hotel that was completely gutted and a collapsed office building. He said, "Tsunami." I asked to stop at a tiny clapboard guesthouse that I noticed was open for business. He shook his finger and drove on to the Sulthan, assuring me, "It's a good hotel. All the foreigners stay there." The guest house was now permanent residence for dozens of families who lost their homes in the tsunami.

A uniformed porter carried my heavy bag up as we rode a slow elevator to the top floor. Down a hallway with soiled, torn industrial carpeting and hardly any light, he showed me a tattered room with a slight sewage stench. Unfortunately, I learned, accommodation was rare in Banda Aceh so this room was my only choice. After I put my fingers over my nose, the porter carried my bag back to the lobby. I showed him how to roll it on its wheels, but unfazed, the slight man chose to struggle with it by the handles.

When I handed over my passport, the front-desk clerk informed me that the smelly room was reserved and the hotel was full. My ride had left, and I was stuck, so I simply refused to leave, asking the same question twenty different ways until the clerk coughed up an accommodation. "We have a simple room that you can take, but only for one night."

The porter, a good sport, carried my bag down another spooky hallway. The next room was miniature, like a walk-in closet with a lock that didn't work. Its door didn't even latch. Before paying for the room, I insisted, "You have to change the lock."

After they had a chance to make repairs, the sweetly patient porter took me back to the room. This time I found myself stuck inside with no way to *unlock* the door. He radioed the desk, and a repairman came and took the lock apart. Eventually, I got my room and was even awarded a two-night stay. They told me the poor condition of the hotel was because the wave had reached the upper floors. Guests were spared because they were sent to the top of the building; the wave reached the fourth floor, but merely soaked the carpet.

I strolled a broken main street that was lined with tightly shuttered shops, searching for something to eat and pondering the same question over and over—"What am I doing here?" Hoping to find an answer, I opened my backpacker's guidebook. It explicitly warned foreigners not to go to Aceh, saying they were in "grave danger" of getting caught in the crossfire between the GAM (Gerakan Aceh Merdeka, translated as Free Aceh Movement) separatist guerrillas and the TNI (Tentara Nasional Indonesia Special Forces), who had been sent by the central government to crush the rebellion. I calmly assured myself that this information was out-of-date.

Back at the hotel, I ordered a cup of tea in the lobby café and called Octa's phone number several times. Meanwhile, I eavesdropped on conversations about Iraq, Bosnia, and Chechnya between members of a BBC camera crew and aid workers. Like belly dancers when they get together and talk shop and discuss the intricacies of Middle Eastern music and hip isolations, these authoritative-sounding people discussed disaster areas, failures of relief coordination, and local corruption.

I spotted two young backpackers who had come in off the street. They quickly devoured huge ice cream sundaes, which were bright with artificial pinks and greens. The tousled duo, Ross and Dan, had come from Ireland to volunteer at a small NGO called FBA (Forum Bangun Aceh). Its motto was "Survivors Helping Survivors."

Ross explained, "Not much gets done around here. Most of the big NGOs get caught up in bureaucracy. The FBA is modest. Mainly locals who help people in a small way, but at least they accomplish something." I asked what they did, and Dan told me, "Mostly microeconomic assistance for small businesses and scholarships for kids. There isn't a lot we can help with, but we're working to build their website. Ross is designing a method for transporting clean water to one of the villages." They gave me a phone number for the FBA and I made an appointment to meet and discuss what I could do to volunteer.

Octa arrived in a shiny SUV, and soon we pulled into Taman Putroe Phang. It was a former fairground, now full of mud and broken cement walkways. Vendors were selling everything from cheap plastic toys to fruit and water, and had set up a few food stalls. Under plastic tarps, some booths displayed photos of tsunami destruction that were taped onto cardboard, making them look like school projects. Everyone displayed their logos and some gave away bumper stickers, T-shirts, and other promotional materials. In the few structures in the fairground that had been left standing, groups like Islamic Relief, the Red Cross, Red Crescent, and USAID had set up ambulances and gory photo and film exhibits. Some had barkers with megaphones. The atmosphere was gruesome yet carnival-like. It had me puzzled. I called the FBA to see if they had a booth and got a laugh from the other end. "Of course not! That's expensive, and it doesn't help anyone."

Islamic Relief's big house was dominated by a movie screen where a film loop of the tsunami ran endlessly—injured people being pulled from rubble, dead bodies floating down river-like streets, and a woman telling her emotional tale and sobbing. Emotion-jerking music was so loud it made the five-foot-tall speakers tremble and distort. Inside, local people were packed tightly together, some crying and others watching with grave expressions.

Octa introduced me to the top people from Islamic Relief, a pleasant enough assortment of men from Lebanon, Palestine, Macedonia, Kenya, India, Bangladesh, and the United Kingdom. The most outgoing and outspoken was a Palestinian from Los Angeles named Abdusalam. He was plump and jolly, a public relations man in an Islamic Relief T-shirt, handing out Islamic Relief bumper stickers to passersby.

She then introduced me to a handsome Lebanese man named Jihad. I wondered to myself why anyone would name their son after holy war. I later learned that the word *Jihad* means 'directed struggle,' which can be religious or personal, social, political, or defensive. When a Jihad involves combat, it is supposed to be defensive and in accordance with strict rules forbidding the harm of innocent bystanders, women, and children. Property and non-Muslim places of worship are not to be destroyed. Taking hostages, kidnapping, and bombing public areas are condemned by Islam. The Prophet is said to have declared that 'the supreme Jihad is against oneself' as a struggle against ego, greed, and desires. Like the Western names of Constance, Hope, or Faith, it is the kind of virtue that parents would pick as a name for their child.

Octa talked easily with everyone, whether male or female. At age twenty-four, she was comfortable with her authority within the organization. She called the men "brother," and they called her "sister," which reminded me of the movie *Malcolm X.*

At first I was intimidated by all her layers of clothing, and I wondered if I could ever get to know the person underneath, whose vision of life must be so different from mine. I thought maybe she covered so much because of working with so many men. Later, when we grew to be friends, she told me her story.

"I love Islam very much. Since junior high, I wanted to cover up." (Half Acehnese, Octa grew up in the Indonesian capital of Jakarta, where it wasn't as common to wear a headscarf.) "At the age of seventeen, I read a book about death and pondered how fleeting life is." She quoted, "You never know if you may die today, tomorrow, or several decades later, but the worst thing is to die without following your heart." It was in her heart to give herself over to her faith. For her, that included covering as much as possible. Octa was so attached to her big jacket, a gift from another aid worker who had gone to Sarajevo, that she rarely took it off even though Aceh is in a tropical jungle. The neck cord holding her cell phone said *SARAJEVO*.

At one end of the exhibition grounds stood a big lavender and peach painted amphitheater with arches and ornate latticework carving. People in the audience kept asking me "Where from?" Some brought tiny children to look at the foreigner. One woman approached, wearing a nun-like cotton headpiece gathered under her chin with elastic, speaking fluent English. She held her kids up to see me and to shake my hand. "Can you come to my school? I am an English teacher, and I'd like the kids to meet a native speaker."

Several women in matching bright yellow headscarves and brightly patterned caftans filed onto a stage, singing Islamic songs. Another ladies' chorus, clad in purple and pink, followed. I'd heard that in conservative Islamic countries such as Saudi Arabia, a woman's voice is considered provocative, so only men may sing religious songs. Not so in Banda Aceh.

Rapa-ii geleng is a trance-like combination of dance, drumming, and Islamic chanting. A group of young boys took the stage, wearing gold headbands and big shirts, pants, and fabrics wrapped at the waist. They played rapa-ii in elaborately coordinated unison, hitting the drums with their hands, then on the floor, to the front and to the sides, and tossing them into the air and trading them. All the while, an older man chanted religious songs, and the boys answered back in song. Their heads tossed wildly, at an ever-increasing speed.

Another group of small children did a calmer dance with elaborate hand and arm movements. They were seated on the ground, each wearing a banner that read "Orphan."

On my way to meet with the FBA, I looked around to see how people from Banda Aceh transported themselves. Motorbikes were a popular option, and some contained families of up to four people: father, mother, child, and tiny baby. I hailed a becak with a colorful little carriage on the side, which served as a taxi. It took me all the way to FBA headquarters, a simple house in the suburbs. The director and founder, whose name was Azwar, had been working (volunteer) nonstop since January and was burnt out, so he'd left town for a while. A man from Jakarta named Wawan interviewed me. Other than Dan and Ross, he was the only non-Acehnise in the group. We sat on the front porch sipping water from plastic cups as Aznawy, another key FBA figure, breezed in, looking dashing in the traditional hat and dressy clothes that he'd just worn to pray in the mosque. He said a quick hello and excused himself, then returned as an ordinary young guy in a T-shirt and baggy pants.

We agreed that I could move into the house the next day and try to find a use for my English skills. Wawan suggested that I help with the wording of proposals and e-mails. The Irish guys said I should go to local schools to teach English, and one of the workers asked if I would teach English at the house. Aznawy said, "It's okay for you to stay, but we're too busy to provide you with work to do." He gave me one assignment: "Try to come up with two to three donated used laptops so FBA workers in other villages can input data and bring it back to the office." This FBA stint was going to be mundane, I realized, but at least I would be living among local people. If I could help the cause by rounding up laptops, pushing papers, or correcting grammar, I was willing.

During my second and last night at the hotel, a French psychologist named Lawrence asked me, "Have you been to the tsunami area?" I wasn't sure. I thought the town was it. "No," he corrected, "an entire coastline of villages were leveled." He added, "Visit this area in the afternoon. You'll see people who go there to remember and cry."

Lawrence said he spent much of his time attending meetings (one of the most prevalent pastimes for those flown in to help) and captivated me late into the night with his French accent and tales of bureaucratic woe. "Doctors sent from India and many other countries were left in the Sulthan Hotel lobby, waiting for instructions. They weren't allowed to start working without authorization. Medical care was desperately needed, but no one directed those who came to help."

He then explained the dilemma of how to dispose of unwanted donations—winter clothes from Argentina that are useless in the tropical jungle climate or long-expired medicine from the Vietnam war era— "The cost of disposing of a tanker full of expired medicines is prohibitive for those who have it, so it becomes a giant hot potato that can be passed off as a good deed."

Another of his intriguing stories was about lack of timber for building homes. "So many were destroyed that there is not enough wood to rebuild them all." He told of a mysterious cargo ship full of unidentified wood that a building company had bought with aid money. It had been supplied by the Indonesian army who had been stationed at a protected forest area to make sure nobody cut down any trees. It was later learned that the military guards cut down the trees themselves.

The single most urgent problem, he said, was fresh water. "Water is polluted because the wave of salt water was so strong that it seeped into the ground. Then too, there were the dead bodies of people and animals rotting into the water."

I asked Lawrence about GAM, whose fighting with the military put Aceh off-limits for such a long time. "The military didn't catch suspected GAM members and try them," he said. "They simply gunned them down in the street. Thousands of people were killed as a result. Some were guilty and others only suspects." He continued, "Acehnise are tough adversaries and the military from other parts of Indonesia are afraid of them."

A taxi took me and my big duffel bag from the world of expats-on-a-mission to the FBA house on the outskirts of town. I would be living with twelve local guys. Saturday was their day off, so the only person around was a sleepy man named Bustami reading the newspaper. About forty years old with a turned-up mustache, Bustami was a problem solver. If the lights didn't work, he got them on again. Too many mosquitoes? He had the right chemical to spray.

Bustami stood by a scooter and circled his hand, "around?" Not one to pass up an opportunity to ride a motorbike, I hopped on the back and we rode to a construction site—a school that an Irish company had donated money for, that FBA would build. It was scheduled to open in less than two months. Bricks were being raised to the second floor in a plastic pail on a rope. It was a slow process, but the building was taking shape.

We rode on, through a wasteland of rubble and graffiti-covered remnants that, on first impression, looked like a sea of unfinished construction. "Why has he brought me to this place?" I wondered, doubting my wisdom in blindly trusting a stranger. Finally, it dawned on me, "This is the tsunami area."

I felt numb and couldn't imagine that people had actually lived there. A few skeletons of buildings still stood, but it was impossible to tell what they had been. We were in the rubble of a village that had been called Ulee Lheu. Now it was an endless, surrealistic disaster area. The reality of what I was seeing was unfathomable. My feelings of confusion were compounded by the fact that everyone I saw was friendly and cheerful. They often greeted me, a stranger, with a cheerful "Hello," and tried out a few words of English. Politeness was the norm in Banda Aceh, whether with friends or strangers. Most people had a gentle, open demeanor. "What," I wondered, "makes the people of Aceh so resilient?"

Some of the land had sunk because of the tsunami, forming stagnant salt lakes. Other areas that should have been sea were now exposed land. The only building still standing for many kilometers around the former village was a beautiful mosque that was being used as a Kuwaiti Red Crescent facility.

Fishing boats had been carried far inland, where some of them were now being used as houses. Houses were underwater, and tents with NGO logos served as semi-permanent housing amid the debris. Lines of clothing were strung from tent to tent, and people cooked on fires outside. An occasional lone child in a school uniform walked home along the dirt roads. Several women in bright clothing with long flowing headscarves piled out of a van, walked solemnly to an empty spot of land, looked around, and got back in the vehicle. "Had they once lived there or were they remembering someone who did?" I wondered and could only guess.

The strangest sight was the "port," which was no port. It had been a hub for passengers from many different areas. Now, a brand new ferryboat, painted shiny blue and white, waited for passengers to go to the resort island of Sabang. One of 100 islands in Aceh, Sabang was spared by the tsunami and remains a local tourist attraction—the most cosmopolitan and tolerant area of Aceh, where women can even wear bikinis for swimming. Amid debris and destruction, the ferry looked as out of place as a spaceship. Apparently the port was not only destroyed, but the area where it had been was now on an island, because the land surrounding it had almost completely washed away.

As time went by, I came to realize that there were two types of people in this world—those who had gone through the tsunami and those of us who hadn't. If we were not among them, we could not possibly imagine the terrible moments they lived.

Some of the twelve guys I lived among at the FBA house had lost everything. Musafir, a tall, gaunt man in his late twenties with giant black eyes, had lost his parents and all of his brothers. His family had owned twenty furniture stores in Banda Aceh. Like many Acehnise, they viewed banking as un-Islamic. Instead, they invested in gold and kept it in the house. Everything and everyone was lost in the tsunami. Musafir was utterly alone. Azwar had encouraged him not to lose hope, and he soon began working at FBA. Living in the FBA house, and with the help of one of his suppliers in Medan, Musafir was slowly able to open one of his stores again.

Musafir set up a meeting for me with his girlfriend, Fifi. She was a beautiful, petite dancer, wearing hip-hugger jeans and a cotton T-shirt with special gauntlets. These were sold in all the markets, so women could wear short sleeves without showing their arms. Made of thick cotton-knit fabric, they were elasticized on the upper arms and gathered with a ribbed band at the wrists. She wore a *jilbab* (headscarf) and never took it off.

Fifi and I exchanged dance classes in my steaming-hot, unventilated room. She showed me several combinations of *Saman*, a dance where you kneel and hit yourself on the shoulders and thighs in elaborate combinations while tossing your head and chanting. This is usually done in groups and is known as "body percussion." She explained, "Saman is also known as 'The Dance of a Thousand Hands.' The purpose of this dance is to give messages on history, spirituality, and how to better one's life. Rows of people, usually women (or sometimes men, though never both together), kneel on the floor, thrusting their heads and chests, singing poetry and hitting their hands against their bodies in complex patterns. They join hands to make wave-like movements with their arms and bodies."

After Fifi taught me four combinations, she said, "You can add so many combinations that one dance may take up to two hours. There are eight to twelve parts of the dance. The first four are basics. After that you can create and do spontaneous improvisations."

We took a rest and she explained, "To write your book, you must learn as much as possible about Islam and understand the tsunami."

She said, "The tsunami came from Allah, who was angry and fed up with the never ending war." According to her point of view, people had drifted too far from God with their indiscriminate killing. "The tsunami brought peace," she opined. "Aceh's hatred and sociopolitical issues were overshadowed by the tsunami tragedy. World attention became focused on this isolated area where outsiders had not dared to enter for so long. Foreign NGOs came to help people. With all of these foreigners (referred to as *turis*) in town, the killing had to stop. The focus shifted from war to survival."

Other people I spoke with offered another angle: "The sinners lived on, and those who died were taken away from this misery to a better place." Either way, the common sentiment was that the tsunami came from God, only God decides when we must die, and we must accept his decision.

Fifi also told me, "I love Islam and want to follow everything it says. It gives me strength, love, and backs me up so I have the power to do anything I want in life." For her, covering was comfortable. "I don't have to worry about something slipping, showing, or to be shy about my body." She also divulged her own little secret: "Being covered protects the skin and makes it more beautiful."

Her explanation for the importance of praying five times a day was that it gives inner peace in regular doses throughout the day. "There is always negativity, frustration, and problems in life. And when you pray, you can ask Allah for help, strength, insight, or anything you need to make life better."

I let my mind wander, imagining what would happen if the powers-that-be on the world's political stage actually communed with God with such regularity. How many lives would be saved?

Sitting in a small tea house, I requested *teh susu panas* (tea, strained through a cloth bag, with lots of condensed milk) in my best Bahasa Indonesia. People didn't respond well to my attempts at speaking Bahasa in Banda Aceh, and I never understood their responses either. It finally dawned on me that they were speaking something else. A diminutive young woman sat across from me, introduced herself as Kade, and explained, "We speak Acehnise, but I'm learning English, and I would like to practice with you."

Whereas, in Bahasa Indonesia one, two, three is *satu, duo, tiga*, in Acehnise, it is *sa, dua, leh*.

I learned a new conversation:

Pue kah me jak kamewe? (Do you want to go fishing?)
Na. (Yes.)
Terimeung geunaseh. (Thank you.)
Saban saban. (You're welcome.)

We didn't go fishing but did become friends. I took my tea to go. Take-out tea was poured into a plastic bag and fastened with a rubber band. The bags were thin but somehow they never melted.

Kade was studying medicine, and I was cooped up in an office, so we regularly met to take escapades in becaks around town. She helped translate my interviews with everyone from merchants to musicians.

We passed dozens of gas vendors along the roadsides. Their gas was stored in large plastic containers, scooped up by a gas can, and used to fuel motorbikes. One day, we saw a man who, instead of using a gas can, poured the gas into a plastic bag and rubber banded the bag at the top. Just like my bag of tea, it didn't melt.

One day, Kade snuck me into the Grand Baiturrahman Mosque, a noted landmark of Banda Aceh. This white marble building, regarded as one of the most beautiful mosques in Indonesia, was built by the Dutch.

Originally, there had been a square, wooden, Indonesian-style mosque on this site. It was here that the Acehnise fought off the Dutch invaders, showing that they could not be colonized. Aceh has always been a staunchly Islamic kingdom, and people were deeply offended that their land was attacked by outsiders and that their beloved mosque was destroyed. Once the Dutch declared the war over, they built the Grand Baiturrahman Mosque as a sign of reconciliation. Its architecture was from British-colonial India and was unfamiliar to them. Initially the Acehnise rejected it, but later generations liked the elegant appearance, and the mosque became a symbol of hope and pride.

The interior of the mosque was a maze of beautiful columns and spotless marble. Study groups gathered to read the Qur'an and children played, chasing each other and giggling. Many adults prayed alone, and some people took naps. The atmosphere was free, except for one thing: non-Muslims were not allowed to enter. A sign outside read "Muslim Dress Area," and a man at the entrance asked, "Muslim?" Kade told me to cover completely with my scarf, and passed me off. I felt a bit conspicuous but was able to get an insider's view.

The people I met in Indonesia didn't claim to judge us Westerners or our way of life. Even Kade, when she could get online, admired my belly-dance website, which opened with me lying on the floor in an elaborately embroidered and jeweled bra and hip-hugging skirt with my stomach exposed. She showed it to her friends from college, who were all very covered and religious. When they met me, they said, "I saw your website. Beautiful!" Many people I encountered, from the men at the FBA to teachers and shop keepers, made it clear that they were firm in their beliefs, who they were, and how they wanted to live. One day, Aznawy told me, "What other cultures do is fine, as long as we are allowed to live our lives in accordance with what we believe."

In 2004, *sharia* (Islamic law) became the rule in Aceh. Before that, women were not required to cover their heads but most of them did so by choice. Now, there are "sharia police," who sit on motorbikes watching to make sure couples don't display too much affection in public and ensuring that women have their hair covered. This only applies to Muslim women. Others are exempt. If a Muslim woman doesn't cover her hair, they can shave her head. Zakiah, the only female working at FBA, explained: "They make sure unmarried couples are not behaving scandalously, kissing in public, touching each other, or getting sexual under the trees. If they are caught, their cases are written about in the newspapers, and they will be taken to a public area, where someone on a loudspeaker announces what they have done and they are beaten for everyone to see."

I asked what she thought of this and she replied, "It's the law. They have sinned and should be punished." Marriages were not arranged, but Zakiah shared many people's sentiment and felt that "kissing before marriage is a sin." In Banda Aceh, the women I spoke to, in various walks of life, from teachers to dancers, students, and housewives, embraced the laws of sharia without question.

I found that there are deeper meanings to the word. "Sharia" means "way" or "path," and is the Islamic legal framework that deals with many aspects of day to day life. People often think of it as legislated modesty, but it also governs politics, economics, banking, business law, contract law, sexuality, and social issues. It is very complex and detailed.

One day, as Kade and I were roaming around town on a becak, a tremendous noise of sirens, drums, and singing on scratchy loudspeakers grew nearer. It was a huge parade announcing the coming of Ramadhan, the important period of fasting that is a requirement for Muslims the world over. Since the moon's position determines precisely when Ramadhan should start, no one was clear about the exact date when the observance would begin. Some said October 3rd or 4th. Hundreds of women, covered in white scarves, sang as they rode past in vans and on motorbikes. They passed out flyers informing the public that the correct date of the beginning of Ramadhan was October 5th. Children and adults waved colorful flags, and there was an air of celebration. The street was lined with people who came out of their homes to watch.

We were still on the becak when serendipity struck. Kade said, "Maybe I can find a dance rehearsal for you to watch." The driver took us to a rehearsal hall.

Inside, the musical setup consisted of a Western-style drum set, electric guitars, and a keyboard. Two guys were asleep on the bare floor, and a few more milled about. The scene didn't look promising. Kade went outside and spoke with an older man on a motorbike who said, "Follow me."

Ever since I saw his concert, I'd been looking for some way to meet Rafly. We ended up walking into a stage set where a music video for another singer was being filmed. This singer performed a variation of the rock-folk fusion that Rafly is famous for. Syek Ghazali, a stout man dressed in a traditional hat and vest, approached to introduce himself. He was the main purveyor of music in town and happened to be one of Rafly's producers. He arranged for Rafly to pick us up and take us with him to the Governor's House that evening for a show.

On stage, Rafly looked larger than life. Up close, he was shorter than me, gently masculine, and extremely charismatic. A throng of fans surrounded him as we stepped out of the car and followed him all the way to the stage. He greeted each of them and warmly shook their hands like long-lost friends. Instead of acting important and taking them for granted, he never stopped showing appreciation that they'd come to see him.

The Governor's House was actually a hall in a village outside of Banda Aceh where many townspeople were invited. Preceding his performance, women performed a slow but celebratory folk dance, enacting a party. We sat through an unending series of long speeches by men in beautiful batik silk shirts and traditional hats, mostly about the tsunami. Kade said, "The tsunami didn't reach this village." The evening was excruciatingly boring, but Kade and I waited patiently, and at long last, Rafly sang three songs, greeted his crowds on the way out, and gave us a ride to the FBA house.

The boarding house where Kade rented a room closed at 11 PM, so I invited her to stay with me. It's taboo for a local woman to stay in a house full of men. Even Zakiah, the only woman working at FBA always went home at dusk. Kade wouldn't leave the bedroom, not even to use the bathroom. In Indonesia, the women I met kept their headscarves on, even at home, but Kade removed hers to sleep. I imagined all of these girls with long flowing hair, but hers was short and looked like she cut it herself. She said, "Less hair makes the headscarf more comfortable, and nobody sees my hair anyway."

The teacher I'd met at the NGO fair took me to her high school. It was one of the few schools that hadn't been completely destroyed. She introduced me to her class as a dance teacher, and all the kids asked excitedly, "Salsa?" I said, "My dance is a little different."

The subject of salsa came up several times. Luckily, I could teach the basics. Boys danced on one side of the room, and the girls on the other. In return, the girls performed Saman—the dance Fifi had started to teach me—sitting on their knees, chanting, hitting themselves, and clapping.

These boisterous, giggly kids were similar to teenagers everywhere, except that the boys wore uniforms that made them look like security guards, and the girls wore shapeless long skirts, jackets, and head coverings.

The second time I went there, it was to another teacher's class, but she simply left. The kids were completely unruly and out of hand. I didn't know what to do with them, but after some boys absconded with my camera, I did whatever it took to get them calmed down. They weren't interested in English, so I got their attention by teaching Spanish instead, with a few salsa steps sprinkled in.

☾ ☆ ⁎ ⁎ ⁎ ⁎

Zakiah, Bustami, and I used to cross the street at lunch time and eat at the same buffet every day. It was a roadside stand with picnic tables. Blue plastic tarps served as windows. Choices were limited, but there was always *nasi* (rice) with *sambal* (refried chili), and some sort of lukewarm fish that had been sitting in the sun for hours, or a little piece of vegetable scooped out of a plastic bowl.

A lot of restaurants were destroyed by the tsunami. But on the other hand, there was a growing need for prepared food because of the foreign aid workers, so new eateries were cropping up.

Aside from the downtown stalls selling mee goreng and the roadside stalls with stenciled writing "Nasi Goreng," *satay* is one of the more popular side dishes, consisting of several tiny shish kebabs on toothpick-thin skewers. These are made of beef or chicken and come drenched in spicy peanut sauce. I doubted that a person with a peanut allergy would be able to eat much in Indonesia. Peanut garnishes are part of most rice dishes, and peanuts are used in so many of the tasty sauces. I loved *den den*, the Acehnise version of beef jerky, which is sun-dried, spicy beef that is crispy rather than chewy.

Aznawy and a visiting Japanese student delegation took me trudging through a forlorn side street on the edge of downtown to eat *rujak*. The place was famous for fresh fruit goodies, evidenced by the opulent display of tropical fruits outside. A man was scooping the insides out of a fruit I had never seen before. It had a hard outer covering and jelly-like brown fruit inside. He mixed it with soy sauce, peanuts, palm sugar, bits of other fruits, and hot chilies. We took fruit from a bowl of mixed varieties covered with shaved ice, and each of us dipped pieces into the unusual, brown, sweet, salty, and sour sauce.

In Indonesia, cucumbers and avocados are considered fruits. Cucumbers are often served in sweet soup, and in the case of rujak, they were included in the array of fresh fruits. We quenched any remaining thirst with coconut water mixed with lime juice and palm sugar, which had pieces of young coconut floating in the glass.

I tasted a wide array of fresh juices: avocado, tamarind, star fruit, mango, papaya, dutch eggplant (a sweet pink drink), cucumber, and melon. Decadent *es campur* was the drink I loved best. It combined dark brown palm-sugar syrup and coconut milk with ice, beans, and "jellies" in the glass. Jellies are popular, colorful, and chewy—all texture and no flavor. "Grass jelly" is black; it's a thick gelatin made from some sort of plant. There are some jellies without color, but I especially liked a firm red one, which was molded into circular-shaped pieces.

The most controversial fruit was *durian*. It is an oversized, lumpy, yellow and tan fruit known for its aphrodisiac qualities. When durians were cut open, a pungent aroma filled the air, which would make Ross and Dan leave the room. Durians were sold in big piles by the roadsides, an indication that people could overlook the smell long enough to dig into the soft custard-like fruit that clings to its big black seeds.

One day, after spending many hours helping translate some paperwork from Singapore, Bustami motioned "around" with one finger, and "motorbike," making fists with both hands and bobbing them up and down as if tilting the handles.

Before leaving Banda Aceh, Ross and Dan said I must try something delicious called *martabak banka*. I had no idea what it was, but Bustami's eyes lit up when I uttered the words.

A soft breeze blew into our faces as we plied lush, fauna-laden back roads, past a chaotic mix of mansions that would have fit in Miami Beach or Los Angeles (some housed international aid agencies and had a plethora of fancy vehicles outside), clapboard shacks, and simple wooden homes.

The neighborhood I was staying in, Geuce Meunara, had not been hit by the tsunami. Rather, it had served as a storage area for rotting bodies awaiting mass burial. Such a disturbing image seemed impossible as we crossed an idyllic green stream, which looked best when not inspected closely enough to see the floating garbage.

Turning a corner, we arrived at a busy intersection of food stalls and fruit stands. I read the word "Martabak" written across a pane of glass. There, we ate the thickest pancakes I had ever seen: about nine inches in diameter and so fat that the batter had to be poured into a metal mold to cook. They bubbled up to an inch in height on a smooth flat metal grill. I videotaped as condensed milk and chocolate pieces were poured onto mine and durian squished all over Bustami's. These deep-dish pizzas of the pancake world were then folded in half like sandwiches, cut in pieces, and wrapped in leaves.

On another occasion, everyone from FBA piled into cars and onto motorbikes to attend a party. Aznawy stopped at the house where he was renting a room to pick up a huge bowl of raw fish, each several inches long and recently pulled from the water. As usual, I had no idea what to expect. We waited in the parking lot of a large orange-colored hotel where an oversized eagle sculpture loomed over the front entrance. The place, surrounded by devastation, looked fresh and unscathed, another example of what people often called "the will of Allah." It meant that those who had done especially good deeds in their lives were spared, and their homes and businesses remained standing.

Discussions ensued about whether to have the party in this parking lot or elsewhere. Finally, we went to a nearby house, also one of the rare unscathed structures, and laid down mats in the driveway. Aznawy and several other guys from FBA built a huge bonfire on the driveway and set about cooking the fish in metal basket-like contraptions. We all shared the duties of chopping peppers and onions, mixing them with soy sauce and spices to dip the fish in.

It seemed a good time to hear some scary stories, so a couple of guys told me about a sort of Acehnese magic passed down through the great-grandfathers. Highly spiritually evolved individuals were able to time travel, make themselves invisible, and send their souls out of their bodies to visit other lands. One man commented, "The Indonesian military is afraid of that magic."

I was scheduled to teach a belly-dance workshop in Jakarta, Indonesia's capital, which was four hours away by airplane. My friend Devi, an Indonesian belly dancer and social worker who lives in Hong Kong, planned to fly in and meet me at the airport in Jakarta.

Jakarta's Sukarno-Hatta International airport looked provincial and poor with no escalators and dirty, unkempt bathrooms. On the island of Java, Jakarta is the largest city in Indonesia. With a metropolitan area containing over twenty-three million people, it's one of the world's most densely populated cities.

There were no chairs in the airport waiting area so I donned my Walkman headphones and sat on my suitcase waiting for Devi to arrive. When I looked up, a man was watching me, talking intently. Upon removing one ear of my headphones I realized that he was espousing the virtues of Islam. This was surprising because Jakarta, although it is predominately Muslim, is not nearly as strict as Aceh. He was baffled when he asked my religion, and I said, "Unidentified." In Indonesia, you have to register as one of four legal religions: Muslim (90 percent), Christian, Hindu, or Buddhist. Many people in remote areas are Animist, but they must claim to be one of the above four.

How ironic that the conservative, very Islamic people in Banda Aceh didn't proselytize, accepting different ways of thought, but this man, who looked quite Westernized and lived in the big city, insisted that Islam was the only way.

Devi and her family are Muslim, but not all of them cover their heads. Her mom hired a driver to pick us up and then showed me around town. She said that the wide boulevards were normally traffic-choked by day. They looked lavish and sparkly by night. Her home was a pretty two-story gated structure with a small cell-phone business on the first floor. The streets of this middle-class area were like tiny alleys and quite atmospheric.

Around the corner from Devi's house was a dingy satay joint. The food was great though, and it was one of those places full of childhood memories that she had to visit immediately upon arrival. We munched on satay, rice balls, and dried tofu.

The next day, we did fabric shopping at Tanahabang, a crowded textile market full of batiks and lace fabrics. It was hot and claustrophobic, with no ventilation. People carrying trays of drinks or huge bundles of merchandise constantly bumped into us. Aisles were wide enough for one, but had to accommodate two or three. Outside, we bought jack fruit, cakes, and sticky fermented black rice from street vendors and ended up bogged down with bags of food and fabric and ready to go home.

On the streets, Jakarta offered many different types of transport, none of them speedy or efficient. Anyone who could afford it hired a driver. Although they were planning to build an elevated sky train, when I visited neither a subway nor any efficient form of mass transportation was evident. People got around on motorbikes for hire, like independent taxis that you jumped on the back of, or tiny homemade-looking trucks called *badjas*. They appeared to be soldered together, then finished off with a lumpy coat of paint, and they puffed out pollution at an alarming rate. They had protruding round lights, giving the odd little vehicles the cartoonesque appearance of bugs with eyes. There were a few taxis and some buses, which people said were a good place to get your pocket picked.

Wide boulevards accommodated this chaos of humanity. We took a tiny *bemo*, which are little vans that hold ten passengers on two benches. People hunch over because the roofs are so low. We barely fit and couldn't see anything but the floor and each other.

The Nikko Hotel was grandiose and luxurious, with sumptuous decor. It surprised me because I'd been roughing it for so long. I'd been getting accustomed to bathing with a pitcher and slapping mosquitoes all night, shedding layers of my comfort zone.

A pretty Chinese woman named Christine arrived, took one look at Devi and me, and said, "You must be belly dancers. I can tell from your hips." Dressed in a black business suit, she was Jakarta's belly-dance pioneer. It was her goal to set straight any negative misperceptions people might have about our dance.

My workshop was in a spacious ballroom, hidden behind a storefront tailor shop in the Chinese district. Oddly, not one student was Indonesian. They were Chinese or European: career women who were just as comfortable wearing business suits to high-powered meetings as they were in a dance studio, baring their stomachs and wearing jingly scarves. "It's a question of economics," Christine explained. "Indonesia is a poor country and most people can't afford the luxury of taking dance workshops."

Before coming to Indonesia, Devi had Googled "Arabic music and belly dancing in Jakarta," and up popped a disco called De Leila, which reportedly had both.

De Leila was a beautiful club with Arabic decorations and a live band, all Indonesian, playing Arabic hit songs. There weren't many women in the crowd, but nobody bothered us, and the music was good. After the band, a DJ played Saudi Arabian and Kuwaiti songs, and the place filled up with prostitutes wearing skimpy, South Beach–style outfits. The woman at the door informed us that it was "Ladies Night." Prostitutes far outnumbered the Arabic men, and both sexes seemed to ignore each other as they danced in separate groups. Later, the music changed to hip-hop, and three go-go girls in bikinis did writhing American MTV imitations. "Could those be the 'belly dancers'?" we wondered.

In the morning, we visited Mesjid Istiqlal, the largest mosque in Southeast Asia. The government had built this modern mosque in 1984. It had chrome pillars and space for 120,000 people to pray at once. Combined with surrounding areas, it could accommodate 250,000 worshipers. As an attendant gave us a tour, we passed hundreds of people sleeping in the mosque with their laundry hanging in the stairwells.

We visited a modern shopping mall where a guy yelled promotional slogans into a megaphone as we passed his display of Ramadhan foods. Traditionally, breaking fast meant eating a handful of dates, but some well-off Indonesians modernize that to mean "anything sweet will do." In malls and parking lots throughout the city, there were "Ramadhan Special" displays of Oreo cookies and other American-brand junk foods.

Her fluffy little white dog named Naughty greeted us as Christine led me up the marble staircase in the center of the mansion where I was to live for a few days. It was a treat, and a contrast to the Indonesia I had experienced so far.

Christine had been sent to live in Australia at the time of the anti-Chinese riots, from 1997 to 1998, and she explained how the Chinese, who made up only three percent of the population, became scapegoats for the country's economic woes. Although they comprise much of the wealthy business-class, most are small-scale traders or regular workers.

In 1997, Indonesia's currency, the *rupiah*, was devalued by 600 percent, and wages didn't rise accordingly. Many people struggled in abject poverty. Riots erupted across Indonesia. The chief targets were the shops and stores owned by ethnic Chinese, who had lived in the country for generations but were being blamed for the rampant inflation.

Indonesian-Chinese relations have historically been tense. In 1967, President Suharto's regime mapped out policies for the "solution" to the Chinese "problem." They closed Chinese newspapers and schools, outlawed Chinese writing in public places, and urged those of Chinese heritage to take Indonesian names and to limit any religious practices to the privacy of their homes. Some of these policies are still in effect. Despite the fact that their families may have lived in Indonesia for several generations, Chinese Indonesians don't have the same rights as others. They must carry special identity cards and are prohibited from entering certain careers or holding some government positions.

Discussing the strife of the late 90s, Christine said, "Rioting was at its worst in Medan. Tensions were so high that many Chinese families still won't buy a home without two doors: an entrance in the front and an escape exit in the back."

There was plenty of concerning unrest while I was in Jakarta. The government lifted gasoline subsidies overnight, causing prices to more than double. That affected the entire economy, because all goods and services became more expensive, and this wasn't compensated for with salary raises.

It created a special hardship for freelancers in the transportation industry. The meager profits of bemo and badja drivers, as well as taxis and motorcycles for hire, would be eaten up by these price increases. Thousands of people clogged the city streets, demonstrating and protesting.

One night at dinner, an Italian belly-dance student that I was eating with received a text message from abroad. Three suicide bombers had blown themselves up in the main tourist area of Bali, killing twenty-three people. After that, all hotels, public buildings, and embassies in Jakarta were on alert for terrorists and bombings. The U.S. government put out a travel advisory for Americans to stay away from Indonesia, warning that it was highly volatile and unsafe. Luckily, I didn't know about that warning until weeks later, when I was already leaving the country.

After I'd spent a few days in Jakarta, Arief called and said, "Meet me at the train station. We'll go to Cirebon and visit my family." Did he know I'd slipped into the lap of luxury and been derailed from my mission to learn about the realities of life in the Islamic world? He was flying halfway across Indonesia, so after a nice dinner among dancers, with wine and chocolate cake for dessert, I bid goodbye to Jakarta's burgeoning belly-dance world.

I later crossed the city, taking an extensive detour to avoid blocked streets full of demonstrating transportation workers.

Outside of Indonesia, nobody talks about Cirebon. Arief was from there and felt proud of its many historical sites. These sites had been involved in the spread of Islam on the island of Java. He said, "Java was Hindu and Buddhist until the 1500s. Sunan Gunung Jati (one of the *Wali Songo* or 'Nine Saints of Islam,' the men who introduced and spread Islam through Java) converted one-third of the island to Islam and founded the independent state of Cirebon." That was my history lesson for the day. There were many more to come.

I realized how lucky I was to meet Arief; he had taken a sincere interest in this book and was committed to helping me gain an insider's view of his culture. He took time off work to travel with me and trusted me, a virtual stranger, enough to introduce me to his family.

After we got off the train in Cirebon, rows of colorfully painted bicycle rickshaws waited outside the station. They looked like huge, backward, old-fashioned tricycles: the two wheels and a metal seat, not quite big enough for two, were in front; the driver pedaled from his high seat with a huge wheel behind. We arranged for two—one for us and the other for our bags.

Arief's parent's house was spacious. The huge living room was carpeted in the center, Arabic-style, and had bean-bag chairs strewn about. A giant, old-fashioned grandfather clock cuckooed periodically in the corner. Bathrooms were the usual: squat to pee, and bathe with pails of cool water. Dining was done outside in a garden. His brother, very pregnant sister-in-law, and their five-year-old son shared the home. There were several bedrooms, some off the living room, others looking onto the garden. We entered the home through a room full of sequin-and-lace jackets and batik sarongs.

His mother was a wedding planner, which included renting costumes to the bride and groom. Cirebon is on the border between two cultures, Javanese and Sundanese, and has its own, called Cirebonese, so she offered wedding attire in three traditional styles. In addition, she provided gold-painted backdrops; did bridal makeup; and hired photographers, videographers, and entertainment. While sewing jasmine flowers together to make elaborate shawls for the bride and groom, she popped in a video of one of the weddings she had organized, which was for Arief's twenty-six-year-old cousin.

The young woman in the video looked beautiful in gold and white brocade fabrics, but her impeccable makeup was put to test when she cried throughout her own ceremony. I asked if this was common, and Arief said, "Most of the time they marry for love but have lived at home all their lives. And when the bride must leave her parents house and move in with his family, her tears are both happy and sad."

☾ ☆ ٭ ٭ ٭ ٭

Ramadhan began the day after we arrived. Lasting a month and taking place once a year, it begins according to the Islamic (lunar) calendar, which recedes about eleven days per solar year. This makes Ramadhan rotate through the four seasons.

Although non-Muslims are not expected to fast, I planned to, out of respect. Arief's mother kept telling me, "You will be hungry." She told me, "My husband is exempt from fasting because of health problems, and my daughter-in-law because of pregnancy, so you won't be eating alone." I wanted to fast anyway, and Arief thought it was a good idea because I would understand more about Islamic life. He explained, "Fasting makes one appreciate food and drink that is usually taken for granted."

He went on to say, "During Ramadhan, one is also expected to give more to charity, thus the quantity of beggars on the street is greatly increased. You should do as many good things as possible for other people and realize when you have hurt others and apologize to them. Life should begin anew by the time Ramadhan is finished."

During Ramadhan, you cannot eat or drink any liquids during daylight hours. The *muezzins* (who call for prayer from mosques) sing to inform people when to eat and when to stop eating and pray. The worst part about fasting was not drinking water. It was really hot and humid, and I had not drunk water during the night or eaten any breakfast. My thirst became too intense, and I felt like I might pass out, so I cheated on that first day and drank a bottle of water.

The local mosque was not near the house, so the singing was not loud enough to wake me up. I asked Arief to knock on my door and wake me for breakfast at 3:30 AM. I heard people talking at 1 AM, and then I awoke in the daylight, at 8 AM. "Maybe they just didn't take my desire to fast seriously," I thought, but Arief knocked on my door and told me his sister-in-law's baby was born at 3 AM. They had just gotten back from the hospital.

When we went to visit, the hospital was bright and cheerful, but I felt concerned when I saw the tiny new mom laying there, hooked up to a bottle of blood. She was too petite to have the baby naturally and had to have a cesarean. The hospital bed was just a narrow raised cot with a thin mattress. There were no machines in the room to monitor anything. She looked so frail.

☪ ⭐ ⁎ ⸰ ⁎ ⸰

We visited the sites that Arief had told me were significant to the spread of Islam in Java. The Grand Mosque, built in the 1500s, was Java's oldest mosque. Its many pillars were made of wood carved in a distinctly

Indonesian style. Being a non-Muslim, I was not allowed into the old-est part, but we explored the outer rooms. This historical mosque is said to be magical, and people travel from afar to pray there.

I saw a lot more sleeping than praying going on, though. There were people sacked out all over the place, which is common in mosques. You see people praying and sleeping and children playing all at once.

Later that night, special prayers were held for the first night of Ramadhan. The mosque was crowded with hundreds of worshipers. Women wore white head- and body-coverings. These are special over garments for praying that look sort of like big capes. Usually, women pray behind the men so as not to distract them from their worship. In this instance, they prayed in a completely separate area. It was spec-tacular to see hundreds of women dressed alike, moving in unison—standing, kneeling, sitting, and standing again—like a huge choreo-graphed dance.

Near the mosque, we entered a driveway that had a scraggly herd of sheep in the front yard. They belonged to the sultan. This *kraton* (palace) was his home. Called Kraton Kesepuhan, it was eclectic with blue windmills etched into Dutch tiles on the walls. A throne with nine colorful curtains behind it represented the *Wali Songo,* or nine saints, who had been responsible for the introduction and spread of Islam throughout Java. There was a colorful chariot belonging to a sultan from the 1700s. Its unique gold-leafed design had wings (for Islam), a dragon (for Buddhism), and an elephant (for Hinduism), representing the religions of all the king's subjects.

We went to the royal graveyard, a place where both Muslims and Chinese Buddhists prayed. One of the first king's wives was from China, and she was buried in the graveyard. Arief's mother knelt to pray to the spirit of Sunan Gunung Jati, one of the renowned Walis. I thought Muslims could only pray to Allah, but she explained, "There are three types of existence: Being alive, which doesn't last for long in the grand scheme of things. Then, there is paradise, which happens once the world ends. People are chosen to go there based on how good they were in their lives. The other dimension is that of being dead, and waiting for the end of the world, when paradise will open up. It is during this time that you can pray to the great people as a go-between from you to God."

After returning home, it was finally time to break the fast. Arief told me, "We break the fast with dates, as they did in Mohammed's time." His mother brought out a crystal bowl full of dates imported from Saudi Arabia. After Arief prayed, we went downtown to eat a Cirebonese specialty called *nasi jamblan*. A lady stood behind a big table surrounded by plastic stools right in the middle of the sidewalk. It was piled high with plates. We could choose whatever we wanted from the *tempeh* (fried fermented soybean cake), potatoes on skewers, tofu, and the fish that had been cured in so much salt that it had become hard and tasted like a salt flat. There were about thirty dishes in all. The feast began with a leaf, which was topped by a dollop of rice, and then all the goodies were put on top.

The next day at 3:45 AM, it hardly seemed like a time to be eating breakfast, but at least I woke up. We ate eggs, rice, and sambal, then went back to sleep.

Later in the day, we went to what Arief translated as "the cave," which was an odd fortress. Made of lumpy stones, it had been built so that the royal family could relax around an artificial lake. The building was now in ruins, the water gone and the grass brown. Graffiti and litter added to the forlorn appearance but it was interesting nonetheless.

The guide told a story of how the Dutch government wanted to kill a king: "This king and another holy man fasted and meditated for forty days and forty nights, which put them in a highly elevated spiritual state. The Dutch thought they had them cornered in a small room. Instead, the men meditated until they disappeared, body and all. One went to China, and the other to Mecca."

I later asked an Islamic scholar about the significance of forty days, and he explained, "Forty days and forty nights is from the Old Testament, in which Moses spoke with God for that length of time." He also said: "There are some mixtures with Hinduism and Buddhism in Java. Some of the mysticism comes from that. There are sacred numbers in Islam, including 7 (seven heavens), and 40 is another special number. They say that there are forty prayers in Medina (the city in Saudi Arabia where Mohammed escaped to and where Islam was able to flourish in the early days). If one can do the forty prayers in a row, uninterrupted, five times a day for eight days, he will be free of hypocrisy. Five is also special in Islam, as people are expected to pray five times a day." (40 is also important in Judaism and Christianity.)

One of Arief's mom's side-businesses was buying batiks from a local village and selling them in Jakarta at a profit. We went to Trusmi, a village outside of town, where most families make batiks as a home industry. At a home, four men laid white fabric on a table about fifty-feet long. They smoothed out the fabric, then took four-foot-square frames that had a print, and stamped dye onto sections of fabric. They took another square, and stamped another color and pattern over the first. It was quick, and within minutes they had finished a long piece of fabric and hung it on a line to dry. Stamping, I learned, is the quick and inexpensive way to make batiks.

Behind one woman's home, several ladies sat in the yard painting wax onto fabric. This painting method is more difficult and valuable than stamping. One lady sat by the side in a trance-like state. Suddenly, she motioned for me to kneel then started whisking the spirits and negative energy away from me with her hands. It was a mini-exorcism, and I felt surprisingly relaxed afterward. I asked Arief what this was about, and he laughed, "She's not well, but you'd better go along with it, just in case." I'd had a headache from fasting, but after the cleansing, it went away and I felt refreshed.

In the village, I bought some amazing batiks made of banana-bark-fiber fabric, pineapple fabric, and silk. They were elaborately batiked by hand with tiny, minute details.

Early one morning, we were picked up by a van (which served as collective public transportation) to take us to Bandung, the city where Arief had gone to college. Passing terraced rice fields, pretty villages, and lush greenery, my mind wanted to watch, but my body needed to sleep. Driving conditions didn't allow either. As I sat in the front seat, two lanes of curvaceous road became four. Our speeding driver dodged buses as they changed lanes, facing us head-on. Meanwhile, motorbikes scooted between both kinds of large vehicles, and pedestrians jumped out of the way with only seconds to spare. Our driver loved to tailgate, pass on curves, and dart between cars that appeared too close together to fit us. At one point, he suddenly stepped on the brakes and Arief's five-year-old nephew, Ibrahim, flew into the front seat between me and the driver. I unconsciously moved my shoulder to the right (drivers in Indonesia sit on the right, passengers on the left) just in time to serve as a wedge between the little boy and the window. I told Arief's family that this driver was out of control. They seemed puzzled and said, "He is a calm driver, because he is Cirebonese. The crazy ones are in Sumatra."

We arrived in Bandung unscathed. More affluent than anyplace I'd seen so far, Bandung used to be an exclusive European-style resort, where rich plantation owners came for weekends. Arief explained: "Bandung is a popular place for people living in Jakarta to come and relax. The weather is cooler than in other parts of Indonesia, and there are many tea plantations and volcanoes outside of town."

Bandung is referred to as the "Boston of Indonesia" because it has so many colleges and universities. One of the universities we visited had a beautiful campus of traditional Javanese buildings and lush gardens. We passed well-preserved Art Deco and Dutch-colonial buildings, plus a neighborhood full of Beverly Hills–style mansions.

I stayed in a beautiful guesthouse owned by Arief's friend Sri. Arief and Sri, a woman in her forties, used to work together but hadn't seen each other in ten years. She had great taste in clothing, sporting a white headscarf, finely tailored tunic with delicate lace trimming, and matching pants beneath. The house had belonged to her parents before they died, and Sri lived elsewhere. Her eldest son, Cesar, was a professional chef and managed the guesthouse.

Cesar and I got on well, and he told me about his spiritual master. The seventy-year-old mystic had noticed that Cesar had a special sensitivity and the ability to communicate with the other side. They would meet every fortnight to meditate, pray, and communicate with ancestors. In the West, we call this channeling.

I had thought genies were the inventions of children's storytellers and Hollywood producers, but Cesar said, "No." Genies (called *djinns*) are real to millions of people. Cesar said, "Djinns are born of fire and live in another dimension, so we cannot see them. They have the ability to take on different forms. Like people, they can be good or bad, and commonly appear as a black dog or a snake. Djinns have their own language too." He then went into a trance and demonstrated this language to me. It sounded like Arabic but was unintelligible.

Arief and Sri came over, and we broke the fast with green cassava pieces, which resembled gummy worms, in a brown-sugar soup. They were delicious followed by rice and fish soup. Now, I understood why Indonesians think nothing of having dessert before a meal. For the month of Ramadhan, they eat sweets to break the fast and then dinner, so maybe it doesn't seem strange to do it that way the rest of the year.

After dinner, we went driving to see the nightlife of Bandung. This included a stop in front of a night market. Throughout Asia, night markets open after dark and have stalls selling all sorts of delicious street foods. We sat down on wobbly plastic stools to munch on deep-fried jackfruit, pineapple, and cassava fritters, washed down with hot ginger tea that was thick with brown sugar and had pieces of young coconut floating in the glasses.

We went to a concert of *angklung*. This is a traditional Sundanese instrument made of parallel bamboo tubes, tuned to specific frequencies, which you shake with one hand and tap with the other. Each angklung plays a different note, and if you have eight of them in a group, you can play most any piece of music. This group consisted of children, ages three to fourteen, who also sang and danced. There were at least fifty of them, and their professionalism was amazing.

Many of Indonesia's islands have live volcanoes, so we took a day trip to look at one. Sri drove Arief and me past green, terraced rice fields. The observation point for the arid brown Tangkuban Perahu volcano was on top of a mountain. Part of the live volcano looked like a muddy lake, and other sections had steam seeping out of large crevices. Vendors were abundant, selling everything from pens to fake-fur hats and bags (which they claimed were real rabbit). A man carved trinkets made of "batik wood." The wood comes from a tree that, when sections of the bark are cut, has a batik-like pattern. It seemed like I was the only foreigner they had seen for a long time; all the vendors descended on me at once, thinking I must go to volcanoes to do my shopping.

I tripped along the trails in my fancy shoes with heels and pointed toes. Sri's blue pumps, which were color coordinated with her outfit, weren't much better. We hadn't planned on going hiking, yet hiked for over a mile to a steaming pool. Park employees were boiling eggs in mesh baskets submerged in the pool to show visitors how hot the water was. I sat for awhile with a group of Korean men, dipping our feet in a warm, though not boiling, mineral pool nearby. On the way back, we heard rustling overhead. There was a huge monkey eating from the tree branches.

Sri invited Bambang, a most interesting Islamic lecturer, to the house so that I could ask questions and hear about the religion from a well-read authority. A calm, peaceful man with a wisp of a long grey beard, he explained how the religion has evolved in different ways, incorporating local beliefs and customs. He said, "Java is a long way from the source (Mecca), so there have been modifications."

He continued, "The Qur'an says the world will end, though nobody knows when." He'd read about quantum physics and a parallel universe, and it was his opinion that "Doomsday will only happen on earth. Old interpretations claimed that all living creatures will die, but new revisions say only mankind is doomed. God can create new creatures. We are not that important. It says, 'When the ocean is boiling, mountains exploding, stars falling down, sky turning red, sun rising from the west… when there are forty women per man and no poor people left, those are just a few of the signs that the world is coming to the end.' It may happen in different places, at different times."

He added, "Even if you think the world will end soon, you must still plant seeds and do something positive." According to Mr. Bambang, "Doomsday will come after man's destruction of the land and sea. Destiny will follow our actions, and God follows what we want. There are many different destinies we can choose from."

On another note, he said, "Music is a gift from God. Everything is music: the wind, ocean, birds, and your own heartbeat. Music can bring us closer to God, or give us bad energy. The universe is music and all is rhythm. Man can achieve spirituality with the help of music. The Qur'an is written as poetry and must be read musically."

He mentioned angels, and I asked him to elaborate. He went on to explain that Muslims must believe in six things:

1. God (Allah is the Arabic word for God and is used as such by Arabic-speaking Christians, Jews and Moslems. The exact meaning of the Qur'an is best understood when read in its original Arabic version, so many Muslims of all nationalities use the Arabic word Allah to mean God.)

2. Mohammed as his prophet (In a later correspondence with Mr. Bambang, he explained the use of PBUH after the Prophet Mohammed's name. {We are recommended to spell Muhammad Shallallhu Alayhi Was-salam. In short: Muhammad SAW. It means Peace Be Upon Him, or PBUH. It is an act of love and respect from us to him. We do believe that whoever spells those words will be rewarded with an equal love from the prophet. I suggest you add those few letters after his name."

3. Angels

4. The holy books (Qur'an and Bibles)

5. Doomsday

6. Destiny

"Angels are God's creations and must obey God. Man can choose to obey or betray." He said, "We each have two guardian angels with us. One takes note of your good deeds while the other writes down your bad ones. Angels can take any form, but often they have between two and six wings. They can appear as a common man as well. The last ten days of Ramadhan are called *Layla Tur Kadar*, or 'Nights of Destiny.' This is when angels may come down, especially on the twenty-seventh day."

Hari Raya is the Indonesian name for the celebration of the end of Ramadhan. It is called *Id al-Fitr* in Arabic. He said that after the month of fasting "You should be purified like a newborn baby. Everyone goes to the mosque to pray. They wear new clothes and make lots of food to serve to guests. Before people are allowed to celebrate, they must have given food and/or money to the poor."

He explained that *Id al-Atta* is another celebration, for the end of the Hadj season, which is when people make the pilgrimage to Mecca, Saudi Arabia. Mecca is where Mohammed PBUH was born and also where Islam began. He said, "During Id al-Atta, you must kill a lamb and give it to the poor to eat. Many actions required by Islam are dedicated to helping the poor."

Mr. Bambang had been to Mecca twenty times and was preparing to go again. Usually, people go to Mecca once. The Qur'an says that everyone who can afford it must go to Mecca once in their lives. Mr. Bambang leads groups of pilgrims from Indonesia to Mecca. "About three million people go to the Hadj every year." He commented, "The city of Mecca used to be magical because you could feel the holy place like in Mohammed PBUH's time. Now, tall buildings and luxury hotels have sprung up all around the holy area. It is commercial, modern, and built up."

He explained, "The ritual of Hadj lasts for five days. Starting on the ninth day, there is another ritual in which they throw out Satan three times, return to Mecca, then throw out Satan three times again. During this ritual, pilgrims live in tents so they can feel how the prophet lived."

Regarding women's need to cover, he said: "The Qur'an can be used as a guide, but in Mohammed PBUH's day, there were enemies and hostilities everywhere, so women had to wear clothes to protect themselves. They were to cover all but the face and hands, the same as nuns in Catholicism. This may come from the same source. Also, they were asked to dress distinctively from the rest of the population to be identifiably different from non-Muslims. In modern times, if we feel that this dress is needed, we should do it. Parents can feel safer for their children and it can prevent some dangerous situations. If there is no threat, the dress code need not be so strict."

About women praying behind the men in the Mosque, or behind a screen or even outside, he had this to say, "Men must concentrate on praying, and a woman's beauty might distract them. At the end of prayer, when they say 'Asalam Aleikum' to the person on their left and on their right, they should only see men. There is no segregation in daily life though."

About men having multiple wives, he explained, "If you are not able to be fair, just take one, which is the norm. Some conditions can cause a man to take more. That is an exception. When Mohammed was older, he took more wives, but they were widows with children."

Mr. Bambang adheres to the Javanese style of Islam. He said, "The religion has traveled far from its source, through jungles, and been adopted by many cultures. It came to Java and has intermingled with local beliefs."

"You can get supernatural powers by fasting and remembering God. Doing this takes great discipline and faith because you must leave everything to God, and have no food or drink. Don't think of anything but God. Of course, most people will not do that, and it is not expected. That's why we don't have those supernatural powers."

I asked about Mohammed PBUH's views on different animals. Bambang said: "Since Mohammed PBUH didn't read or write, he had many scribes to record all of his sayings, actions, and daily life. He was close friends with one of his scribes who loved cats so much that they followed him all around the Medina. Mohammed PBUH loved animals and had nothing against pigs, but there was a practical reason why it was forbidden to eat their meat." (I understood this to be diseases, like trichinosis.) "About dogs, he said not to allow them to lick you. If they do, you have to clean off the saliva in a special way." (I'd heard that involved cleaning with soil seven times.)

Lastly, he added, "A good Muslim must stay disciplined within the religion. You must understand the reasons why you are following rules and why they were implemented. Some rules always stay the same, but those that change are called *fatwas*. Meetings are held periodically to discuss updating the fatwas."

Later, I asked Bambang about the subject of djinns. He said, "Islam allows for their existence," and told me several stories he had heard. One involved a woman whose husband disappeared into the dimension of djinns while on a visit to Saudi Arabia, and in another, a djinn moved someone's shoes while they prayed. He explained, "Some people can have a djinn at their command." He said his wife had inherited "Uncle Abdul Karim" from her grandfather, adding, "On one of our trips to Mecca, I left a pair of shoes in Indonesia and Uncle Karim delivered them."

Several days later, I received my first of many letters from Bambang:

Dear Tamalyn,

Today I happened to open up your website, and I am surprised, what a low-keyed brilliant figure I met last Sunday. I didn't know that you had a vast traveling experience and encounters with so many prominent personalities. You've talked with royal families, celebrities, and ordinary people all over the world. Yet you act so humble that anyone you are talking with feels free to tell his or her story. Maybe if I had read your biography before we met, I would have acted a bit cautious and not so spontaneously. Anyway I appreciate you very much. The way you behave will guarantee your success in finishing your book. Insha Allah. And I believe our meeting is not a mere coincidence. It is a meaningful coincidence. I think Allah, the Almighty God, has decided to choose you for an important and beautiful mission. He wants you to guide the American people toward a better understanding about Islam. Your new book will be an unimaginable thing... A book that helps straighten out the American prejudice on Islam, written by a professional belly dancer. Bravo. Do not hesitate to ask me anything about Islam, local Javanese beliefs, or whatever else you need to know for your book. I am available. For your information, I am now the Chairman of West Java Mosque Preacher Council, but decades ago I was a ballet dancer, traditional musical instrument player, and a drummer. May Allah guide you to success.

Yours,
Bambang Pranggono
Bandung

Getting the letter, I was humbled and thrilled!

Arief was headed back to Batam, and I wanted to return to Banda Aceh. Azwar, the founder of FBA, was coming back and I hoped to meet him. Arief said I should visit other parts of Indonesia instead. He suggested Padang, the capital and largest city in the province of West Sumatra. Sumatra is an island with several provinces, including North Sumatra (where Medan is situated), Aceh, and West Sumatra.

After making a few calls, Arief gave me the address for his cousin's friend Ririn and instructions on how to take a taxi directly to her home. On the map it looked like Padang was on the way to Banda Aceh, so it sounded good to me.

I flew to Padang and a taxi took me through lush fields, past greenery and mountains, to the town of Teluk Bayur. I had an address written on a torn sheet of paper, which I thought would be in Padang proper. My unimpressive driver tried his best attempts at flirting with me in Indonesian. All I understood was that he wanted to be my special friend so we could go to America together. I'm good at nonverbal communication when I want to be, but preferred pretending to fall asleep, with one eye open just in case we took a wrong turn. As we entered a land of industrial buildings, muddy streets, and squat cement houses, and then mud and more mud, I realized this was way out in the boondocks.

Ririn was the cousin of a friend of Arief's from many years back. She had no idea who he was, who I was, or why I'd come to Teluk Bayur, but her entire family was waiting and happy to see me. Ririn, a tiny, slender twenty-three-year-old college student, didn't cover her head and was wearing a short-sleeved blouse. I asked her about this and she said that, in her opinion, "You have to earn the right to wear a headscarf and be covered. If one has the discipline to follow the rules, it is not hypocritical to wear a headscarf, but I don't always listen to my parents, so I'm not ready to dress Islamic."

The people of West Sumatra are of an ethnic group called Minangkabau. The Minangkabau are the largest surviving matrilineal society in the world. Their culture is unique because property is traditionally passed down through the women of the family from mother to daughter. They are strongly Islamic but also follow their ethnic traditions, which are called *adat*. The Minangkabau adat was derived from animistic and Hindu beliefs before the arrival of Islam.

I was a bit confused by the complexity of their culture, so Ririn and her father brought me to meet professor Dr. H. Salmadinis of the Islamic University. He explained, "There are two types of inheritances: 'high heritage,' which are big, traditional homes and land that has been passed down through the family, and 'low heritage,' meaning ordinary houses and land that has been purchased. High heritage is passed down through women, and low heritage through the men. There are two systems. The matrilineal is pre-Islamic. The patrilineal came about when the area was converted to Islam. Both systems are in place simultaneously. People are comfortable with that and don't see them at odds."

He said: "Traditionally, a woman's land cannot be sold without permission from her uncle. The uncle plays an important role in a woman's life. If her aunt dies and her uncle becomes a widower, he must move into a small mosque called *suran*, and the niece must cook for him and wash his clothes. Nieces have more responsibility to take care of a man when he is old than a daughter does.

"If a man divorces, he still has sisters to take care of him. The wife cares for her uncle who may find her a new husband. Children go to the father or the mother's uncle. If the father is poor, the uncle provides a home, and the father provides food and daily needs until the child is old enough to earn his own money. If both the uncle and father are poor, the child must depend on the charity of the rich, *zakat*, an obligation in Islam, which stresses helping poor people and orphans.

"In town meetings, where the major decisions are made, the people who have the right to speak up are: Islamic teachers, intellectual leaders, uncles, and women. All have equal rights in the decision making process."

Many people urged me not to miss visiting Bukittinggi, a small town near Padang whose name means "high hill." Ririn and her eighteen-year-old brother borrowed their father's weathered SUV to take me. We first wandered Padang's market, looking hungrily at the produce and jellies. Food was abundant during Ramadhan, but nobody ate until the appointed hour. I liked the horse and buggy transports, which had the horses decorated with huge red pom-poms. After that, we rode two hours through lush green mountains and steep rice terraces, past traditional houses, to Bukittinggi.

Traditional Minangkabau architecture features large, multigenerational houses called *rumah gadang* (big house) with massive roofs that curve upward from the middle, ending in points, representing the horns of a water buffalo. Made of cedar, entire houses are intricately hand carved and painted.

Ririn and her brother left me in Bukittinggi and rushed to get back home. She said, "My brother doesn't have a driver's license, so we have to be home by dark."

On the street, a man made fresh sugarcane juice, which looked tempting after a whole day without eating or drinking. Nobody was buying. He just kept filling little plastic bags and inserting straws into the tightly rubber-banded tops. I wandered around until 6 PM, waiting for a signal to break the fast. While I'd been in Cirebon, it had been broken at 5:50. By 6, I bought the juice then headed to the plaza. Many people sat around, and no one was eating or drinking. Minutes ticked by until 6:10, when I decided that I'd definitely missed the call and that these people must have already broken their fast. I sat on a bench and drank up.

Suddenly, a siren wailed. It sounded like an air raid! People went running, and I wondered what kind of emergency was taking place. They ran to kiosks to get something to drink. I had beaten the bell.

I learned that the way they decide when to break fast in the evening and to stop eating in the morning is very delicate and involves relating the sun's position to the moon. It is variable and changes according to what part of the country you are in. While I was there, Bukittinggi broke fast at 6:13 PM.

Morning was ushered in with a 4 AM call to have breakfast, followed by a call to prayer that lasted over an hour. There were endless Islamic teachings blasted over a scratchy microphone until 7 AM. It sounded like a dramatic radio soap opera, with different characters' voices, both male and female. I wondered when people slept, because I certainly didn't.

I thought I could purchase a plane ticket from Padang to Banda Aceh in a travel agency in Bukittinggi. There was little computerization and even less communication with other cities, so it was impossible. I asked the agent, "What do you do?"

The man replied, "We give tours."

"Strange," I thought, "there aren't any tourists." He agreed that it was slim pickings for a guide, especially after the Bali bombings. Bukittinggi was hours from Bali by plane and one of the most benign places I could imagine. He asked, "Would you like to take a tour?"

When he pointed to his motorbike, I said, "Sure!"

Riding sidesaddle, I held my skirt with one hand and videotaped gorgeous scenery with the other. Water buffalo pulled plows that hadn't changed design for hundreds of years. There were monkeys eating from a garbage bin. Entire villages had pools of water, instead of lawns of grass, for yards. I asked about the pools, in which schools of fish swam about. He said, "Bathrooms."

"People bathe in them?" I asked.

"No," he said, "they go to the bathroom. Fish eat everything, so the water stays clean."

We passed valleys, canyons, and terraced plantations of rice, chilies, spices, vegetables, and fruits. An old couple made brown sugar. Their tired water buffalo walked in circles, fueling a contraption that squeezed juice from fresh sugarcane into a pan. This juice cooked for hours over a fire, becoming a thick brown paste. It was allowed to cool then molded into patties and sold.

He showed me a cedar rumah gadang up close and explained: "The design, shape, and size of a house tells the social standing of the family. Only people who can trace their ancestry to the original settlers are supposed to inhabit these homes, which are considered 'high heritage,' and are passed down through the women.

"When a boy becomes a man he cannot live in the house with the women. He must live in the mosque and sleep on the floor until he gets married. Around the age of seven, boys traditionally leave their homes to live in a *surau* (prayer house and community center) where they learn religious and cultural (adat) teachings. Teenagers are encouraged to leave their hometown and learn from life's experiences, then return home as adults who are wise and useful to society. They can contribute their life experience and knowledge to running a family or as members of the hometown's 'Council of Uncles.'

"In the traditional way, married daughters remain in their mother's home. Married sons are relegated to the role of 'visiting husband.' He spends the night at his wife's house and comes back to his mother's home at dawn in time to help with farming."

Other than the fact that it poured down rain most of the time, causing me to spend a lot of time sewing in my hotel room, Bukittinggi was fascinating. I had promised Ririn that I would be back in a couple of days, and she grew worried when my bus back to Padang simply didn't show up. It was a minivan, and although I had scheduled an appointment, other people wanted to go at different times, so I had to wait until it was convenient for everyone. She called my cell phone eleven times during the two-hour trip back, to make sure I had broken fast, to know if I was hungry, and to ask if the driver was safe or if anyone bothered me.

The only problem was the traffic getting through Padang. It was stormy and the cars sloshed through the water at a sluggish pace. She gave the driver instructions to a restaurant where her entire extended family was waiting for me to eat. They had already eaten dinner and all eleven people sat and watched me eat, commenting and asking questions about America, my travels, and my impressions of Indonesia. I was definitely a rare bird in this neck of the woods.

The next morning, I was off to Banda Aceh again. Although Padang was on the same island of Sumatra as Aceh, getting from one to the other entailed almost two days of travel and included an overnight stay in Medan.

There was a lot for me to do in Banda Aceh this time. I wanted to know more about Rafly and looked forward to meeting Azwar Hasan. His reputation preceded him as the most energetic, outspoken, honest, and motivated NGO person in town. When we met, he was really easy to be around and welcomed me back to the house.

On my first visit, I'd felt a bit useless at FBA, but now Azwar saw potential in having me there. He wanted me to write "survivor success stories" about people who put their lives back together after losing everything in the tsunami. While he was trying to connect me with people in the barracks, I said, "I want to write a success story about you."

Azwar was an effervescent, well-educated man in his early thirties, with salt-and-pepper hair. He had lived through the horror of being surrounded by dead bodies in the tsunami's immediate aftermath.

Originally Acehnise, Azwar had lived in Jakarta until the day after the tsunami, when he rushed home to find his family. What he found was a blacked-out city underwater. No electricity and nowhere to go. The only place with lights was the Governor's office, where the journalists and aid workers who were beginning to pour into Banda Aceh camped out.

He set out on a blind search for his mother and sisters. The Baiturrahman Mosque appeared to be full of sleeping people. He thought, "Maybe some family members sought refuge there." Upon closer inspection, he found that most of the people were dead. Others lay dying, and he was helpless to do anything.

After a few tortuous days, the bodies of his uncle and cousin were found. He learned that his mother and sisters were safe. In all, twelve of his relatives had died or disappeared.

"How can I go back to Jakarta and live a normal life?" he asked himself. Determined to do something, anything, Azwar summoned ten of his friends from Jakarta. Each of them lived with a family of tsunami survivors and learned firsthand what the families needed. Some had food, but no pot to cook it in. One woman had no underclothes. These were simple situations and easy to remedy. Ten more friends came and did the same. They bought what the people lacked and gave it to them.

A donor from Ireland gave $1000, which was used to buy a becak for a man who had lost his livelihood in the tsunami. The recipient waded through the muddy water to his home, which he had constructed himself from debris. He had six dependents, but now with a means of income, he was much better off than his neighbors. He soon returned half the money to Azwar, requesting that he use this to help more people.

Thus, FBA began. At the time of my visit, they had helped restart over two hundred businesses and given aid to about 800 people. With a donation of $150 to $1200, a man or woman could have their own becak or be back in business as a chip farmer, fisherman, street vendor, or kiosk owner. When they gave money back, it went straight into helping the next person.

I looked at the long list of people needing help. There wasn't enough money for everyone, but the idea was to help one person at a time as the money came in, bypassing bureaucracy.

Within a few months, outside charities began to pitch in. A German charity sent funding for FBA to rent a house and set up as a charitable organization. An Irish company donated money for the building of a school in Lampoh Daya, a village on the outskirts of Banda Aceh that had been heavily damaged by the tsunami. (The school opened six weeks after I left.)

The FBA evolved into a multifaceted source of help, with a clean water project, scholarships to buy uniforms and books for orphans and poor children, and an exchange program that sent students to study in Australia.

I went to the computer café to meet Kade. She shared more details about her life this time. Her home village was not affected by the tsunami, but she had been in Banda Aceh when it struck. As the wave carried her, something hit her head, giving her amnesia for several hours. Her parents got a scare, but she recovered completely.

Kade was a beautiful young woman with deep cinnamon-colored skin and expressive black eyes. She had complained of bouts of depression and low self-esteem which I thought had to do with tsunami trauma, but she told me that these problems plagued her long before.

When we hung out together, we usually found something to do because we could eat or drink. This time, during Ramadhan, our options were reduced to nothing. So we took a walk and promised to meet again soon.

I hailed a run-down becak with a skinny driver. We pulled up at the house just as it was time to break the fast. Azwar insisted that the driver come in and eat. He explained, "If you see someone who is unable to break fast, you must give him food."

He brought out rice, fried fish, vegetables, and hot chilies. The foods were wrapped in banana leaves, packaged in brown paper, and tied with a string.

A big American guy was seated at the long table. "Who is this new face?" I wondered. His name was Peter. He was a graduate student, doing his master's thesis on "conflict and coexistence." Having been in Sri Lanka to witness the tsunami's aftermath and study how it impacted their conflict with Tamil rebels, he surmised that it had made the situation worse. In Aceh, he was finding that the tsunami helped resolve the long-standing conflict.

There was no entertainment during Ramadhan, because people

were supposed to concentrate on spirituality and prayer. Azwar decided to teach us his version of Saman. We all knelt on the floor. I and a row of guys, including Peter, sat slapping and clapping while Budi, one of the guys from the house, played "Hotel California" on his guitar.

Each morning, before dawn, Bustami knocked on all the doors in the house. We all got up and stumbled onto motorbikes to head to a restaurant. A self-serve line formed behind the counter for rice, fish, sambal, and some watery curry sauce. The place was set up for those with no families and everyone was male except me.

Azwar sent me out to meet some of the FBA's revolving funds recipients. He was adamant that I say "revolving funds," not "loans," as loaning money with interest is against Islamic principles. He didn't want people confusing his program with any sort of banking.

Aznawy and Musafir accompanied me to a set of "barracks," temporary plywood housing perched precariously on stilts. With no electricity or plumbing, they were built after the tsunami as interim housing. With no other options, people were staying much longer than expected, and some had begun calling the housing "semi-permanent."

Barrack number 13 was surrounded by sunken land and homes flattened into scraps of debris. Much of the land around it was flooded. A few people fished on these sunken, flooded areas. Some built makeshift shacks out of debris and waded through the ankle-deep water to get to their homes. I saw a man walking toward a broken structure in murky water up to his chest. Boats were on land, and houses in the water, but mainly there lay vast expanses of nothing: marshes and endless broken bits of wood.

Sharifa, a direct descendant of the Prophet Mohammed PBUH, lived in a barrack that consisted of twenty small rooms and housed a hundred people. Most of her belongings were in one plastic storage box, with the overflow piled into shopping bags neatly tucked away in one corner of the room. The nearest bathroom was in a mosque, the only structure that remained standing after the water receded. Emblazoned with a big sign reading "Kuwaiti Red Crescent," the mosque served as a place of worship and offered the only bathrooms for miles around.

I was surprised by how beautiful and gracious Sharifa was. Sharifa was thirty-eight years old. She had had four children, one of whom died before the tsunami; the other three died during the tsunami, as did her husband.

When the tsunami came, Sharifa was in the mosque with her three daughters, ages thirteen, nineteen, and twenty-three. The water pulled her away, lifting her high in the air where someone on the roof pulled her from the water.

Her extended family had numbered forty-eight people. All that remained were her brother, a cousin, and herself.

For twenty-three years before the tsunami, Sharifa had been making hand-crafted fishing weights by melting tin and palm oil, then cooking it with kerosene in a pan over a stove. Before the tsunami, she had a factory in a nearby village with twenty employees, including housewives, university students, and orphans. None of her employees survived the tsunami. Both her home and factory were flattened.

Through the FBA, she received three hundred dollars in microeconomic assistance which bought a stove, hammers, pans, tin, and all the other materials needed to start making fishing weights once again. She started alone, selling them in one of the big camps, but in the ensuing months, her business grew to employ thirteen women. They were all housewives who would otherwise have had no way to make a living. This became a booming business, but she still had no home because there were no homes to be had.

Looking out at the mountains surrounding this flattened area, then at the grey waves gently rolling in with the sea, she said, "We remember, we cry, and sometimes we laugh as well." I thought of the strength she must have had to be able to continue living, and how this strength was multiplied by the hundreds of thousands of people whose reality had been washed away. They smiled, showed kindness to one another, and drew strength from the God whose hand they believed created this natural disaster—they lived on.

☾☆ ⁎ ✶ ⁎ ₒ

The last room in the barrack was occupied by Mohammed Yani. A husky man of about thirty-five, he greeted us at the construction site of his new fish-salting factory. Salted fish was one of the favorite foods in Indonesia, and before the tsunami Mohammed's business has employed fourteen people, producing up to 800 kilos of salted fish every two weeks. He had never married and had lived with his parents. There were seven brothers and sisters in his family, of whom only four survived the tsunami. His parents were lost, and ten of his employees disappeared as well.

Immediately after the tsunami, Mohammed had received twenty kilos of rice per month from World Vision, which was redistributing it from the government's social department. Japan also gave rice, which the Indonesian Red Cross distributed. The Indonesian government also gave survivors a lump-sum payment of nine dollars each.

Later, when he had nothing left, he didn't want to ask anyone or any NGO for help. His motto was "If someone offered, I would take it, but I wouldn't ask for handouts." Most people he knew lived by the same principle. Consequently, they often received what they didn't need, and didn't ask for what would have made a difference in their lives.

Mr. Yani got a job as a chauffeur for Mercy Corps and ran into an old customer who said, "I'm happy to see that you are alive." He wanted him to start making salted fish once again, but the smell was too strong for his neighbors in the barracks. With $500 from the FBA, he was able to create an area to keep his fish and start working toward building up the factory again.

Mohammed explained the fish-salting process to me: "First, I clean the raw fish with salt water. Fresh water ruins the texture of fish. Next, the water quantity must be reduced by 80 percent, which is done by putting the fish in a big box with a hole underneath for the liquid to drain out of. Each piece is hung to dry in the fresh air for twenty-four hours then packaged in aluminum foil and wrapped in paper."

Only four of his former employees had survived the tsunami. When I met him, he had six workers and planned to train new employees from among the population left from his village. He said, "I want to experiment with creating new products and build up the production enough to sell salted fish outside of Banda Aceh."

When asked what he wanted to share with the outside world, he said, "I'm skeptical of promises. There are many promises, but people still live in terrible conditions. They need shelter, not promises."

He continued, "I want to prove that life can start again." And added, "A strong belief in God and God's will is what gives the people of Aceh strength. We do not need psychological support because we aren't stressed. It is God who decides who stays and who goes, and we must accept."

Azwar took me to meet another tsunami survivor named Alfi. Alfi started his "One Stop Auto Shop" with FBA funds and wound up employing several guys to do mechanics, wash cars, and reupholster interiors. Like many other tsunami survivors, he and his family lived in a crowded house with several other families. His income was modest, but he said, "I'm happier helping people than being helped." He was helping seven teenage orphans, teaching them skills and giving them food and guidance. He was also proposing a training program that would teach mechanics to orphans.

Alfi's expression became pensive as he talked about Ramadhan. The month of fasting usually culminates in the happy holiday of Id al-Fitr, in which family members unite, forgive each other for any past wrongdoings, and start anew. If a family member has passed on during the year, they go to visit their grave. He said, "This year, there are few family members left, and no graves to visit. Many loved ones are lost, while others are buried in mass graves. What is normally a happy occasion is producing anxiety and sadness for us tsunami survivors."

For another kind of perspective, I wanted to talk with the people at the Aceh Institute. Located in a traditional old home with carved-wood details around every edge, it was created by the first Acehnise student movement as a forum to discuss important issues. Reporters, researchers, and the like visit the institute to find out their take on local issues. I met with a spokesperson named Aguswandi, who had lived in London for the previous five years.

He said, "Many activists have been living abroad because of the danger of expressing their opinions."

When asked about the stringent sharia law, he said, "I am dismayed that it mandates that women cover, since according to Islam, it should be voluntary." He added, "The position of women has deteriorated considerably. Aceh has a tradition of powerful, feisty women, both leaders and warriors . . . recent trends have been accepted and embraced, even by women, because the people love Islam so much. But I see sharia as a form of escapism that has been politicized and is being used as a symbol. Anything symbolic of Islam is embraced without question."

He questioned why the fasting and strict adherence to Islamic ritual hadn't eased the corruption problem, wondering aloud how the people who skim money at all levels can be found at the mosques—praying and going through the motions of spirituality—while missing the point.

The cease-fire was over a month old, and the Aceh Institute was abuzz. A frantic Finnish woman entered, firing questions at all the men. While riding a car that was allegedly stolen, a former GAM member had just been shot on sight by the military. The peace process was very delicate, and everyone, on all sides, wanted it to last. Before the tsunami, 6 PM had been fear time, and meetings of more than five people had been prohibited. People worried that this shooting could botch up the whole process, spinning the area back into war.

Much of the separatism was caused by Aceh being the only part of Indonesia that the Dutch failed to completely conquer. The Acehnise people have always had an independent spirit, and they resented that their natural resources, starting with the oil, were mercilessly exploited by Indonesia. Banda Aceh received little benefit from that money, and it was the last region to get infrastructure and development. Indonesia became the colonizing power.

At the Aceh Institute, people around the table suggested that religion got exploited as way to keep Acehnise quiet and make them feel like concessions were being made. Sharia law made them feel like they were self governed and had their own identity. It was actually a smoke screen, distracting from the real problem, and women's rights suffered as a result.

One evening, everyone from the FBA piled onto whatever transportation was available and headed someplace to break the fast. I didn't ask questions because, as we had been fasting all day and food was involved, that was all I needed to know.

I rode in an Australian NGO's SUV with a muscular guy I'd never seen before. He drove like a maniac. I hoped we would survive the trip, wherever we were going. The FBA entourage wound up at a house with two rooms of men seated on the floor, plus a couple of Australian women milling around the food table. There were several types of sweet drinks, including one with little pieces of avocado.

We were at the headquarters of an Australian NGO where Azwar and Wawan worked in addition to their work with FBA. Azwar and Wawan didn't get paid at FBA, but they had to make a living. They coordinated over one hundred land surveyors who remapped the land, determined what land belonged to whom, and redistributed what was left of this altered topography in the fairest manner possible. Nothing could be rebuilt until this was accomplished.

At the headquarters, I talked with women who turned out to be Australian aid workers. Most of the FBA crew joined the men in the other rooms, where a prayer leader recited the Qur'an for two hours straight.

I had an appointment to interview Rafly at 10 PM and was getting worried that I might not make it. It was nine o' clock and there was no end in sight. Everyone had taken off their shoes, and mine were by the front door. There was no way for me to get to the door, because I would have had to cut through the religious service. Azwar led me through the backyard as we tiptoed through the rain and mud in our bare feet, then around to the front door.

Since the first time I came to Banda Aceh and attended Rafly's concert, I'd wanted to know more about him. He was the superstar of Banda Aceh. I can't equate him to any Western singer. Instead of being a heartthrob—making women scream with romantic songs and sensual moves, like Elvis or Tom Jones—Rafly had a different kind of draw. Though his music was modern, driving, and intense, it was spiritual. His songs were steeped in folk tradition and layered with deep meaning.

On the way back from the show I'd seen at the Governor's House, Rafly and his manager had promised that if I returned to Banda Aceh they would let me ask all the questions I wanted. Since neither of them spoke English, I brought Wawan and Musafir to translate, and I invited Peter, so he could take a break from his heavy subject matter.

I was expecting to find Rafly living in one of Banda Aceh's coveted mansions. Instead, at the end of a dark street, we pulled up to his relatively simple home. Rafly greeted us wearing a winter sweater and a checkered sarong. He wasn't sweating beneath the layers of clothing. I wondered, "Who would even own a sweater in Banda Aceh?" His living room was typical of what one would find in Egypt or almost any Middle Eastern country. It contained no furniture, and everyone sat comfortably in a circle on a big rug. We sipped tea and ate papaya slices while Rafly strummed his guitar. For hours, we discussed music and the meanings of his songs. Rafly said, "They are open to interpretation of the listener, but always contain a message . . . several layers of messages, depending on one's level of perception."

Rafly had shown a photo of his extremely covered wife, so when Musafir mentioned I was a dancer, I pretended not to hear. Rafly asked me to dance to one of his songs and I got worried. Improvising whatever I could think of that didn't hint at sensuality, including turns, stops, and a bit of pseudo-flamenco was fun and a bit scary. Rafly said he would like to do a collaboration and have me dance in a concert, but he wanted to design the costume, which would have to be Islamic. Who knows when or where it would happen, but the world is small and anything is possible.

Rafly said he wanted to start an art school and rebuild his recording studio that was lost in the tsunami. Even being a star, he had a day job as a school teacher.

On my last night in Indonesia, Kade and I met downtown and headed out to dinner. When we started talking about men she said, "I want to marry a turis." (All foreigners are called 'turis' even if they're actually aid workers, journalists, and the like.) I asked, "Does he have to be Muslim?" and she replied, "Of course. It is not possible any other way." I suggested that there are a lot of Turkish people working with Turkish NGOs and some Arabs in town too. She said "No. I want an American or European."

I had also invited Maya, a demure and conservative looking girl I'd met at one of the NGO offices. She called us as we arrived at an open-air restaurant, which had just run out of food because of the fast-breaking rush. All they had left were eggs.

We three ladies crammed onto a becak and moved across town in search of food. Maya and I sat on the seat, and Kade perched on a railing. It was dangerous but fun. We phoned Peter and told him to meet us at Banda Seafood, the fanciest restaurant in town. It was considered outlandishly pricy because a crab dinner cost $5. Although simple by most standards, it had good food. Banda Seafood was frequented by foreigners, so this was the first time Kade and Maya had entered.

Peter was a big hit with the ladies. Earlier in the day, Maya had told me, "My boss complains that I keep to myself and never talk to anyone." Maybe she was making up for lost time with Peter. She was being charming and batting her eyes as she spoke. Kade pouted, "Peter doesn't like me because I'm not pretty." This kept on until I took her to the side and told her to stop. We'd had so many conversations about her negative self image, but by our standards she was very pretty. She would call herself stupid and say "Nobody likes me." I talked to her about positive thinking and how thoughts can create reality, then added, "Look at Maya. She is confident."

We went back to the table, and Kade sat studying the interplay between Maya and Peter. Then she suddenly piped up, "Peter! Give me your phone number." He was surprised and amused, but he did as she asked, and they talked nonstop for twenty minutes after that.

My first forty-day journey in the Islamic world was coming to a close. It was still Ramadhan in this intensely religious disaster area: not somewhere I could have ever imagined myself a year before. Yet Banda Aceh had grown on me and now felt comfortable and familiar. While digging crab meat out of claws, we spent the final night saying goodbye, like friends anywhere in the world. I didn't feel far from home at all.

SIWA OASIS, EGYPT

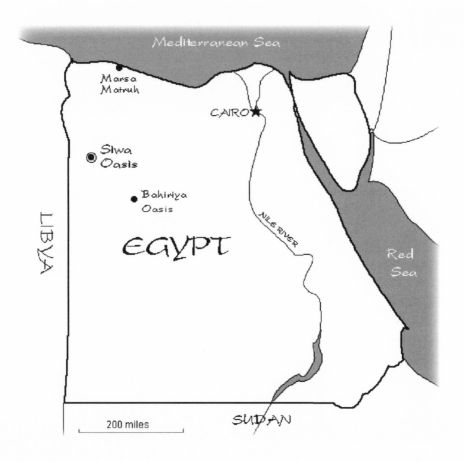

Mediterranean Sea

Marsa
Matruh

CAIRO ★

Siwa
Oasis

Bahiriya
Oasis

EGYPT

NILE RIVER

LIBYA

Red
Sea

200 miles

SUDAN

"THIS YEAR'S GOT A BAD START," Mo lamented. "Lightening just struck a man at a nearby oasis, and the night before, a policeman shot himself in the head. The night before that, three teenage boys killed a man. The forty-seven-year-old married man with children had a young male lover. He would buy the boy drugs, alcohol, and any material pleasure he desired in exchange for sex. Then the man made the boy sign a paper stating that he owed several thousand Egyptian pounds, and that everything was a loan. In retaliation, the boy and his friends drew an agreement stating that the man owed the boy an equal amount for services rendered. They hit him on the head with a stick to 'teach him a lesson,' and carried him to his doorstep. By morning, the man was dead. The boys didn't know he had died, but when questioned by the police, they told all."

In Siwa, there is a long history of homosexual relations. Anthropologists contend that homosexual marriages, which were legal in the Siwa Oasis until King Fouad banned them in 1928 but continued secretly until the 1950s, were accepted because it helped enforce the protection of women and keep the youth isolated. Before marriage, Siwan women are totally off-limits, so, historically, men turned to each other for sex, switching to women after marriage. Long ago, laborers called *zaggalah* (stick bearers) worked the fields, harvested dates, and were paid only by food. They were not permitted to marry before the age of forty and often had no money to marry, thus they stayed with one another.

Zaggalah stayed outside the Shali, a five-story fortress where most people lived, and had a tradition of drinking date wine and partying until the wee hours of the night. Now, alcohol is illegal on the oasis but can be purchased easily in backstreet deals where houses make home-made moonshine out of dates.

The story then revealed another twist; as told to me by a long-time resident, "The dead man was an 'Easterner,' and the others were 'West-erners.'" This rekindled an age-old feud between two sides that used to have wars against each other, and, according to one of the shopkeepers I met, "They had their sticks ready." As one girl explained, "Back in the day, there were Easterners and Westerners. They would have wars, throwing stones at each other until there was no one left."

I didn't have to shield myself from stones because, although there was said to be some uneasiness between the two groups, Easterners and Westerners hadn't had a war for many generations, and the matter of the murder was taken up by a council of tribal elders to find a wise and peaceful resolution.

Over thirty years ago, desert expert Raouf Ahmed Ali was sent by the Ministry of Petroleum to inform the people of Siwa that an asphalt road would be constructed to link them to the cities of Egypt. In re-sponse, the elders reportedly called it "the black road."

Raouf is said to have answered, "Yes, its color will be black."

The elders are professed to have replied, "We did not mean its color, rather the analogy of the word black, for we are a conservative, reli-gious society, endowed with our own peaceful traditions. Disease is scarce. Crime is alien to us, and our young respect their elders to this day. This road is black because it shall allow in attitudes that are con-trary to our values and traditions."

Siwa is Egypt's westernmost oasis, as well as the name of the larg-est of the four towns located within the Siwa Oasis. It lies in Egypt's western desert, sixty-five kilometers east of the Libyan border. In fact, until fairly recently, one could not enter without special permission.

It took more than a thousand years to bring this oasis under the control of the government in Cairo. The Siwans, Egypt's only native Berbers, remained fiercely independent following the decline of the Oracle of Amun, which was famed all over the classical empire.

The Siwan Manuscript was compiled in the mid-1800s to document the history of the oasis and its families. It included information gathered from Arab chroniclers as well as oral traditions passed down through Siwan families. The manuscript was in the hands of one family until the 1960s, but now no one knows where it is or even if it still exists.

In Siwa, where date and olive farming have been the people's livelihood for hundreds of years, an over-abundance of water caused by more and more outsiders coming and drilling into the desert floor is one of the many forces that could drive this remote culture into oblivion.

While I had been unfamiliar with Indonesia until I went there, Siwa was another story. This was my third trip, and I felt like I already had some knowledge and good contacts.

In July 2004, my friend Alexandra and I took an excruciatingly boring ten-hour bus ride from Cairo to Siwa, underwhelmed by the barren nothingness outside the window. One imagines there to be some sort of magic or romance when traversing the Sahara, but no. This was flat with a few stones but nary a camel or sand dune. No tents, Bedouins, or even shrubs. It was truly no-man's land, devoid of any form of life. We looked at each other, saying in unison, "Siwa had better be worth it!"

Entering the oasis was such a welcome respite from the monotony. Dust-covered date palms and mud buildings appeared as we barreled down the road into town. In the plaza, Ahmed, a boy of about fifteen, greeted us. "Where are you going?" he asked.

We looked at each other as he offered a ride on his donkey-driven cart. Hopping aboard, we took a spin around town then settled on a place to stay.

He asked, "Do you want to meet my uncle Mo?"

"Sure, why not?" we agreed. Off we trotted to House of Mo, a little souvenir shop selling an eclectic array of local handicrafts, from simple baskets to elaborately embroidered wedding shawls. Mo, the tallest man in Siwa, asked if we wanted to go on a desert safari. He seemed nice enough, but being two women alone in an oasis, we wondered if it was advisable to run off with this stranger. Fortunately, the other tourist in town, a Dane with a shock of white-blond hair, walked by and we asked him to join us.

The "safari" included baths in several hot mineral springs and a visit to a lake so salty that the bottom looked like ice. Balls of salt resembling snowballs floated on the surface. We watched the sun set behind sand dunes just like the ones in the movies, then stopped to wallow in what Mo called a "natural mud bath." I later learned that it was silt from a farmer's irrigation pool. So much for the Siwan spa treatment.

Anyway, we were duly impacted by the magic of Siwa, returned with a group of belly dancers the following summer, and hired Mo as our guide. In January, 2006, I set out to report on life on the oasis from a more in-depth perspective.

Winters in this part of the Sahara are incredibly cold. When I took the bus from Cairo, it let me off in Marsa Matruh, where I arrived in a pouring rainstorm, lugging two suitcases. The smaller one contained my two prized possessions: an as-yet-unpaid-for video camera, with which I would be continuing my film, and my new miniature Sony VIAO laptop from Hong Kong, with which I was writing this book.

Mo called to say that he heard it was raining and he would be sending a friend to pick me up.

As I descended from the bus, a young voice rang out, "Tamaleen." Hamid, a small man in his twenties, whisked my bags into a white car with a waiting driver. He helped me climb a small fence so I could use the bathroom behind the bus station without stepping into one of many deep mud-puddles. Then he asked, "Have you had lunch?" Hamid and the stone-faced driver, Fawzy, took me to an empty "fish restaurant" called *Samak* (fish). A big fish caked with salt was blackening over a charcoal grill outside in the rain. Out of nowhere appeared a big man who got in the car and drove away with my new acquaintances and all that belonged to me.

Marsa Matruh is a Bedouin city, and I had read that Bedouins have a special code of hospitality for strangers. Even so, my trust was put to test.

As the fish hit the plate, the big Bedouin reappeared and joined me.

He kept promising "Good car . . . good driver." The fish was yummy, with a surprise inside. What I had thought were intestines that hadn't been cleaned were actually hot peppers.

Once we hit the road, with Fawzy at the wheel again, the speedometer clocked 140 kilometers per hour (over 90 mph). I managed to fall asleep.

The weather cleared and I periodically opened my eyes to see the desert colors turning from pink to golden to white, and was too tired to know in what order. Entering Siwa never failed to be a beautiful surprise. Date palms were short, with fronds fanning like huge unruly heads of hair. Mo was waiting in his shop. I began to realize that the life of men in Siwa consists of a lot of sitting, drinking tea, and socializing. The lives of men and women are completely segregated, but as a foreigner, I perceived myself as what Alexandra and I used to call "the third gender," a woman who lives a man's life, gets put on a pedestal when in a group, and completely ignored as if invisible when walking down the street alone. It's much easier for a member of this gender to integrate with the local men. Only through them is she able to get a glimpse of the lives of women. Very few Siwan women speak any English at all, so even when I was able to spend time with women, we either had to depend on the translations of men or have simple conversations: "How old are you?" "Are you married? Engaged?" Or we bypassed verbal communication altogether and belly danced.

Shali, the large ruin in the center of town, was a five-story mud and salt fortress where most of the people of Siwa had lived beginning in the thirteenth century. Three days of rain melted it into uninhabitability in 1926. From that point on, the people of the oasis built homes in the surrounding area. In recent years, tourism and development have been expanding at a dizzying pace, because the western desert areas have been opened up to outsiders. Entrepreneurs from Cairo, Alexandria, and various parts of Europe have set their sights on this oasis as a future hot spot. The Shali, which has lain in ruins for years, is now seen as a landmark and appreciated for its beauty. Floodlights have been added to give it a magical glow as it towers above the freshly reconstructed plaza. Construction vehicles create traffic obstructions. Traditional donkey carts plod around them, and SUVs sit waiting to offer desert excursions.

Since this was my third time in Siwa, certain things were like a home-coming: drinking date milkshakes at the Shali Lodge (the town of Siwa's most elegant hotel), riding Ahmed's donkey cart, and climbing the Shali at sunset to hear the prayer call from mosques. Mosques are scattered throughout the oasis and all have loudspeakers. One call begins, then another, and soon there is a chorus of chants. An old mosque from the Shali still survives as a rustic mud-brick tower that leans slightly lop-sided with a scratchy megaphone atop a bald palm tree.

What a feeling of freedom to bicycle the back roads of Siwa! Dozens of children, both girls and boys, called to me "What's your name?"

I would answer in Arabic "Isme Dallal."

Then more would run after me, "What's your name?"

I asked each one, "Ismik eh?" (What's your name?) The count of Amels, Fatmas, Sofias, Noors, plus the Ahmeds, Mohammeds, and Alis became so numerous that I would never remember who was who. As I rode on, a strong push from behind the bike spun it out of control. A large mentally ill boy was running behind, pushing my bike at full speed. It took all the children to get him to stop.

A tiny girl with brown braids ran to me and said "America?"

"Aiwa," I responded, meaning "yes."

She said with the determination of an expert, "America good. Bush bad."

Other children echoed, "America good. Bush bad."

I pedaled my rickety pink rental bike through blankets of palm trees to the Oracle of Amun, a ruin that was much more ancient than the Shali. A guard showed me around what was left of the collapsing structure, through a maze of passages which led us up several sets of stairs. The ruins contained two ancient Egyptian rooms where the priests of Alexander the Great's day relayed messages that the Gods wanted to send to earth.

Every pharaoh of the twenty-eighth dynasty had traveled to Siwa to be acknowledged by the priests of the Oracle as the "Son of Amun-Ra," the supreme God. Afterward, they would be depicted wearing the ram's horns of Amun on their heads. Alexander wanted to legitimize his conquest of Egypt with this declaration of divine power. It is said that on the journey, his men's water supply ran out. They were rescued by a sudden rainstorm and when his legions became hopelessly lost in a sandstorm, two crows led them safely to Siwa.

Alexander requested a private session with the oracle and from then on was depicted on coins wearing ram's horns.

He vowed to be buried in Siwa. When his body was being transported from Babylon, where he died, it was entombed in Alexandria instead. One day, his body disappeared. Many believe that he is now buried in Siwa "where he belongs."

On my way out, I was besieged by children demanding *baksheesh* (money). Two little girls followed me, asking "Henna?" I agreed, thinking this might get me into their home. They sat me on a step, smoothed a cut-out piece of vinyl with flower shapes onto my hand, and proceeded to slather dark green paste of henna and water on top. As I sat, eight more children came along. They ranged from runny-nosed toddlers to eight- and ten-year-old girls in frilly dresses with sequins and sparkles. Children painted designs on my wrists by dipping toothpicks into the mixture.

Riding my bike through the village of Agurmi on my way back to town, several children followed, screaming, "What's your name?" "Baksheesh," or "Pen," at the top of their lungs. I was stopped by a beautiful young woman with deep brown skin. She did a sewing motion with her hands and urged me to follow her home. I thought, "Either she wants to sell me some handicrafts or show me some women sewing." Behind a wooden gate in the yard of a mud-brick house, several women came out. A large bag of Siwan wedding shawls, baskets, and other textiles was produced. I explained, "Mafish masari" (No more money), and she said "Mish Mushkalla. Bukra" (No problem. Tomorrow). Women and children crowded around me, tugging on the beaded chain of my cell phone and giggling at the screen design. Somebody had switched it to a pink cartoon lion with hearts around it.

The original people of Siwa are Berbers whose native language is not Arabic. Berbers are the people who lived in North Africa before the Arabs came and before the spread of Islam. Like Native Americans or other indigenous people, they preceded the people who later ruled the country where they lived. Their traditions and lifestyle remain distinct from the majority of Egyptians. They speak Siwan, which is only spoken in the Siwa Oasis; there are related Berber languages across North Africa from Libya to Algeria and Morocco. Now, Siwan is heavily peppered with Arabic words. Due to contact with tourists, some of the men speak English. I had been listening to Arabic language CDs in my car before coming to Egypt, which helped me become fluent enough to communicate basic needs. If all else failed, there was always nonverbal communication.

Siwans are divided into eleven tribes, some pertaining to Easterners and others Westerners. The original inhabitants of the oasis lived in the eastern side of the Shali. Several hundred years ago, thirty families were brought from the outside and settled in the western side of the Shali. Some of this social division remains even now. Each group has their own *shaikh* (tribal leader, or elder; this term also refers to religious leaders) who settles land disputes, legal matters, and other issues using Siwan law and the Qur'an. Punishments include beatings, giving alms, paying fines, or banishment from the tribe.

Some Siwans are very dark and look quite African, while others have blue or green eyes and even blond hair, which is always extremely curly.

From childhood until marriage, girls wear long dresses of stiff fabrics with ruffles on the sleeves and below the waist. Sequins sparkle in the sunshine as they walk the dusty backstreets of their neighborhoods. Married women must ask permission to leave the home, and when they do go out, they are covered in a checkered blue garment called *tarfotet*, which is woven in Kerdasa, a town near the pyramids outside of Cairo. These big sheets cover the body from head to toe. Black scarves completely shroud the face, eyes and all. The only inches of skin you are likely to see are dusty, sandal-clad feet.

When women enter their homes, outer coverings are shed, and then they wear loose handmade caftans, often patterned with wide stripes. In a room full of women they merely remove the blue tarfotet and fold back the black fabric.

Young women run the gamut from thin to chunky, but after marriage, which is usually arranged to take place between the ages of fifteen and eighteen, they start having children and blossom into corpulent creatures. Men wear long shirt-like robes with matching loose drawstring tapered-leg pants. These outfits range in color from white to blue or olive green, and I have even seen lavender and mint green. Traditionally, they wear turbans wrapped around the head, and if it's cold a Western-style jacket goes on top.

Many young boys have donkey carts, a major form of transportation around town, as well as transportation for produce from the gardens. These carts are used as taxis as well.

In addition to the Berber population, Bedouins, whose native language is Arabic, have been a presence in Siwa for hundreds of years. Long ago, formerly nomadic Bedouins traveled back and forth from Libya, often invading Siwa, helping themselves to dates and olives at harvest season. Eventually, they settled in the area and now coexist peacefully with the Siwans. They live in villages outside of town. Bedouin women wear black and have more freedom than the Siwan women. Most of the drivers of SUVs that take tourists into the desert are Bedouin.

Other Egyptians, city dwellers from Cairo and Alexandria, come to Siwa to develop ecolodges, usually without much environmental expertise, aesthetic taste, business savvy, or many international connections.

The exception is Dr. Mounir Neamatalla, who started the ecolodge craze. He is an environmentalist and knows how to build in a sustainable way with all natural materials, grows organic food on the land and hires gourmet chefs, attracting a well-heeled clientele that flies in on private planes. When Alexandra and I brought our group of belly dancers to Siwa, she knew someone who knew Dr. Mounir. We lucked out when he offered to let us stay in his exclusive Adrere Amellal Ecolodge. They usually charge $300 to $400 per night, catering to foreign dignitaries, model shoots, celebrities, and an exclusive circle of international jet-setters. Other developers attempted to follow suit. Their "ecolodges" lay empty or half-constructed, waiting for the big boom when the airport opens and well-heeled visitors arrive en masse.

I met Egyptians from Alexandria and Cairo who came as government workers, bankers, military, or as members of the highly feared police (infamous for beating the local population into submission). They seemed to have little interest in the local culture and were more concerned with earning a paycheck. Poor folks from the Nile Delta arrived a couple of generations ago as laborers and comprise the poorest sector of society.

A lot of tourists wandered about town, mostly backpackers, and often Korean. Around the plaza, a slew of businesses catering to them had recently sprung up. Like House of Mo, handicraft shops double as unlicensed tour agencies. Vehicles range from rattletraps to sturdy SUVs. The tourist industry is changing the oasis at an ever-quickening pace. An airport is in the discussion phase, and the government plans to pave the road from Cairo through the Bahariya Oasis and on to Siwa. That will make the journey shorter and much more pleasant. Also, there is a small expatriate community with an interesting cast of Europeans you won't find anyplace else in the world.

The most eloquent person I met in Siwa, Abdella Baghci, is the superintendent of schools. He owns Siwa's first handicraft souvenir shop. Mr. Baghci is one of the few people in the area who has traveled outside of Egypt. There are some who make pilgrimages to Mecca or travel to nearby Libya, but Mr. Baghci has been to the United States twice. One visit, in 1999, was to receive an award that is given to six people every year by the United Nations Development Program. It was on "The Day of Eradication of Poverty." The second visit, in 2001, was at the invitation of the International Visitor's Program. He had also been to France, Switzerland, Italy, and England. In his fifties, with a turban and salt-and-pepper beard, he spoke in polished English about his travels. I asked if his wife ever ventured out, and he said, "Not yet, but I will take her to Mecca."

I asked about the inspiration for his shop. He explained, "In January 1988, tourism was on the increase and visitors wanted to buy things. It pained me when I saw a married woman breaking tradition by standing at her door, beckoning male and female tourists to enter her home to buy handicrafts. ('Tradition' meant the complete seclusion of women.) I decided to open my shop so that women could make money but keep their dignity."

He showed me a big book where every consignment item in the shop was recorded. "Women decide the price of their work, and I add 10 percent as a commission." It was interesting how he made assuring that the women stayed indoors out of sight of the men sound sensitive and politically correct with the same demeanor as an NPR radio commentator.

"Now, there are many shops along the same order," he continued.

"Some are owned by outsiders from other parts of Egypt. Before, everything was genuine, made for personal use, but now most of the goods are for the tourist market."

I asked about a hand embroidered wedding dress that was hanging on the wall. "Poverty makes them sell their wedding dresses," he replied. "There is a lot of poverty in Siwa."

One of the most typical items associated with Siwan handicrafts are black wedding shawls with orange and yellow embroidered geometric Siwan symbols. "If only decorated with embroidery, they were for every day. For weddings, they traditionally added mother of pearl buttons or shells. Now, mother of pearl is hard to find, and they have started using sequins. The lines of embroidery on shawls are always in an odd number, with a maximum of forty-seven lines." I asked if women still use embroidered shawls for daily use, and he said, "Not since thirty or forty years ago."

Siwan wedding jewelry was traditionally made of silver, but the silversmith died years ago without passing on his craft. Abdella elaborated, "Since World War Two, nothing was made of silver. Recently, three boys went to Cairo and learned to recreate traditional Siwan designs. Now, they have a small shop behind the tourist office."

I mentioned, "It seems that gold is the metal of preference now. Do any of the women want to use the traditional silver jewelry?"

He said, "No. They will never go back. Silver is only for the tourists."

"Has any Siwi woman broken tradition and become independent?"

He said, "Yes. Her father, the most important man in Siwa after World War Two, wielded extreme power in the Western Desert. She went to the university in the faculty of agriculture and still works in Marsa Matruh. She paid the price, though, and had to marry an outsider."

"What changes have you seen in Siwa in recent years?"

"Architecture is the most notable. With underground water getting higher by the year, mud houses cannot survive. In 1985, there was a big rain which caused many houses to collapse. Now, they use more concrete, which is horrible because it holds the heat in summer and stays cold in winter. Siwa started losing its unique identity, so a rule was made that you cannot get a building permit unless you paint it the color of mud."

There were some mud houses under construction outside of town. He explained, "The permit is easier to obtain if you build of mud in the traditional way. Nowadays, many people take shortcuts and want to finish quickly. The proper way is to let the mud and water mixture ferment for at least forty days, or to put palm seeds in the mud and wait until they sprout. People don't follow these methods anymore so the mud doesn't dry completely, and they have problems.

"The quality of workmanship is deteriorating in every way. It's due to commercialization. Embroidery is getting more slapdash and the baskets are woven with bigger stitches. Green palm leaves should never be used, but people no longer wait for them to dry."

"How do you envision Siwa in ten years?"

"It will be facing a flood of modernization. I hope we don't lose our identity because there will be more and more outsiders. We are fighting against building an airport in Siwa and asking the government to build it in Marsa Matruh instead. Visitors should travel at least three hundred kilometers through the desert to appreciate our oasis.

Due to so many people digging deep wells, the water level is rising dangerously. The government is trying to curb this, but nothing has worked yet. Siwa will be drowning. Not the town, but the gardens. It will be disastrous for farming and harmful to the economy. People in Siwa are scared!"

We spoke about education. He said, "Now, in every village, there are good schools and enough teachers. The illiteracy rate of only 5.5 percent is lower for women than for men. In the rest of Egypt, illiteracy is over 35 percent. More than thirty female [Siwi] teachers work in the public school system, teaching boys and girls, and working alongside male teachers."

I asked, "What will happen if they get married?" He replied, "If they marry an outsider, they can keep working, but if they marry a Siwi, they will have to stop."

Abdella Baghci explained some of the ways education has been molded to meet special needs of Siwan society, especially where women are concerned. "Adult education has been very successful. Women will not leave the house, so we find a well-known and trusted person in each area who will lend us his sitting room as a classroom. A local daughter is the teacher, and all the women attend class. There was a problem that they would take the classes but not the final exam, because they couldn't go to the school where the exams were held. We adapted to that too, and now the exams are in houses. We have made the system flexible because it's not fair to break tradition."

"Why educate women who would never leave the house anyway?"

He responded, "At least we will have educated mothers. I want children to learn how to deal with tourists in a proper way, and for this training to start in kindergarten."

The subject of pedophilia was delicate, but I felt it was important for the superintendent of schools to address. He replied calmly, "There was a foreign website that said 'People will deny the existence of homosexuality in Siwa, but if you want to know the truth, just ask a young donkey-cart driver.' Now foreigners come and take advantage of our boys. We stopped this custom a hundred years ago, but tourists approach the donkey-cart boys, and since our boys eat a lot of dates and are easily excitable, they respond and get paid a lot of money. What worries me is the day when one of our young kids gets the first case of AIDS."

Time takes on a different meaning in Siwa, where the day is measured by when the sun sets and the week by Friday prayers. As a foreigner, I was blinded by the magic of nature: pink sunsets beyond the Shali or over the sand dunes, and pure night skies resplendent with stars. There are many hot springs to bask in. The tourist trail is a world apart from the Siwa of locals.

Scattered about the Great Sand Sea are fossilized sea shells. No visitor to Siwa should miss zooming up and down the sand dunes at sunset. Bedouin drivers let air out of the tires and drive around dunes that change shape daily. Hassan, one of the guys who drove my women's group last summer, found a big dune. Slowly inching to the top, it looked like the jeep would fall over the edge of a cliff. Repeatedly, we dove into the abyss, experiencing a momentary thrill and winding up at the bottom in one piece—a Saharan roller coaster.

We stopped at a hot spring and took a dip under the moon and stars. Siwan women never bathe in the springs. Foreigners are expected to go in fully dressed. That meant being very cold and wet all the way home. It was amazing to be inundated by silky smooth thermal water with tiny bits of algae floating about. The hotter the water, the more one feels the cold air upon exiting.

I was invited to crash a party at a desert camp. These were often set up for tour groups, who could order a lamb to be cooked under the sand and musicians to play long into the night. Local guys crashed as well. Penny, an English woman, and her three kids came along in the back of a jeep. This family had survived the tsunami in Sri Lanka and had been living in Siwa for several months. Their story was an inspiration because they chose to live outside the box, renovating homes in out-of-the-way villages in Croatia, Romania, or wherever the local culture captivated them. The three kids were growing up with such an expansive view of life. I told Sasha, the oldest, that she was very lucky. Her mom chided, "Keep telling her."

Sasha laughed, "I thought Siwa was boring, until I went back to England. Then I couldn't wait to come back."

Groups of Siwan and Bedouin men sat around the campfire, singing and hand clapping. Different types of drums were played. One man drummed on a blue plastic olive-oil container. It sounded great. Then there was the *def*, which is a common frame drum used all over Egypt. The *simsimeya* is a round instrument, with a triangle shaped neck and five strings. When the simsimeya stopped, another man started to play a *tashibept*, a small, strong-sounding horn brought to Siwa by the Bedouins, which is used to play sad songs. Later, with the *nay*, a reed flute, the songs became happy.

I danced with Sasha and could tell by her earthy style that she had spent time with local women. I asked Penny's opinion of raising daughters in a society where women are secluded, and she told me "Siwan ladies are the strongest, most feisty women I have ever met!"

Various men got up, wrapped their *galabeya* (long robes) above their knees, shuffling through the sand with hips gently pulsing forward and back. That was the typical Siwan men's dance, although they have other, more elaborate, varieties done in groups for the harvest. Traditionally, the zaggalah of days gone by would play music and dance outside the town, past earshot of the women "because of respect."

Ahmed did a wilder dance, shuffling through the sand, lifting his feet with pelvic movements, getting on his hands and knees, doing the same, and finally in a push-up position, mimicking the sex act. Another man in a striped woolen robe with scarves wrapped on his hips performed an amazingly smooth and sensual version of belly dancing.

Desert nights are cold even in the summer, but January was bone chilling! Located near the plaza, another of Mounir Neamatalla's projects, the Shali Lodge, is stylish but a lot cheaper than his exclusive ecolodge. A toasty indoor fireplace burned olive branches. I often attempted to type my journals while warming my feet by the fire, but my work would get disrupted by conversations with interesting people. Sometimes it was Dr. Mounir's friends and employees, visiting from Cairo and always hinting gentle reminders of their class superiority. I even saw women wearing diamonds and fur coats!

One night, a film crew came to town and stayed in the Shali Lodge. While networking with one of the producers, who was more interested in a woman for the night, I met Lorraine. He tried to lure me, then her, but he would have had better luck sticking to business, because both of us were inquiring about the cost of making instructional videos. Tall and statuesque, and of South Indian descent, Lorraine spoke with an Aussie accent. She taught workshops in "success through inner awareness," and "finding one's purpose in life." On this blusteringly cold oasis, where everyone and everything is limited to earth tones, Lorraine stood out. Her clothes were vibrant shades of pink and yellow. Her life's work involved traveling to sacred places and giving motivational workshops. She had connected with an Austrian traveler named Cristof, who was a landscaper back home. He took time off when the gardens were snowed over. We spoke a while around the fire and promised to team up for some excursions. I recommended Mo as a good guide.

Knock knock.

"Who is it?" I asked impatiently. No answer. The alarm on my phone went off, but I had no idea why. It was Mo. I jumped up with a start. Time to go! Gara awaited.

Cobwebs in my head, I could only think about the cozy covers, but soon we were off to experience a glimpse of Siwan life as it was before being "discovered." Gara is one of the smaller towns on the oasis, relatively untouched by outsiders, and one must have a permit and military escort to visit.

Lorraine, Cristof, Mo, and I boarded Kamel's jeep, picked up a soldier, and barreled off-road through the desert, bumping and swaying from side to side. I had the crazy idea of trying to sleep but realized that I was more likely to get a damaged vertebra. Kamel, the driver, brought lots of food. When Mo tried to sleep, he laid his head on one of the bags and broke the uncooked eggs.

After several jarring hours, a salt lake appeared, then a ruined fortress. Mo explained, "They had a Shali here too, but it was much smaller than the one in Siwa." The village of Gara is small, just a cluster of mud homes. News of our arrival traveled fast, and dozens of children ran to greet us. Mo had collected money from us to buy pens and sweets. We were embarrassed when he told us to pass them out to the children, who wound up fighting, hoarding them, and hounding us for more. We came to a consensus and explained to Mo that these handouts give the wrong message and foster dependency. We suggested that he not encourage tourists to pass out goodies in the future.

We paid a visit to Shaikh Hassan. He was the head of the local tribe, and we were expected to sit awhile. Men of the village joined as we sat around the room. Peanuts, candy bars, and donut-shaped crackers were placed on a table. Everyone watched us eat, and we presented a package of sweets to the shaikh. One man whisked away flies with a small broom-like swatter, while another made tea on a gas fire. Bags of local handicrafts emerged in case any of us wanted to buy, and Shaikh Hassan handed us a thick guestbook to sign.

We climbed around the Shali, visiting the tomb of Sidi Yaga, a Sufi Saint. It was decorated with strings of ostrich eggs hung across the ceiling.

Kamel drove us to an old garden that had been an olive and date farm until one night when twenty-five springs emerged. Mo said, "Where there is sweet, hot water, there is salty water nearby." The overabundance of saline water killed most of the olive trees, but the garden had small streams running through and was a scenic place for a picnic. Lorraine had us go from tree to tree, giving them hugs to feel their energy.

Hot water gushed from the ground. Grains swayed softly in the breeze and glowed eerily in the setting sun. It was an idyllic place to lose oneself in the moment.

In the middle of the desert our jeep broke down. Kamel said, "Bathroom break." Upon exiting, Lorraine and I marveled that everything happens for a reason. The sky was so full of stars that it looked like they were going to snow down at any moment. They weren't twinkling against a black sky. Rather, the sky was alight with layers behind layers of stars. So many that we saw more stars than sky.

Whenever foreigners go deep into the desert, they must get a permit from the government. It wasn't clear whether the motivation was the $12 it cost each person, or if they must keep track of us as a matter of safety.

Mo showed me an odd photo of a mushroom-like white rock formation in a land of chalky white soil. He asked, "You don't know about the White Desert?" and said that four Koreans wanted to do two nights camping, visiting the oases of Bahariya and Farafra, plus the White Desert, Black Desert, and Crystal Mountain. There was plenty of room in the jeep, so I gave my $12 to Mo and told our plans to Lorraine and Cristof.

Departure was delayed because Lorraine, Cristof, and Mo were having a heated argument about the money. Mo added the cost of going to Gara and this trip together and gave them an exorbitant price. Lorraine talked him way down, to the point that I didn't think it was fair for Mo. He agreed to her offer, but was really angry. He had a habit of talking in circles and being evasive. We were never sure what he meant to say. If he had just quoted one price from the start and stuck with it, there would have been no problem. Lorraine tried to give him a lesson on "the correct way to do business," which made him angrier.

She said, "He should be thankful, because if he changes his business practice, he will have more customers." Saying "thank you" was the last thing on Mo's mind.

The morning started off negatively, and things got worse from there. We stopped for breakfast at Abu Shrouf, a clear warm spring with fish swimming around. I had an uncomfortable feeling in my gut and wanted desperately to stay in Siwa, but I never imagined the upcoming desert safari to hell. Not wanting to further disrupt the journey, I kept my mouth shut.

Mo kept adding passengers, to be dropped off at various points along the way. We were crammed together amid camping supplies, backpacks, and food. Weather went from miserably cold to below freezing. There was absolutely nothing to see all day. The jeep had three flat tires and ran out of gas twice. Kamel lost both his wallet and his cell phone, then Mo claimed that it was Lorraine's fault, that she had "jinxed the trip" with her "magic" (meaning he couldn't understand the previous day's tree hugging, and then sitting on scraggly sand dunes to meditate). The jeep had four gas tanks and carried extra cans of gas on the luggage rack up top. Mo and Kamel connected a plastic hose to the canisters leading to the tanks when they needed filling.

We had lunch at one of the five military checkpoints, which opened my eyes to the dismal reality Egyptian soldiers endure. Four young military men lived at this freezing spot. There were three windowless shacks and the outhouse had only three walls. A blanket was laid on the dirt in the third hut, which consisted of broken fiberglass walls and had most of the roof knocked out. A dirty, scrawny cat begged for our food as we ate tomato salad, tuna fish, and pita bread. The desert was unbearably cold and not attractive at all. These poor soldiers stayed for thirty or forty days straight, then got a few days off and started over again.

I tried to sleep as much as possible in the jeep. Sometimes there were roads, and other times not. Some roads existed, but Kamel drove off of them because he knew the terrain well and knew where roads were broken.

We set up camp long after dark. The cold was bone chilling, and even the campfire failed to provide warmth. Each of us sat lifeless, bundled up and hunched into tight human balls. Three small tents were pitched, but some of us opted to sleep under the stars. While I was asleep, Mo swept me up in his arms and started running across the sand. I laughed and asked, "What's your problem?"

He said, "There is a type of humidity between the hours of three and six in the morning during the winter that can make you sick if you sleep outside."

Mo tripped and dropped me in the sand. I was still in my sleeping bag, so he said, "Start jumping!" With every hop up the sand dune, I fell further back. I had to exit the sleeping bag and run up the dune in my socks.

Mo had been flirting with a man named Kim, a tall Korean university student, who had forewarned him that he wasn't allowed inside his tent. Instead, Mo was stuck sharing a tent with Kamel and me. I asked what would happen to the other four figures huddled into blankets under the stars, but fell back asleep before hearing the answer. Mo dipped under a couple of thick wool blankets and proceeded to snore at fever pitch all night. I had to get up and punch him regularly to tone down the noise.

"Today's another day," as Lorraine put it. She proceeded to turn her face toward the sun and say, "Aaah. Life is good." The general mood was much lighter as we rode the rest of our way to the oasis of Bahariya.

Bahariya looked like a dreary truck stop. I couldn't imagine why anyone would go there. Suddenly, Mo became cross with Lorraine and Cristof and demanded that they pay more money or get off the trip right there and then. He said that since Kamel had lost his wallet he needed more money.

I said, "You can't do this to people! I haven't paid yet, so let me pay and that should help him."

Mo responded, "Maybe you won't have to."

I was puzzled. Anyway, he gave Lorraine and Cristof such a hard time that they left.

I hated the trip so far, but Mo insisted the best was yet to come.

Since there was no public transport back to Siwa, I had to go back with the group so I stuck it out. The other option was busing several hours to Cairo, then ten hours back to Siwa. Kim was tall and looked like one of those Korean actors that Japanese housewives go wild about. Mo continued to hound him throughout the day, looking him in the eyes and saying silly nothings in broken Korean.

At one point, I sat in the front seat between Mo and Kamel, dodging the gearshift. Mo piped up, "You shouldn't mix with any of those people. You are on a much higher level. You are an artist." I was amused and tried to explain the concept of backpacking. Travelers can be from any walk of life. Two girls on an earlier leg of the trip were medical students. I thought about how, in Egypt, a doctor starting out might make $100 a month, while a successful belly dancer earns a relative fortune.

He went on a tirade about my book. "You shouldn't talk about what you do . . . some people in Siwa don't want you to write your book . . . you might be stopped and you won't have enough pages . . . there was a Swiss lady in Siwa trying to write a book for fifteen years. People spread rumors and got her in trouble." I pooh-poohed his concerns, but he continued, "They could easily say you are a spy."

I replied, "That would make interesting reading. I'm trying to write this book to promote friendship. I don't like to suffer, but if I came to this little oasis and was accused of being a spy, it would just go in the book and I would sell more copies."

That shut him up for awhile, until he piped up, "Am I going in your book?"

The next item of contention was about me dancing at the camp fire in the desert with Sasha and assorted tourists. Apparently, that was the talk of the oasis. "What about other people?" I wondered. Tourists are a source of income and can do what they want, but stick around too long and you have to start following the rules. He vented about how badly people see belly dancers.

Females in his culture never perform with men present, but in tourist parties, everyone is encouraged to dance. I discussed the differences between the Western view of belly dancing as an art form and good exercise, and the local view. According to Mo, "All people here know is Dina, and she's a prostitute." Dina is the most famous belly dancer in the world. She is also known for wearing outrageous costumes and having surgical enhancement.

Mo said, "You know about the video. That proves Dina is a prostitute." I didn't want to continue this discussion, but here's the scoop on the Dina controversy: Commanding fees of up to $10,000 a night, Dina was famous for bypassing modesty rules with her skimpy outfits. According to news sources, when her businessman husband fell out with the Egyptian president's son, police raided the couple's apartment and found compromising videos. Her husband had recorded them without her knowledge. They were then released onto the internet. Several people went to jail, but she was not one of them.

I said, "It's just a dance, and dance is simply movement. It is innocent. Who the dancer is, what she does in her life, or even what she wears doesn't change anything." I offered to have a dialogue with the Siwan men who were judging me for dancing and to give them my point of view, as a dance teacher.

I asked about his recent pilgrimage to Mecca, knowing from my Indonesian experience that after a pilgrimage people are expected to live a clean and vice-free life forever after. The Mo I saw chain smoked and hadn't given up smoking hashish. When I asked what he got out of going to Mecca, he replied, "There are no real Muslims. Islam is good, but the people calling themselves Muslims are the problem." His goal was to leave Siwa, which he could no longer stand, and find a way out of Egypt. At the moment, he was juggling two women in different countries and said, "One of them might find me work as a supermodel." I wished him luck.

We visited the Black Desert and climbed a mountain overlooking sandy hills covered with black rocks. Next, we stopped at Crystal Mountain, which consisted of huge crystals that had been picked apart for years leaving only some still intact. Mo complained that "people like Dr. Mounir have taken away most of the crystals," then went on a verbal rampage against the wealthy businessman.

The White Desert looked like a Salvador Dali dream and made the journey worthwhile. Out of the earth sprung huge white mushroom-shaped rock formations, and there were others shaped like birds, heads, and other familiar objects. The sun was setting as we drove deep into this otherworldly environment to set up camp. Several more jeeps had camps in the distance. Each camp, including ours, had brightly patterned fabric set up to block the wind. Several mats were placed on a rug, with a campfire treacherously close.

Kim brought out his laptop computer and downloaded photos he had taken throughout the day. He had a great music collection of American oldies. We sat by the fire amid surrealistic chalky stone figures, listening to Nat King Cole croon in Spanish while looking at photos on a laptop.

Come morning, Mo was experiencing another mood swing. We were supposed to visit the Farafra Oasis and a hot spring, but the Koreans were stone faced and Mo informed me that the journey would not continue. They wanted to be taken to Bahariya and put on the next bus to Cairo. Everyone was mum on the ride back.

The Koreans caught a bus, I went into a hotel for a shower, and Mo and Kamel disappeared. They had promised to get me back to Siwa that night, which didn't seem possible.

I crossed the street to have coffee and something to eat, and then Mo stepped out of a Land Rover. "I told Kamel to get your permission documents yesterday. Now it's Friday, and the office is closed. He can't get them until tomorrow, but he has to leave today"

I said, "This is your responsibility. You said you had all the permissions. You got me here and you have to get me back, tonight."

He was really nervous and pointed at a beige station wagon. "Get in the car. We're going to have lunch."

"Where?" I asked.

"At my friend's house with his family" was his answer.

He tried to whisk me away, but I protested, "At least let me finish my coffee."

When I got into the car, something felt wrong. The driver, a rough-looking man in Western dress with greasy curls, didn't look at me and we weren't introduced. Mo walked away and I got out. He came back and said tersely, "Get in the car."

Kamel and Mo were having a heated discussion. I refused to get in the car. Finally, against my better judgment, I sat in the back seat with Mo. We were driven outside of town to an ugly block of apartments. The vehicle parked in a puddle, and we stepped over mud and garbage. Mo and his mysterious "friend" led me up five flights of stairs to a room that looked like a cheap, ugly disco. It was painted garish blue, had a sound system, lots of plastic flowers, and fluorescent lights. I stood, looking around at this strange scene, feeling certain there was no family living there.

Mo said, "Don't stand. Go in the other room and stay there."

The next room was a bedroom with one small unmade bed.

The man left. Mo spewed angrily, "You had to take a shower in a hotel. You could have taken it here." Then he went in the bathroom and took a shower. I felt stupid, realizing that my trusting nature had deceived me. Now the question was how to get out and where to go. I hadn't brought a lot of money with me. Kamel had my passport along with my permission to be in the desert (it was normal to leave one's passport with the driver, who showed it at the military checkpoints). I couldn't even manage to open the locks to stand in the dirty stairwell and get air.

I felt stupid, realizing that I should have listened to my feelings. I was disillusioned with Mo—all the signs pointed to the fact that he was a creep. Now I was in a pickle but was determined to get out of it unscathed. A peculiar calm came over me, and when it would have been normal to panic, I became unnaturally cool and collected.

Mo came out of the shower and I sat him down. "So, what's the plan?"

He said, "Kamel will be here in two hours."

I retorted, "I'm not waiting here for two hours. You have to take me back to town now!" With a serious look, I bluffed, "I am very famous in America." He stayed quiet as I continued, "Every three days I am expected to check in by e-mail. It has already been four days. Today is the fifth. If I am not back in Siwa tonight, they will call the embassy and send the police looking for me. That means they will be looking for you, right?"

The magic word was "police." The greasy haired guy came out of nowhere with a bag of eggs. Mo said something in Arabic, and they rushed me down the stairs through the mud and garbage and into his car. We sped toward town and pulled up behind Kamel, who came to the window and handed me my passport with all the money I had paid for my trip, plus an extra twenty English pounds. Mo opened the passport, showed me, and said, "See. More money. Get it?"

At that moment, the minibus carrying the Koreans drove back into town, stopped, and opened the door. We were off to Cairo.

Kim told me they were driving through the desert when the minibus suddenly made a U-turn and headed back to town. I was still too stunned by my narrow escape to think straight. I should have stopped ranting about my bad experience and asked why they didn't finish the trip.

During the never-ending ride into the dusty metropolis of Cairo, I checked several numbers programmed into my phone, trying to decide whom to call first and hoping that my prepaid minutes and uncharged battery would hold out. I could have caught a bus back to Siwa, but it would've been wise to let someone know what happened. I rang Raqia Hassan, the most famous belly-dance teacher in Cairo. She said, "Go to the tourist police. We cannot let this happen to foreigners in Egypt."

Once in Cairo, I was led into an office where a big man listened to my story, then kept repeating the facts back to me wrong. He seemed more interested in whether I had a laptop and where it was. Then a man in uniform asked, "Do you have permission to write a book in Egypt?"

I sensed a great possibility that I would be the loser and doubted their ability to protect me. The big man gave me an address and told me to go there and make a report. I went, unsure how much information I wanted to give. It was a wild goose chase. When I finally entered a police station, it was only a little room with two officers who didn't speak English and had no idea what to do.

Meanwhile, my phone rang and a young woman's voice said, "I was in Raqia's house when you called. Do you need a place to stay? I have an extra bed in my hotel room." She was Sabriye, a belly dancer who worked in Dubai and was staying in Cairo. That was all I gathered, but I accepted her offer without hesitation.

In Cairo, traffic is always a hodgepodge of cars speeding between lanes and people dodging traffic while trying to traverse many lanes without aid of crosswalks or lights. We sped to the posh Pyramisa Hotel. I entered as a wedding procession wound its way through the lobby, complete with music, *zagareets* (calls of celebration), and lots of people dressed in their finest. With matted hair and covered in desert dust, I carried nothing but a folkloric bag from Siwa decorated with multicolored pom-poms.

Sabriye met me in the lobby. It turned out that when I was one of the original Bellydance Superstars, we had performed together for the CD launch in Los Angeles. What a small world!

She had recently graduated from the University of California at Berkeley. In the Middle East, it's assumed that dancers have few options in life and that is why they become dancers. Yet the pay for a belly dancer in Gulf hotels is comparable to that of upper management. It's an odd contrast, considering that society thinks the dancer is outside the norms of social acceptability and thinks that she dances because something has gone wrong, forcing her to take up this shameful life. This is the image of professional dancers throughout the Arab world.

The locals of Dubai constitute only 14 percent of the population. The rest are guest-workers. Many of these workers make a pittance, especially if they are from poor countries like India or the Philippines. The workforce is so international that the main language is English.

Sabriye told me "Men at the hotels where I dance get my room number from the front desk, when they shouldn't, and call my room. They try to impress me with what they have and what they can offer." I was laughing when she told me of a man that bragged over the phone "I'm a pilot."

She replied, "I'm a belly dancer."

He kept repeating, "I'm a pilot," and she repeated, "I'm a belly dancer."

In his mind, she was supposed to be impressed. We mused about how belly dancers are some of the freest women in the world. We have a network and a subculture that is global. Anywhere a belly dancer goes, whether it be China, New Zealand, or Montana, she can meet up with other dancers and be welcomed into a circle of friends. People who think that we are dancing to please men have no idea of our reality.

I planned to leave the next morning, but instead Sabriye and I ended up at Raqia Hassan's apartment. Among the most renowned belly-dance teachers in the world, Raqia Hassan is a grandmother. Her apartment is cluttered with gold leaf baroque furniture and knick-knacks. She took us into the dance studio next door to demonstrate some steps.

Wearing baggy double knit stretch pants and holding a cell phone in one hand, she moved with such spice that I kept thinking how dance has to ripen and mature to reach its full beauty. She tossed her hips and undulated in patterns that drew their energy from the earth, creating magic through her body.

Making sure we ate, Raqia led us back to her apartment, where some of the movers and shakers of Egyptian belly-dance society sat. Her wheezing old white dog slept in one of the ornate chairs. I recognized two men as former members of the Reda Company (Egypt's famous folkloric ballet) who now coach belly dancers. These were kindly look-ing elderly men, who nobody would ever imagine teaching women from all over the world how to belly dance. The third man was Dr. Mo Geddawi, a recently retired Egyptian physician based in Berlin who is another of the world's top belly-dance instructors. He now travels ten months a year to teach workshops around the world. Sabriye asked where he lived, and he replied, "Nowhere at the moment." Sabriye replied, "Me neither." I chimed in, "My cat lives in Seattle." Welcome to the global belly-dance subculture.

I had to get back to Siwa. Staying in Cairo was easy, and it was comfortable to avoid the long bus ride, especially when I didn't know what reaction awaited upon my return. I considered the possibility that people didn't want my book to be written and that locals had sent Mo to distract and stop me. Raqia favored that hypothesis. One of the men suggested that people might think I was Dr. Mounir's girlfriend and want to give me a hard time. My mind wandered, wondering if they believed I was famous like Dina and wanted to set up a porno video shoot or if maybe the tacky room was a makeshift brothel.

The bus ride back was smooth. I sat next to a nice Palestinian wom-an who fed me cookies as we watched colorful crazy Egyptian movies on the overhead TV. They had music, dance, comedy, men dressed as women, women dressed as men, and lots of drama. Belly dancers were depicted as sex kittens, giving seductive looks to the men as they over-powered them with their dance while the men made silly faces, fell backward, and acted like helpless buffoons. At one of the rest stops, I introduced myself to a strawberry-blond haired woman named Sal-ly. She was American but had lived in Egypt for over twenty years. Sally was a colorful character with a loud mouth who bossed every-one around in screeching Arabic. She claimed to be the only American hostage ever held in Libya, and after a couple of hours, I realized why they'd released her.

As if my experiences in Bahariya weren't scary enough, Sally could make anyone paranoid. She said, "We're in the world's largest un-marked minefield. There are mines in this desert left from World Wars One and Two. If you step off this road to go to the bathroom, you're likely to get blown up." I thought back to when we brought the belly dancers on a retreat to Siwa and was glad that no one wandered off.

(In reality, any leftover minefields are marked and fenced off.) "Don't flash your video camera because the duty on cameras has gone up so much that stores can't afford to carry them, so they are fair game for thieves." I wondered if this might explain the Bahariya incident. Maybe Mo wanted my video camera for the black market. After she kept suggesting more scary scenarios, I figured I was better off not knowing and could only hope my laptop was still in my room at the Palm Trees Hotel.

Once I got to Siwa, I stayed up until 4 AM writing, then tucked myself in for a long sleep. In the early morning hours, the manager knocked at the door. He informed me that I would be sharing the room for a few days. I mumbled something and went back to sleep. All the hotels in town were full because of a huge influx of Egyptian tourists. It was like spring break in Florida as bus loads of college students descended on Siwa.

There was another knock on the door. Dina stood, holding a backpack and sleeping bag.

This was not Dina the belly dancer. Rather, this Dina was a yoga teacher and former Peace Corps volunteer from San Francisco. She had a place where she didn't live in Kathmandu, and was another of us nomadic souls. I told her about the desert trip and Mo's escapade, fearing what might happen upon my return to Siwa. She explained a bit about life in small communities, gleaned from experiences living in a small Nepali village. "People have to see each other every day, so nothing is said directly. Everyone beats around the bush. If someone wants to ask you a question, they go through someone else. If there is a conflict, they simply don't talk about it." She said, "People won't react openly. But everyone will want to know what happened." We also conjectured that if the tables were turned, and a foreign woman who didn't speak English found herself alone with some American guys in the desert, anything could happen. It might be much worse, and she wouldn't have the option of scaring them with talk about her embassy sending out police.

On the street, several people approached, asking, "Have you seen Mo?" or, "Where have you been?"

While I shopped for an embroidered Siwan wedding dress, the

store owner Abi said, "I'm waiting for Mo. Do you know when he's coming?"

I asked, "Mo who?" Whenever I got the chance, I casually mentioned that I was doing papers with the embassy in Cairo or attending embassy parties. If some sort of word was getting back to him, I wanted it to be that I had protection or, as they said in Siwa, "backside."

On my way to type at Abdu's (the most popular restaurant in town), another shopkeeper caught up with me and asked, "Don't you know that he wanted something?"

"Like what?" I asked. He refused to elaborate, but from the smirk on his face, I could guess he meant sex.

I said, "At least I had a great time in Cairo, especially at the ambassador's house."

In the evening, Dina and I went by the fire at Shali. The big, mean hotel manager brought up Mo's name as I walked out, hoping to elicit a reaction or some sort of story. As I showed Dina my favorite wedding shawl in one of the shops, Mo entered. I only saw a large shadow dip in and out, but Dina said he literally ran out the door. As we hit the street, I saw him slip into an all-male coffee shop. We laughed until our bellies hurt. He was literally running away and hiding from me. I realized that I had nothing to be paranoid about.

Shazli, a deaf teenager who ran errands for Mo, caught my glance and motioned "tall man" and shook his finger "no good," then made a typing motion and gave a thumbs-up. I later learned that he was referring to Farid, a man who came to work out of Mo's shop.

In search of an authentic cultural experience, I had hoped to stay with different local families, both Berber and Bedouin. Long before the ill-fated camping trip, Mo had taken me to his family's home. His house was depressing and dirty, which I accepted as normal until seeing other places and realizing it was an exception. He had led me through a maze of rooms, some leading into gardens and courtyards. Ceiling beams were of split palm trees connected by dried palm fronds. The walls were made from mud brick and cracked stucco and painted varying shades of blue and white.

Mo's sister Hadia was rolling pieces of pastry on a low wooden table with a wooden stick. Her three-year-old daughter tried to help. Mo put the round layers into a pan and topped them with oil and a meat mixture until the pan filled up, and Hadia took it to the oven. One imagines these mysterious women behind blue shrouds to be some sort of forbidden beauties, or at least to look different from anyone we would know in our world. Hadia was a thirty-one-year-old single mother in a sweatshirt and housecoat, with frizzy black hair tied into a bun and wire rimmed glasses. She spoke some English, and I felt like she could have been anyone's sister in America. Mo told me, "Hadia is not a lucky woman." I asked why, and he explained that she had been divorced twice and each of her children was from a different marriage.

Back then, Mo kept mentioning an apartment outside of town that his mother owned, which had no water or electricity. His father said it was fine for me to stay in the family home, as long as I paid. But suddenly he had to go to Cairo for medical treatment. A police officer approved my stay but later gave me a heads-up and warned, "Mo plans for you to be in the apartment, not his family's house." (Mo conceded that his mother objected to me living in the house on the grounds that I was a belly dancer.) I remembered the movie *The Sheltering Sky*, in which Debra Winger ended up secluded in the middle of nowhere in a remote North African village, and I started pursuing my plan B.

So that's how I came to stay at the Palm Trees Hotel, a large cement structure of simple but functional rooms with balconies and hot-water showers. People from all over the world stayed there. One of the managers was a young man with a sweet demeanor named Anwar.

Every night he sat around the outdoor campfire, making sure we had plenty of mint tea and swapping stories until the last tourist went to bed. He said I could stay with his family.

Several people told me that the police wouldn't let a foreigner stay at a local house. The commentary was "Anwar's okay, but Siwis never do something for nothing."

Another guy said, "A British girl who went to stay with them only lasted two days. They wanted to marry her to one of their sons." I'm too old to get married off to one of their kids, so I set a time with Anwar to meet his family. He walked me to an old four-story house by the Shali. It was really picturesque, the type of place I had imagined living in when I came to Siwa.

Up two winding medieval-looking staircases, I entered one of many small rooms and sat on a piece of a broken chair with his mother, Farida, seventeen-year-old sister, Amel, and a couple of tiny toddlers. They patted bread dough into round balls on a metal disc that looked like a giant pizza pan with flour at the bottom. Each ball was rolled with a small rolling pin, and the round pita breads were laid out on a six-by-three-foot piece of cloth on the floor. When that was full, they set another cloth on top and did the same until the sum of pitas reached eighty. Upon seeing my phone, Amel whispered, "Telephone?" I showed it to her, and she proceeded to dial and sneak off to a quiet place. She motioned for me to keep quiet. I found Farida lounging in a small room with cushions on the floor. Her husband came in. He was a tall, handsome man with a white beard and a turban. Amel brought lunch: pickled lemons and rice cooked in beef fat with chunks of fat floating in it. We ate out of communal bowls, each person with a big spoon. Anwar's father opened a small trunk full of family photos. Some featured women of his family, and others showed the men or foreign guests who had visited their home.

When Farida and Amel left the room, he asked if I was married, then said, "You must marry in Siwa."

"I think I'll marry an American," I replied.

"No. Leave America. Bush is bad."

"But there are many good American men."

"I will speak to a neighbor woman who can find you a husband." After some thought, he added, "Marry me."

"You're married," I reminded him.

He was unfazed. "I can marry two."

I shrugged off the idea, hoping that he was joking.

Three of his kids came home from school, and another woman named Mabruka entered to help bake bread. Amel took me on a tour of the house and we ended up on the roof. Chunks of fatty meat were hanging to dry, along with laundry and bales of hay. Amel asked for my phone over and over throughout the day. I sensed a potential drama in the making, and whatever the secrecy was about, I would be an accomplice. I urged her to finish quickly. Going down the stairs, I tripped on the elastic bottom of my harem pants and tumbled all the way down, face first. I landed on my chest and my knee, which hurt so much I couldn't stand. Luckily, nothing was broken. I just had a big bruise and a scrape, plus my pants were ripped. The little kids kept trying to make me feel better by patting my knee with their hands. Ouch!

Since ancient times, Egypt has been known as "the land where people eat a lot of bread." Mabruka and Farida urged me to sit with them while they baked bread. Farida fed the fire beneath the mud stove with dried palm fronds, as Mabruka threw rounds of bread into the oven and watched them puff into pillows, turned them over, and took them out. This all happened very fast, and it didn't take long to bake eighty pieces.

Amel wanted dance lessons and was fascinated by how many parts of my body could move in isolation. She could already do a head slide with a tray full of bread on her head, so I showed her how to make head circles, then use the shoulders, chest, hands, and arms. I promised to bring my computer to play music the next day, but had second thoughts because it could easily be seen as a play toy for little hands or a curious teenage girl. She reached inside my sweater, grabbed my bra strap, and asked me for my bra. I told her "No," so she insisted that I bring her another one instead. The family wanted me to spend the night, but I wasn't comfortable. I wanted to stay with a family, but my gut said that between the probability of a telephone scandal and losing my bra, and then having dear old dad talking about marriage, it wasn't a good idea. Finally, I decided that staying at the hotel gave me more freedom to meet people from different parts of the Siwa scene and settled into my little room for the next few weeks.

"No, Dorothy, it's not Kansas, and Tamalyn, you're not in Indonesia," I thought as I lay in bed, pondering this modern-day version of Oz. Feeling foolish for mistaking Mo for a Siwan version of Arief and thinking that everyone in the world actually wanted to be written about, I tried to pry myself from between the covers once again. I had learned the trick of making a "Siwan electric blanket"—filling plastic water bottles with hot water and crawling beneath the covers with an armload of books and chocolate-filled dates.

Somehow, I had thought that everyone in the Islamic world wanted to be understood, that they would want to clear up misconceptions and share their culture. Siwa gave me a thump on the head, and I woke up with the realization that some people could care less about the concept for this book. Too late. If I had known, I would have gone to Timbuktu instead, where one of my students owns a guesthouse and invited me to stay, but now my tight time schedule and finances didn't allow for a change in midstream.

I went through different phases of thought during my time in Siwa. First was the naiveté, thinking that this was an innocent little oasis and since there were a lot of praying and calls to prayer, the Siwans must be like the people of Banda Aceh. How silly of me to think that 20 percent of the earth's population would all have the same way of thinking just because they believe that "there is only one God, and Mohammed PBUH is his prophet." It's like equating Canadians with Bolivians just because they have church bells.

Later came intimidation, because I realized how much people watched and gossiped about one another's every action. I was concerned about making a misstep or offending the locals. Unfortunately, local sensibilities had been trampled on for years. The Siwan culture is seriously endangered. All I can hope is that, instead of keeping silent and completely whitewashing my experiences (though I have been extremely cautious and tactful), this book will help someone in some way to make decisions that will keep the best parts of the culture alive.

One tradition we could all learn from is Id al Siaha. Literally translated as "Tourism Festival," it has nothing to do with tourists. It is actually the annual reconciliation feast, a tradition that began over 200 years ago, held at the foot of Dakrur Mountain. Some say the festival celebrates peacemaking between the Easterners and Westerners. It coincides with the full moon during October or November. Other factors that determine the exact days are Ramadhan and the date harvest. Id al Siaha was started by a Sufi who ordered all of Siwa's men to come to the mountain, reconcile their differences, and pray for lasting peace. Now it is a three-day festival involving men, unmarried women, and children who pitch tents and camp out in empty houses built specifically for the holiday. They slaughter many animals for the elaborate feast, play games, sell foods and handicrafts, and have religious ceremonies. At the end, men come together dressed in white, carrying flags with verses of the Qur'an, and chant together.

I wasn't in Siwa during the festival, but one summer I was part of another interesting event in Dakrur. Therapeutic sand treatments are said to cleanse the body, help people with rheumatism, and make one look younger. For three days we were wrapped in blankets and buried in the sand to sweat, then led to tents under heavy blankets in hot weather to sweat some more, given special soups and teas to cleanse the body, and ordered to rest.

Unfortunately, I became aware that much in Siwa was hidden from view and it would have taken years for me to be allowed into enough confidence to be able to experience it fully. Tourists are usually seen as cash cows, to be milked, then held at arm's length. Writers are okay, as long as they write tour guides or study uninhabited ruins. At least two female authors I heard about were run out of town over the years, so I think that experiencing as much as I did was an accomplishment and opens our eyes to some of Siwa's many truths.

Internet has taken Siwa by storm. The computer I used faced a fluorescent green wall that was so bright I wondered if it would glow in the dark.

I had some trouble downloading an important application for a yearly grant to fund a festival and theatrical performance that I write (in my other life), and enlisted one of the more upstanding men in town to help me. He asked what I was doing, so I showed him last year's application, which he read with great interest. I mused, "He must think I'm so smart and be impressed that I could write all this, organize budgets for a nonprofit organization, and implement festivals and multimedia productions."

Oops. My delusion. He walked out, turned around, and came back to say, "Can you give me one hundred dollars?"

"Why?" I asked.

"I might go to Europe or someplace else one day, and I will need dollars."

Truth was on my side as I said, "I didn't bring dollars. I go to the ATM, and it gives me Egyptian pounds." To avoid more inquiries, I lied, "All the money I take is from a company, and it has to be accounted for."

He said, "Okay," and that was it.

The incident made me think how foreign and different I was. At first I felt disappointment, but then I realized that this experience made Siwa even more compelling. People's thoughts can be so different. The way we process information and our reactions to it are based on our own life experiences. Whereas I thought a fairly important and intelligent guy might be impressed by my wits, he merely looked at the dollar signs on our organizational budget and wanted some too. When there is a communication gap, that's when people have problems and countries have conflicts. It would be easy to judge and say it was bad that a strange man would ask so boldly for money or that women are covered from head to toe and locked away. It's more interesting to try to understand the behavior of a culture that has recently been forced out of isolation and now has to navigate an onslaught of new ideas.

Ali Wazir, the local olive oil man, smashed wrinkled black olives into small pieces by hand near the ancient Shali, pressing them with a handle that rotated in a circle. I'd seen something similar in other countries, pulled by mules or buffalo, but he did it with one hand. This slight man wearing a thick wool coat over his robes was sixty-nine years old with weathered skin and soulful blue eyes. He wrapped the pieces of olives and seeds in woven fiber and transferred the bundle to a press, extracting a small amount of oil. Remains of the olives were set aside as feed for livestock, and the oil was put in warped plastic water bottles. He poured a capful for me to taste. This "real" olive oil had a strong earthy olive flavor, nothing like the supermarket variety I was used to in the states. It dawned on me that I had seen this man and his rustic olive press in a European documentary about Egypt. He'd actually been featured in several such films. I later tasted a dessert made with dates and olive oil.

He wanted to introduce me to his twenty-year-old daughter Samia, who spoke some English and taught computer programming at a school for girls.

His home was neat and tidy, decorated with rugs on the floor and flat, colorfully covered cushions to sit on. Samia had opted not to get married yet. She said her "spinsterhood" was because she wanted to help take care of her mother, who was diabetic, nearly deaf, and had kidney stones. She worked teaching women how to use computers.

It is unusual for Siwan families to allow their girls to leave the oasis for any length of time, which negates higher educational opportunities. Siwa doesn't have a high school or university, so anybody wishing to continue their studies must leave home and stay in Marsa Matruh until they finish. While some young men are able to, it's out of the question for young Siwan women. Consequently, their formal education stops, so girls rarely progress beyond junior high.

The government started an initiative to train several Siwan women in the use of computers and to send them into the community to train other women. This program involved living in Cairo or Alexandria for three months, but it had to be condensed to accommodate the Siwan custom of not letting the girls leave home. Samia studied eleven hours a day for seven days and was pronounced a teacher, which entailed some serious cramming!

She was a pretty girl with a round face, dressed in black with a black wool scarf on her head. We spoke awhile in the bedroom, where several mattresses were piled up, then she had to leave. There was a potluck dinner where women brought meat and vegetables to another village, cooked it outside, and all ate together. I was invited and wanted to go, but it was a hard choice because I was also fascinated by Samia's father. A big pan of spaghetti cooked in meat soup was already placed on the table between us, which clinched the decision. There were two plates of tomato and cucumber salad and some large spoons. Mr. Wazir brought out long hot green peppers. We broke off pieces of pepper to eat with our pasta. There were no plates; rather, the meal was eaten directly from the pan.

As we sat, Ali Wazir told me he used to be a "magician," meaning a wizard who does magic spells. There is a lot of traditional magic in Siwa, much of it not the nicest kind. I was later told, "Relatives have to sleep in the graveyards for at least three days after a person dies to make sure that practitioners of 'bad magic' (usually women) don't rob the graves of body parts."

I was curious about djinns (genies). The word "djinn" literally translates as "concealment, invisibility, seclusion, or remoteness." Djinns are frequently mentioned in the Qur'an, and it says that the prophet Mohammed PBUH was sent as prophet to both humanity and the djinns. It is said that they have communities, similar to human societies. They eat, marry, and die. Although djinns are invisible to humans, they can see us. Some say they eat bones and have the power to possess people. Their strength is greater than ours and they live longer lives.

Mr. Wazir recounted one of his experiences. "I was walking with a man who appeared to be a local shopkeeper. Upon opening his shop, he grew to seven meters high, and I fainted. I was taken to a place to rest and attended by a kindly woman. Instead of her eyes opening sideways, like everyone's do, they opened from top to bottom, right down the center. She told me, 'Stay away from us,' and I realized that I had entered the dimension of the djinns."

He was so frightened that he went to the strongest wizard in Siwa, a man who lived to age 115 and had a different djinn at his disposal for every day of the week. Though humans are not supposed to have this knowledge until they reach middle age, Ali Wazir was only twenty-five at the time. The wizard told him, "Give up using djinns to carry out magic, and only to turn to the Qur'an for spiritual guidance," which is what he did from then on.

I heard that "the man with all the music in the world" was coming to Siwa. Unfortunately, he was selling his discs from House of Mo. Fortunately, Mo was hardly ever there, so I peeked my head in. Shazli indicated the tall man with a turban by winding his hand above his head, then waved his hand away, meaning "far away."

The serious man seated at Mo's desk looked intimidating with his piercing black eyes, rough features, and straight hair. I hesitated, but Shazli pulled up a chair and motioned for me to sit. On the desk were a mysterious looking black box and an old laptop, several times the size and weight of anything normally used today. Barely looking at me, he clicked on downloads of Lebanese belly dancers. Libyan Bedouin music was dubbed in that had a completely different sound and feel from what these glamorous women were doing. He mumbled, "What do you want to hear?" and poured me some tea.

I replied, "I'm open."

This solemn stranger, who finally introduced himself as Farid, proceeded to play songs from remote and unexpected corners of the world. A lot of his music was obscure, classical, folkloric, or just plain old. It was clear that he had a refined and educated taste.

He clicked around between the music of Banda Aceh and vintage songs from Egypt's "golden age" and finally asked, "Do you want to hear the music of Zanzibar?"

"Why not?" I mused. "Zanzibar. It has a nice ring to it." Upon hearing one song, I said, "That's the perfect belly-dance music! What is it?" The song sounded old and classical, with complex patterns and organic instrumentation.

"It just says, 'Music of Zanzibar.' That's all I know." He promised to make a copy for me.

"Where exactly is Zanzibar?" I asked, and we both agreed that it must be off the east coast of Africa. He played music from Yemen, Iran, and Qatar. I was fascinated.

After we'd traversed the world's music on his computer and the town went to sleep, Farid opened up. The words held inside for so long streamed out, revealing a self-taught intellectual who could talk music, culture, and history in-depth. Gossiping and sharing spooky stories came just as naturally.

We stayed up until the roosters crowed, telling ghost and djinn stories. Farid told tales of local magic. He said, "Some men wanted to kill Ali Wazir and waited in a dark alcove by his house. He never came home, but a dog passed by and peed on one of them. The next day, the magician went to the police to press charges against the men for waiting to kill him. He said, 'That dog was me.'"

He told of two friends in Marsa Matruh who wanted to marry the same woman. The loser commissioned a magician to cast a spell on the groom, rendering him impotent.

What an interestingly contradictory man. Some people said he was Libyan, while others said he was from Marsa Matruh, but he was definitely a Bedouin, with some Bohemian hippy mixed in.

Farid invited me to his garden. He had a chunk of land in town, easily accessible by foot. The first floor of his homebuilt duplex contained an apartment that he rented to a likeably eccentric Spanish woman named Lina. He lived in the unfinished second story. The roof afforded a beautiful view of the floodlit Shali by night, and a meager offering of dates was spread on the roof to dry. He explained that the dates would be used as animal feed.

Next door was the shell of an unfinished house, whose restoration in the traditional style with local mud (*kershef*) had been aborted. Farid said the owner was grumpy, so he used this argument: "I have two floors and a roof. You have one story. Anyone who comes to my house will be able to see your wife in the courtyard from above." Thus the man was convinced to sell it to him cheap. He filled this picturesque abode with a family of goats. I met his chickens, saw their eggs, and watched ducks waddle past. The unkempt gardens were prolific with dates, eggplants, onions, and loofahs.

I thought loofahs grew in the sea, but he peeled what looked like a huge, dried out cucumber. I said, "In the U.S., I buy these in the supermarket to scrub myself with." He shook out the seeds and handed it to me.

We sat on palm-fiber furniture, watching the sunset from his roof, drinking tea and talking for hours. He explained the historical problems between Siwans and Bedouins. "The Siwans would hole up in the Shali when the nomadic Bedouins traveled through. Of course, the Bedouins helped themselves to all the dates and olives they wanted, and nobody came out to challenge them."

Back at House of Mo, I came and went as I liked, to visit Farid. Mo stayed away when I was there. He had become the butt of jokes between Shazli and Farid. These two unlikely characters communicated easily, to the point that Farid made the same grunting noises as Shazli, who couldn't speak, and they shared jokes nobody else understood. One day, I saw both of them poking around House of Mo with suspicious smirks on their faces and a sugar bowl in Shazli's hand. Their latest pet peeve was that Mo never bought sugar for the tea but invited half the men in town to drink, using what Farid bought. Shazli hid a bag of sugar in a hanging basket, then, with a sly grin, mixed what was in the sugar bowl with salt, handing it to Farid to taste and getting his nod of approval. Farid said, "Next time Mo serves tea, it will be mysteriously salty." Shazli's face scrunched to show the distaste Mo and his friends were soon to experience.

Farid invited me to dinner at his home. This could be construed as the closest thing to a date in Siwa, other than those growing on trees. Male-female relations are taboo for the locals, but Farid was a special case. He had a rebellious streak. Long ago, in avoidance of his military service, he fled to Siwa, which was obscure enough to be a good hiding place. Finally, so many years had passed that he could freely travel home to visit his family, no longer having to hide.

The evening of our "date" was extremely cold and windy. The campfire that usually burned in his garden was reduced to a few crimson coals, so we cooked in his unfinished abode. As could be expected of an intellectual hippy, his place lacked furniture. Books and bedding were strewn everywhere. Farid busily cooked on a lopsided gas stove, lit candles on an earthen dish full of sand, and took some red-hot coals indoors. He cooked the shish kebabs on skewers propped between a wastebasket and earthen jug, with the fire below. We had a candle lit feast of kebabs, baba ghanoush, yogurt and cucumber salad, "potato salad" (mashed potatoes with lemon and olive oil), fried potatoes with lemon, and green salad. It was the most delicious meal I'd had in Egypt, and he was a perfect gentleman.

On his computer we watched footage of the 2002 Ahlan Wa Sahlan Cairo Belly Dance Festival, the one Raqia Hassan organizes every year. I pointed out some of my friends in the audience while marveling at how Farid could take the burning coals beneath a boiling teapot and toss them back and forth with bare hands. He showed me a video of a man eating a red-hot coal, another sewing his face together with a needle and thread without bleeding, one pulling a bus with his teeth, and one doing some nails-up-the-nose tricks. Unconvinced, I pointed out how easily these tricks could have been manipulated with editing.

My curiosity was piqued because every day a steady stream of local men would buy CDs and DVDs from Farid. I doubted that they were beating down the door to buy vintage songs from Zanzibar and Banda Aceh. One night he became extremely agitated when Mo made off with his black box. What did it contain that was such a secret, I wondered. Later I asked, out of curiosity, what kind of movies he was selling. He gave me a sly little salt-in-the-sugar grin and poured some more tea.

"The police do what they want. If they want something, you have to give it to them for free," was one shopkeeper's take. More than one person told me of a room in the police station that was infamous for being used to force information and confessions out of people, and I often heard stories of Siwans being brought in for beatings. According to local tradition, discipline was to be carried out by the shaikh or, in more serious cases, a tribunal of shaikhs and usually involved a fine or lashing. The police weren't Siwi or Bedouin; they were sent in from other parts of Egypt.

Once my tourist bubble burst and I realized there were social issues and realities behind the magical oasis facade, I started noticing the predominance of uniformed men, both military and police.

Hamid was second in command at the police station. Lorraine had given him a new age healing therapy one night as we were sitting around the campfire at the Palm Trees Hotel. He was with one of the Caireens who had come to develop an ecolodge. My vibe on Hamid was bad, maybe because of his perennial frown. Lorraine said, "He's actually a good guy."

On my way back to Siwa from the Mo incident, I called Lorraine, and she called Hamid, convinced that he would be "understanding" and watch out for me during my stay.

I felt like I was dodging a minefield because I might need him but such an association might completely alienate me from the locals. Since, upon my return, I didn't sense anything more dangerous than gossip, I never called . . . until the ATM incident.

There was only one bank in Siwa, and it had an ATM machine. I took money out many times without a problem, until one day, when I really needed it, the machine processed my withdrawal—but didn't give me the cash. I tried again, and the same thing happened.

Along came Lina, Farid's tenant. She told me in an unintelligible mixture of English, Spanish, and Arabic, "Este machine haram!" (This machine is bad.)

"Hmm?" I asked, without taking my eyes off the machine.

Her pitch rose as she screamed, "Ladrones!" (Thieves!)

I spoke with her in Spanish and finally got the scoop. Several days before, she had used the ATM, which took the money out of her account but didn't give it to her. The ATM's printer was out of ink, so the receipt was blank. Inside, the officers refused to give a receipt and, after much to-do, handed over a faded photocopy of something handwritten in Arabic which, upon translation, turned out to say nothing.

I went inside and, between translating for her and explaining my problem, got an unproductive runaround and no receipt whatsoever.

Agitated, Lina resumed speaking her special language that nobody understood. I made her sit and be calm. "I can call this guy I know. He's the second in command for the police in Siwa."

When I dialed Hamid, he said, "Stay there. I'll send someone." Suddenly, a man emerged from behind the counter and escorted me outside to the ATM and I got my money.

When I returned, Lina said, "The police came, spoke a couple of words to the manager, and left again." I resolved my problem but, promising to help her too, called Hamid again.

He put me on the phone with the officer, who claimed, "I talked to you on my way in and my way out." Lina said he didn't even speak to her, so I insisted that Hamid come in person.

He spoke with the manager and explained more nonsense to us, suggesting that her problem should be taken up with her bank in Spain. "The Egyptian bank cannot be held responsible."

I told Hamid, "The police should look into this because a lot of tourists could be losing money, and they wouldn't know until they got home, especially if they were like most people and only stayed in Siwa for a couple of days."

"This is a government bank," he insisted. "They would never cheat people."

He then escorted me outside and I knew what was coming. He asked about the Mo story and said I needed to make a report. I said, "This is not a police matter. It's good enough that he hides from me. I don't need to do anything, neither do you."

"Anytime you want to get him back, let me know," Hamid said. "This isn't the first time people have problems with Mo. I've had his ass kicked before and would be happy to do it again."

Soon after, Mo told a good friend of mine his version of the camping trip from hell. Although one could get a permit to take tourists from Siwa to Bahariya, it was very difficult to obtain one to bring them back. We had paid for permits, but there were none, so, since I was the only one left, he figured I could be smuggled back to Siwa under a pile of blankets, and if the military found me, he would simply pay a small bribe. The car belonged to Kamel, who wanted no part of the scheme. I knew nothing about his cockeyed master plan, and he didn't want to attract undue attention because what he feared most was the police. I was simply being locked away because he didn't know what else to do with me. Mo wanted time to figure a way out of this predicament and couldn't understand why I wasn't cooperating. I can't believe I was so intimidated by someone so stupid!

On a different occasion, Farid was kind enough to lend me one of his bikes indefinitely. I liked renting a hot pink one from down the street, though it rode like it had been run over by a donkey cart. But Farid was concerned for my safety and insisted that I take his.

Since my arrival, people had been telling me "there is no stealing in Siwa," so I thought I could leave Farid's bicycle outside the hotel. One morning, expecting to ride around town, I noticed that the pedal was broken off and nowhere to be seen. I guessed that someone needed a pedal and couldn't afford to buy one. Luckily, there was a bike repair shop next to the hotel, and it only cost a dollar to fix. The owner's adorable three-year-old daughter was playing outside, and he told me to go with her, motioning to "take photos."

I followed the tiny girl behind a blanket like curtain, and blood spattered before me. Her mother was in the process of killing a duck. I'd eaten plenty of meat and worn leather shoes all my life, but this was the first time I had witnessed an animal killed with my own eyes. I had to keep from wincing and not allow nausea to creep in. The child brought me into a tiny earthen room. Mattresses were folded against the wall, and her brother and sister were playing on the floor. It was clear that the family of five lived in this humble room. Most Siwan homes I visited had many rooms. They might not be furnished, and could be partially painted and old, but there were rooms to spare. I suspected these people were from someplace else. Nazira, the mother, entered in her bloodstained caftan and served tea and homemade cake. She said they were from a small town in the Egyptian countryside.

When I told Abi about the missing pedal, he insisted, "Nobody stole the pedal. It's impossible."

"I don't mind," I said, "it was cheap, and I met a nice family."

He added, "A big policeman probably took it for a ride and broke the pedal."

I thought that was a weird hypothesis but agreed, "Anything is possible."

When I told Farid about the pedal, he thought a moment and said, "I saw a policeman riding around town on my bike. They think they can do anything they want and take anyone's things. I asked, 'Where did you get that bike? It's not yours,' and he said a lady at the hotel gave him permission to ride it. He was fat, so he probably broke it." I guess Abi's logic was right—or, more likely, he saw the policeman but didn't want to tell me.

Some of the most interesting people I met in Siwa were foreigners. Whoever left the comforts of the Western world and made their home in Siwa, braving the gossip and cold winters, had to have a unique perspective on life. As soon as I saw Frederic, I wanted to become his friend. This unique man, bundled in layers of sweaters and scarves with Coke-bottle-thick glasses peeking through, flashed a big smile and some dry wit, and I was hooked. He had gone through many incarnations during this lifetime in Egypt. Starting out in the civil service of one of the European governments, he then became a famous artist. He said, "I am now in the farming phase."

"Life on the oasis revolves around interpersonal relationships," Frederic observed, "so that's what they spend most of their time discussing."

Then he added, "Life in Siwa is like peeling an onion. You want to stay between the layers, not become one of the layers, so you won't smell."

I didn't know what he meant, but I kept it in mind.

"Have you seen the men dance?" He asked.

I had seen them around the campfire and replied, "Yes, but I'd like to see more."

He told me about his New Year's Eve party and advised, "Tourists can hire them, but they won't do a good show with tea and cucumber sandwiches. In order to see them relaxed and dancing for themselves, they need plenty of alcohol and hashish. If you really want to see them dance, I can arrange it."

"Who'll buy the inebriates?" I asked doubtfully. I had read that in old times, date wine and hashish were part of the culture and that zaggalah partied heavily.

The oasis was dry, but homemade date wine was readily available. Frederic said, "When they start playing music they're cold, but if there is alcohol, they drink it as fast as possible for the express purpose of getting drunk. That's when you get the real music and dance."

Traditionally, men only played music and danced outside of town, amid the gardens and out of earshot of women. In those instances, absolutely no women were allowed into this exclusive world of men. For me, a woman, to be part of this cultural experience, we needed a venue outside of town but inside four walls.

Frederic asked if I wanted to see the place he had in mind. As he drove me outside the town, a hitchhiker hopped onto the back of his pickup. We stopped at what had been a prison run by Italians in World War II. Most of it had been torn down and a modern house built on top. There was a front room with lots of space, plus a traditional room with rugs and cushions, two charcoal braziers, candles, and hanging lamps with lights under blowing cloth that looked like faux flames, the kind you find in novelty shops in the U.S. He showed me a former torture chamber, now a cellar, which remained locked "to keep the ghosts at bay."

Frederic said, "When I moved to Siwa eleven years ago, there were only three cars in the oasis. Now there are many, but donkey carts are still a primary mode of transport." It was considered unlucky to have a female donkey, so the males fought a lot. Mostly it was heehawing, which at first I thought was just donkey talk, but was told that they did it because they didn't like each other. Since nobody wanted to have a female, they couldn't breed and sell donkeys in Siwa, so all the donkeys were bought in other areas.

Frederic had a very special donkey cart. It looked like a nineteenth-century carriage of black leather and handcrafted wood. He explained, "This is like the horse carriages in Alexandria, but I had mine specially made to fit a donkey." He didn't drive his donkey cart anymore, "One day, my donkey attacked another donkey. I was caught between the donkey and the seat. Once I separated them, I got myself loose and crawled into the bushes."

On the night of the big party, he arrived at the hotel to fetch me in a donkey cart. It was not his fancy one, but still it lent an air of old-world charm. Officers outside the Palm Trees Hotel were duly impressed. Some of the hotel staff came out to watch, and there was much discussion as we trotted away.

This former prison now resembled an Egyptian temple, with high ceilings and columns and traditional Siwan architecture, a small pool in the center, and an adjoining sitting room full of Bedouin carpets and cushions on the floor. Frederic built two fires in charcoal braziers, tossed some frankincense on top, and lit two trays of candles secured in sand. The room was toasty warm, and we sat eating dates and sipping hot chocolate, waiting for the band to arrive. Frederic had warned me, "Be very careful who you invite. Absolutely no children."

Ali was bringing the musicians, and they were late. He said, "Many uninvited guests kept trying to hop on the truck. It was a battle to get rid of the hangers-on." After the band arrived, there was a line at the door of people he had to turn away. It was like a New York City night club, and Frederic had to choose who entered and who didn't. Malek, a dashing young man who had the only motorcycle in town, was admitted to the party.

Thirteen men with turbans and one dressed as a woman filtered into the room and shook my hand. They hooked up a scratchy sound system and proceeded to play some songs on the tashibept, with drums, singing, and hand claps. Frederic said, "Wait till they break out the date wine." The man dressed in a woman's wedding dress with a belt wrapped around his head belly danced as Frederic explained, "The chap in a woman's dress is engaged to Ali's daughter."

They took a break to drink date wine. Water bottles of the homemade brew were opened and poured into tiny shot glasses, downed in one gulp. They tried serving me shots, with which I just moistened my lips, then made a face and gave back. This caused amusement. The main server took it upon himself to try pouring shots down my throat. It became a game as I evaded the brew, which then made its way down someone else's throat. The party got wilder, and they pulled me up to dance. I kept my steps simple and often sat down on cushions until they pulled me up again. I must admit that being surrounded by what was now at least twenty-five handsome men in turbans, exhibiting full masculine energy with their music and dancing, was a pleasure. In keeping with tradition, though, their male sexual energy was directed at each other.

Much dancing was refined, soft, and sensual, similar to belly dance. Some men used African-looking steps as well, and there was the inevitable laying on the floor simulating the sex act, layered in twos and threes. They sometimes put their hands against the wall above men who were seated and writhed over them, or placed hands on each other's shoulders or waists with similar moves. Frederic thought I would be shocked, but I found the whole scene interesting. It was masculine homoeroticism, but without any show of skin and with none of the violent or aggressive overtones found when sensuality becomes enmeshed into American dances.

One man opened an orange and burned something in the peel. I wondered about the aftermath of this party and its effects on the carpets. Piles of peanuts had been placed around the room as snacks, and orange and banana peels had been squashed into mush with the peanut shells by the dancer's feet.

Sometime around 1 AM Amir, one of the star lead dancers, put on his jacket. He bid goodbye. It was sudden, and the band followed. I asked Frederic if everything was okay.

He laughed, "Of course. There's no more booze, so they leave as fast as they came."

One day I got worried because I was looking for Frederic and my calls wouldn't go through. He drove into town and told me how one of his sheep had just birthed a lamb, but the ram got between her and her baby, and she was rejecting it. He separated them and had to get the mother to feed her lamb or it wouldn't last the night. We went to see his goats and a herd of sheep. The little lamb was so cute, running after his mom with thick legs and almost adult-sized hooves. The mom was more interested in joining the other sheep than taking care of her baby, and Frederic was concerned.

"She's young, and her lamb was unseasonably late. I hope maternal instinct will kick in." Three goats escaped by forcing the gate open. Frederic sent me out with a stick to herd them back in. I tapped one on the butt. He said, "You need to hit harder." I tried blocking a little one's escape with my hip. Frederic made special goat-calling noises with his mouth, and they eventually returned to the pen.

We drove through some olive groves to a mud house Frederic was rebuilding as a picnic retreat and summer home. The government makes getting a building permit easy if you build onto the framework of an old structure in the traditional mud style. Three brothers were taking mud from ground that had been dried for several generations but had not yet turned to sandstone. They were chipping it into pieces that fit the wall, stacking them, and holding the pieces together with fresh mud. Slathering mud on top made a natural-looking finish. The house contained several rooms, two bathrooms, and a roof that we couldn't go onto because the mud stairs leading up to it were still wet. The ceilings were made of palm and bamboo.

Siwan fences are made from dried palm fronds standing straight up and tied in a row. Frederic's fence had a hole in it, which he explained was due to the local men using his property for drinking parties.

He said, "Since the house has been abandoned so long, they have been using this spot for generations. They do clean up after themselves, though."

While I was eating lunch with Penny and her family, a steady stream of people came in and out: little girls, bigger girls, and finally a man in a crisp white robe. Tall and slender, his bone structure and black eyes could have had Hollywood casting him as an ancient Egyptian pharaoh. His name was Malek.

He didn't take his eyes off me, but it wouldn't have been culturally correct for me to return his gaze. Malek's family were the landlords, and he was one of eleven brothers and sisters who had been traipsing about. The grandson of a prominent tribal shaikh, he spent his time overseeing workers of the family gardens. He proposed all sorts of ideas—introducing me to the women of his family, having his ninety-year-old grandmother demonstrate the real Siwan women's dance, and hosting a garden party on one of their farms—none of these ever materialized, but he became my faithful stalker.

Stalking is illegal in the U.S., and a stalker is usually seen as a deranged menace. In Siwa, dealing with the opposite sex isn't a skill one learns, nor is there any precedent. To a man with a lot of time on his hands, persistence is the only tactic.

I often sat in an outdoor area of Abdu's restaurant, which was the meeting place for all walks of oasis life. Pecking away at my little computer a couple of hours each day, I would inevitably look up and see

Malek lurking about, watching me from a distant table. Half the town noticed before I caught on.

He regularly offered me rides on his motorbike. I loved riding, and this man was definitely eye-candy, but I didn't want to fuel the rumor machine. I still held hopes of getting a deeper glimpse inside this closed society, so I said, "No."

At the end of Frederic's party, which Malek had schmoozed his way into, the musicians were being picked up by the truckload. Frederic and I had to wait for everyone to be dropped off before the truck would return for us. It was cold and he suggested, "Don't wait. Let Malek take you home."

Fully aware of the scandal that would ensue if I was seen riding around town on the back of his motorcycle at one in the morning, especially after the crowd formed outside the hotel to see Frederic and me ride away in a donkey cart, I shrugged and said, "I guess there will be enough talk in the town after this party anyway." Frederic told him something in Arabic and explained that we should take the back roads. I said, "Leave me off a ways before the hotel."

I had to wear a helmet to disguise my face. "Everyone will recognize my fuzzy black coat," I said. It was lush, fashionable, and I'd been wearing it every day. He gave me his jacket and proceeded to put my coat on. I protested, "That will be worse!" So he rode through the biting wind in only his long white robe. Mission accomplished. Only one farmer saw us do the coat exchange, and I walked the last hundred meters to my hotel.

Finally, the preposterousness of such limitations hit home. If Malek was going to turn into someone I couldn't handle, he'd already had his opportunity. If people wanted to gossip after such a wild party, they had each other to gossip about.

The next day at Abdu's, I let Malek catch my eye. He jingled his keys. I stopped worrying about public opinion and nodded.

"Do you want to see the sunset at Fatnas Island?" he invited. Fatnas is a famous island with a hot spring. When we arrived, the island was messy and partly underwater. We motor biked on dirt roads across sections of the salt lake. Roads were falling apart, and I thought we were going to wind up in the water. Fatnas Island had been a scenic spot in the past, but now the area seemed to be drowning. The sunset was beautiful, as all Siwan sunsets are, but I was saddened by this flaming example of environmental destruction.

Amir, one of the principle dancers at Frederic's party, possessed a unique blend of chocolate skin, light eyes, and chiseled features. Frederic invited him to dinner, and Malek showed up too. Frederic seated Malek on my left and Amir on my right.

At Frederic's party, Amir had appeared larger than life—an amazing dancer, drummer, and singer. In this totally different setting, he seemed so young! Toying with his cell phone throughout the evening and answering at least a dozen calls, he acted like a teenager. He was smaller than I remembered and a bit thin. I asked his age, and he replied, "Almost twenty-six." He worked all day in his garden, liked to drink date wine and sing by himself, then go straight home, sitting far from his parents so they wouldn't smell the alcohol on his breath.

Amir's father was a famous Siwan who had sung for the president. He had a collection of hundreds of Siwan poems written down, and Frederic had been wanting to have them recorded for awhile. I offered to record with my video camera, which had great sound, and then clean them up in a recording studio and send him the masters. Excited about the project, Amir invited us all to his home for lunch the next day and to his garden afterward.

Amir's family lived in a four-story medieval-looking mud house with a maze of large rooms. His mother prepared a delicious lunch of soup called *shorbit*, made with vegetables and some sort of internal organs. There was also a salad of tomato, cucumber, parsley, hot pepper, and lemon, then *mulukhiyya* (a dark green soup made of a slimy green Egyptian herb) along with pita bread, rice with tiny noodles, and tea.

After lunch, Amir escorted me into a room with his mother, who started pulling clothes out of her closet. I thought she might be trying to sell them. She laid out her wedding dress and wedding shawl. The dress was like a large white shirt, heavily embroidered with silk, shell buttons, and assorted amulets. I said, "I already have a Siwan wedding dress." Amir insisted I try it on, then put the elaborately embroidered shawl with sequins and bright tassels over my head and brought me into the room where the men were drinking tea. He changed into a farmer's outfit and posed with me while everyone took pictures using their cell phones. Our "wedding photos" became wallpaper on his family's and friend's cell phones.

With my video camera, Amir filmed his mother patting out bread dough; he skillfully focused on the bread without showing more than her hands. Frederic said, "We should be going to the farm, or it will get too cold."

Earlier in the day, I'd watched a boy drive his donkey cart with two donkeys, one was an adult and one was a cute little baby. Now Frederic's custom-built chauffeur-driven donkey cart had two donkeys. He explained, "Donkeys hate to be alone, so a few days ago, I bought mine a baby. He'll walk alongside his new brother until his legs get strong enough to pull the cart himself."

At his garden, Amir showed me a spring and the Jacuzzi-sized pool of hot water it created. It looked really tempting, but it would have been uncomfortable to bathe in denim palazzo pants and a turtleneck. We sat on a straw mat in the garden while Amir fixed tea over a plate of coals. Siwan tea contains mint and a lot of sugar spooned into a tea glass. Tea was poured into the glass, and the contents were poured back into the pot, then back and forth repeatedly.

I mused to myself that this new circle of friends was a step up from some of the characters I'd met in Siwa previously. I had not been begged from, proposed to, talked to about sex, or subjected to gossip all day. That was about to change.

Frederic caught me alone and said, "Malek wants to marry you."

"What?" I responded, knowing that Frederic had a quirky sense of humor.

"I told him you wouldn't be likely to agree. I said, 'She's been around the world a few times, and I doubt that she would settle in Siwa.' He says that it is not Siwa you should fall in love with. It's him. He has a plan, which I must warn you about." I listened, sensing more silliness in the making. Frederic explained, "He asked me to invite you to my house, then, in the area where I had wanted to put a statue of Alexander the Great, he said he will come out and stand without any clothes. He is convinced that if you saw him in the nude, you would fall in love and marry him."

I told Frederic "Stop pulling my leg."

Soon after, while we were on a bike ride home from an evening of belly dancing with his little sisters, Malek queried, "Did Frederic tell you?"

"What?" I asked innocently.

"That I want to marry you." (He didn't mention anything about posing as a Greek conqueror.)

I explained that I live in America and have to travel for the next year to write my book and I was too old for him.

"Age doesn't matter," he said, "I love a twenty-year-old, but I will give her up for you because you are perfect."

That was flattering, but I assured him it wouldn't work.

We rode a ways, then he broke the silence. "I love you and want to help you. There is a designer named Tony from Italy. He is seventy-four years old."

"Seventy-four?"

He thought a moment and said, "I mean forty-seven. Like your age. He's single. I don't know when he's coming, but maybe you can go to Italy to meet him. You can marry him and be happy." I appreciated his concern and assured him that there were plenty of men to marry.

Shazli made a series of gestures that I interpreted to mean I was invited to a wedding. He then led me down some alleys to a tiny mud-walled room full of women. It was his sister's henna party, a traditional celebration where women beautify the bride by decorating her hands and feet with elaborate henna designs. The bride, about twenty years old, was having leather pieces of cut-out patterns placed over her hands and feet. Women of the family packed a paste of henna on top. Girls applied these patterns on one another, being extra careful not to move and cause their decorations to flake off. The henna must dry first. Then you rub it off, making a big mess, and remove the leather relief design, ending up with orange patterns on the skin.

Young women wore ruffled, frilly, long dresses of lace and sparkly fabrics, topped off with Islamic headscarves. Married women entered, their blue tarfotets draped over their shoulders like shawls and the black facecloth flipped back. Underneath, they wore knitted shawls on their heads and loose caftans over other layers of clothing. I felt like I was living in an old painting.

We sat crowded and crunched against each other. Each woman spoke louder than the next, and most had husky voices. Even the little girls had deep raspy voices and shouted over the others to be heard. What looked like a cushion to sit on was actually a baby wrapped in heavy blankets. It's a good thing I stepped carefully.

One of the girls rewound a twisted Egyptian cassette and inserted it in the broken front of a boom box. Scratchy sound wafted through the room as several women tied scarves around their hips, started to dance, then chickened out after a few seconds and pushed someone else into the center, who would chicken out too. All eyes looked at me.

To their surprise, I could dance. After that, inhibitions were released. All the unmarried girls took turns dancing with me. I would start just to get them up and then pull back and watch. A lot of clapping was going on, but an old woman came in and told everyone not to clap. They were still a noisy bunch, and the warped music continued. Twisting headscarves into a ropelike shape, they took turns tying them tightly under their buttocks. The movements were sharp and strong. All with the hips and nothing with the upper body, hands, or arms.

Shazli was the only man allowed to enter the room. I was told it was because he couldn't speak, so he wouldn't tell anyone what he saw. The bride invited me to her wedding the following night.

I arrived on time for the wedding, but a man turned me away. "One hour," is what I thought he said. I went to see Farid, who was sitting nearby. He said I should go in with Shazli.

Unfortunately, an elderly aunt didn't want a foreigner at the wedding. Farid asked one of the bride's brothers and came back with the explanation, "Yesterday, it was just the family, but now, all the women of the town will be here. They're afraid some people wouldn't like a stranger to see their women." I sat outside. All the men of the town filed by, descending from bicycles, trucks, and donkey carts. Shazli motioned something about my video camera, so I showed him how to use it and watched him head for the wedding. He returned unsuccessful; they didn't allow him to film.

It was customary for the bride's family to invite all the men of the town for a meal. Farid said, "I'm going in to eat. I'll see what I can do.

Anyway, it'll just be a few minutes." They basically eat and run. The next day, the men visit the groom and also eat, but they have to pay, and the amount each one pays gets written down. I never got to go in, but it was interesting to watch the entire town come and go from the house.

My luck improved thanks to Penny. Abdu's daughter was getting married, and Penny asked if I wanted to go. The bride was fifteen. Her wedding was a surprise—even to her. From what we could gather, her fiancé, whom she had been engaged to since childhood, was leaving Siwa so they had to get married right away. Most girls were engaged through an arrangement around puberty or before, and married in their teens.

We entered a long room crowded with women in traditional dress. A typical wedding lasts three days. Day one: the henna party. The next day: the bride wears a white dress similar to those in the Western world. Women gather round, dancing and socializing. Everyone then packs into cars and trucks to drive around town and take the bride to the groom's family's house to consummate the marriage. The third day: the bride wears a Siwan wedding dress with all her gold jewelry, and an entourage accompanies her on her final move to her husband's family home. I heard various versions, but this was how Abdu's daughter's wedding took place. Penny said, "She's a tomboy, and I can't imagine her getting married."

When we saw her sitting on a chair, elevated above the others like a queen in her throne, Penny couldn't believe the transformation. Her hair was streaked blond and woven with silk flowers into an elaborate do. She was fully made up, with lots of gold glitter on her eyelids. The dress was of beaded satin with a big hoopskirt. Underneath, she wore white tights and grandmotherly looking shoes.

Some of the young married women wore large tunics of white lace with beaded pieces of wedding shawls inserted into panels near the bottom. They had white fringe shawls on their heads and wore at least ten solid-gold bracelets on their arms, and large gold beads and pendants hanging from their necks. Others dressed in the typical Siwan married women's tarfotets over caftans and black face-coverings flipped back. Unmarried girls wore frilly dresses, but some had modern flared jeans underneath.

Penny and her kids told the bride "This is Tamalyn. She's a dancer."

The women played a tape of nondescript Egyptian pop music on a huge boom box and made everyone in the room sit. It was show time.

I did the usual—hip circles, eights, and shimmies from the old-time Egyptian movies, with no hand or arm movements, keeping it simple. Then, women took turns tying scarves around their hips and dancing either alone or in pairs. They asked Sasha to do an "English dance." She looked at her mom with a shrug asking, "What dance do we do in England?"

A French girl got up and they told her to do something Moroccan.

Women took turns dancing in a small space, while one of the women sat holding the large tape player, shaking it back and forth, keeping time with large sweeping movements. I was ducking the flailing boom box when Penny said, "They like to see something different." When the bride's mother made me get up again, I decided to use my hands and arms, doing some slow movements. She made me dance facing the bride for a long time.

Suddenly we were on the move. Everyone in the room stampeded through doors and crowded their way into a caravan of vehicles. We were packed onto the back of a pickup truck, standing, screaming as if on a carnival ride, and falling over each other as the procession barreled down the road to a village. All the carloads of people gathered together, and the bride was escorted into the groom's house. People threw candy from the roof for the children to scurry and collect. They had done the same at the bride's house. I wondered whether Spanish piñatas had evolved from this custom.

One local guy, whom I considered somewhat of a rogue, told me that he had been beaten by a shaikh because a 13-year-old boy accused him of forcing sex on him. This man insisted; "But I paid him." This same man expressed concerns that one of his young relatives was interested in women and felt that this boy should stick to men until he gets married.

Over the course of my stay in Siwa, the topic of premarital homosexuality came up repeatedly, from a variety of sources.

Wanting to make sure I wasn't being misled by people who might be the exception rather than the norm, I asked one young man who seemed decent and not involved with local gossip. He explained—

quite candidly—"There are no women available here, so we f---- each other." He wasn't ashamed, nor did he use the F-word with the violence or aggression usually attached when English speakers say it. For him, it was simply a word to describe an action. "When a man sees another man he wants to f----, he asks 'Do you want to f----?' If the other agrees, there are two ways to do it. Either you f---- him and then he f---- you, or if you only want to f---- him, you have to pay." He went on, comfortable and very matter of fact, "Sometimes a man will be very drunk and take another man by force. If the second man goes to the shaikh and complains, the first man must pay one thousand pounds [about $170 US at the time], and the shaikh beats him eighty strokes."

Reactions to the subject of men with men followed a distinct pattern. Single men said it was common practice. Their stories usually included far fewer lovers than rumors would indicate. Married men often denied that it happened anymore and said it had stopped long ago. Some married guys bragged about extramarital affairs with great exaggeration and a lot of wishful thinking thrown in.

One night, at the Shali Lodge, a guy was joking about a man who stamped his feet as a signal to his wife that he was in the mood. Everyone laughed uproariously, but it fell flat when translated to English. They discussed how romantic love wasn't part of the culture, and neither was kissing or being openly affectionate with your wife. The only exposure they had to romance was in the movies. Some said that, in order to express themselves in that way, it had to be with an outsider.

Another subject that came up repeatedly was that of getting a foreign woman (or man) to buy expensive gifts, or marrying a woman to get a visa out of Egypt. Often, intercultural romances were so intertwined with material conveniences that it was hard to decipher what the relationships were about.

I asked how the women felt about their meanderings. Of course, according to the men, they're completely innocent. I could sew, watch them bake bread, or dance with them, but to speak about more than name, age, married or engaged, I would need a man to translate. My window to the women was through the men. In subsequent visits to Siwa, I was able to spend more time with women. They knew little of the outside world and seemed fairly content, though many were divorced at least once, often at a young age. No one that I met questioned her status in life or complained of a lack of freedom. Social lives among the women were vibrant, and I didn't sense any waves of dissent. More often, I learned, it was the men who had been exposed to the outside world who expressed dissatisfaction. Several young men wanted the restrictions to ease up on the women in their families. Others didn't want to marry a girl with little education or worldly experience. Clandestine pornographic movies from the West were widely available in Siwa, serving as the only teachers of sexual practice available on the oasis. This, combined with an influx of tourists—some in search of young boys to exploit and others merely unmarried couples traveling together and wandering the plaza hand-in-hand—created confusion among young men. Women stayed home, with little exposure to the outside world, so they seemed the more grounded and secure gender.

Richard, an Englishman sitting around the fire at the Palm Trees, was a photographer who specialized in documenting soccer fans. The Pan African soccer playoffs were finishing up in Cairo. This was akin to the Super Bowl in the United States. He had been there for some of the games and then came to Siwa to get shots of the men cheering from coffeehouses. Egypt won that night, so the coffeehouses were on fire with enthusiastic shouts.

Another of his projects involved photographing the overabundance of water in the middle of the desert. He wanted to know what was being done to slow the flow. His inspiration was spawned by purchasing a bottle of Siwa water in a local shop in Bristol, England.

Apparently, 100,000 liters a day were bottled in a plant just outside of town and sold all over Egypt—and in European markets too. He thought, "How odd to find water imported to Europe all the way from the Sahara," then learned that there is an oversupply of water in Siwa. Most of it is saline and not saleable. Siwan deep-source fossilized mineral water is the purest in Egypt though. The Siwa water plant is going strong, and there is another company in Siwa called *Hayat* (Life). It was good to know the drinking water didn't come from the Nile!

I thought about the paradox between Banda Aceh, which was surrounded by water and got a lot of rain but had a freshwater shortage that had reached crisis proportions, and the abundance of water here in the middle of the Sahara. Flooding, a major method of irrigation, poses drainage problems. Excess water sat in the soil creating water-logged land and high salinity.

Farmers have been using the same methods for hundreds of years, but the many newcomers and their projects are tipping the ecosystem off balance.

A driver from our hotel, who had taken Lorraine, Cristof, and me on an excursion to see tombs a few weeks before, approached me and said, "Remember when we went to my land and you saw some workers in uniforms?"

I responded, "Yes."

"They were from the government and they cemented over my spring. That spring took four years to build."

Rapid development has been increasing groundwater extraction. This is accompanied by continuous lowering of the water table, leading to depletion of the aquifer and increasing the groundwater salinity, which is ruinous to crops. Cementing over wells is one of the ways the government attempts to control the water problem that has environmentalists and farmers scared.

The exclusive domain of women, embroidery is one of the more visible aspects of Siwan culture. Everything from heavy coin, button, and shell-laden wedding shawls to wedding dresses and tarfotets is elaborately embroidered.

Abi told me about his cousin who makes extra money embroidering for a European designer. I invited Dina, and Abi invited Penny's nine-year-old daughter, Claudia. We all followed Abi to a home and were introduced to nineteen-year-old Hoda, a plump girl with dark skin and light eyes. She showed us the work she does on flowered mesh fabric. *Harir* is the name for embroidered symbols made with silk thread, and *tercher* is the name for work done with sequins and beads. Often tercher is done on top of a piece of fabric already embroidered with harir. Hoda showed us her wedding shawl, which weighed ten kilos. Replete with every variety of sequins, beads, buttons, cowry shells, coins, and antique jewelry, it was extremely heavy and made jingly noises. Around the edge were long tassels of bright multicolored wool. Claudia and I asked if she could give us embroidery lessons, and we arranged to meet the following day for our first class.

Abi said we'd have to bring our own beads, which they call *bayed*, and silk thread. We asked where to buy these things, and he directed us to a local lawyer's shop. It was closed, but a young boy motioned for us to ring the bell next door. Out came a swarthy looking man, his face darkly stubbled. He opened the "gold store," which had a few sets of earrings and some bracelets in a meagerly stocked display case. Everything was dusty and dark. We asked, "Bayed?" and he took us to a locked backroom. It looked like all the beads, sequins, and little plastic flowers in Hong Kong all condensed into one tiny room. I was amazed that all this had made its way to Siwa. Drawer after plastic drawer were brought out and shown to a steady stream of women who came and went through a separate entrance. As we looked around this opulent but obscure shop, veiled women filtered through a side door, purchasing large amounts of plastic beads and sequins. Against one wall were cosmetics, hair products, and boxes containing lingerie.

We returned to Hoda's for our sewing lesson. More productive than the sewing was the amount of English we taught Hoda and the Arabic she taught us.

As in every home I'd visited, we removed our shoes and sat on cushions on a floor of simple rugs. There was only one piece of furniture—a dresser with a TV and two remotes. Hoda asked Claudia if she had a satellite dish where she lived, then proceeded to switch on the TV and channel surf through programs of many nationalities before switching it off again to resume sewing.

We asked about music and dance. Hoda said, "Wait until my father goes out." Then her brother brought in a broken tape deck and a cassette of Egyptian pop music. Along with a 12-year-old neighbor who stopped in, we took turns tying a headscarf around our hips and dancing. Hoda danced well, with sharp hip movements. After her brother returned and took away the tape deck, she told me "Younger Siwan women get most of their movements from Egyptian television shows and have given up dancing to Siwan music."

Rashid was the only tour guide I met with business cards, e-mail that got checked regularly, and a cell phone permanently attached to his ear. I wasn't sure whether to trust him or not, since he was often seen flanking Rico, a loudmouthed developer from Alexandria with a gravelly voice who took on the airs of a gangster from a bad movie. Basking in Rico's shadow was a plump, nondescript guy with pants low enough to show the top of his boxer shorts. They spoke tough-guy English together, as if they were in an action movie, peppered with four letter words. Surrounding these two were always a few local guys, including Rashid.

Since my arrival in Siwa, Rashid had offered to take me in his jeep to see a women's sewing class, but not wanting to end up in another weird situation, I was hesitant. I measured my fears against the possibility of experiencing another aspect of life with Siwan women and decided to take the chance.

As we sped far out of town in his jeep, I got nervous and said, "I thought this was in Siwa."

"No," he replied, "we're going to Maraqi." He sensed my discomfort as we passed an unfinished shell of an ecolodge and headed past mountains of Greek and Roman tombs. "You don't trust me," he observed as I sat on the edge of my seat.

We pulled into a small village and entered a typical mud house with a maze of unfurnished rooms. Rashid's mother greeted us, then his sister and several other female relatives. They took me to a room where ten teenage girls sat on the floor, practicing embroidery on squares of muslin ten inches across. We exchanged names—many were Fatma and Leila— and shared our ages. They asked if I was married and told me whether or not they were engaged. With each visit to women, I learned a few new words, like *ghani* (they wanted me to sing). I tried to express that it wasn't in their best interest to suffer through my attempts at singing.

One of the girls took a plastic pail and started drumming. Headscarves went on the hips, and we took turns dancing. These girls had a different style of belly dancing—more earthy, with an African flavor. I guessed that they watched less television than the women in Siwa. Their musicality was evident as a thirteen-year-old girl led songs and drummed. As everywhere I'd been, the girls were loud, shouting over each other. It was a bit dizzying. Their strong, deep guttural voices belied Western images of secluded Muslim women as meek, mysterious creatures behind their veils. Rashid translated as his mother said "Dance is supposed to be done by old women, only on special occasions, not as an everyday social thing." I was intrigued but, unfortunately, never got the opportunity to see the older women dance.

Two girls showed me the gardens and wanted to videotape me. Their customs prohibited them from being filmed, but they liked playing with my camera. I heard some foul English and sensed that Rico and sidekick were nearby. What a way to mess up the vibe of this little village! Either they were trying to impress me, or they just liked listening to their own vocabulary, because the girls had no idea what they were saying and paid them no notice.

Back in town, Elena, an Italian girl, was in charge of overseeing a room full of young women who sewed sequins onto jeans and embroidered blouses for Tony, the Italian designer. Thanks in part to him, Siwan embroidery has been making it onto the runways of Europe. Though I never met the man, I learned that he commissioned a lot of embroidery in Siwa. What the women in this workshop were doing was not Siwan. It was outsourced embroidery with contemporary designs. When I entered to speak with Elena, everyone stopped sewing to comment. Seeing a foreigner wearing her hair in two braids brought squeals of delight. I think of braids as being American, but they are traditional in Siwa and Siwan women often asked if I did them myself or if a Siwan braided my hair.

On the edge of town stands a particularly unsightly "Olympic Stadium" and an empty attempt at a five-star hotel made of cement— both fizzled government projects aimed at developing Siwa as a tourist destination.

Nearby, a prefabricated metal building housed a carpet factory. Hoping to meet more women, I wandered into this factory full of teenage girls. It was one of the first initiatives by the Egyptian military to get women into the workforce. Soldiers stood guard as a stubby foreman sat supervising dozens of girls between the ages of fifteen and eighteen who were not yet married. I was such a novelty that the girls fought over whose loom I should sit at. I tried tying a few knots, and managed to communicate my name, age, and marital status. In all, about 200 women worked there, dyeing yarn and weaving rugs.

Asked about the designs, the Egyptian foreman explained that he creates the patterns, which aren't Siwan. The giddy teenagers were so excited by this break in monotony caused by my presence that chaos overtook the factory. After awhile, I heeded the cold stares from the soldiers and said "Mas salama" (goodbye).

One freezing night I stayed up until 3 AM, typing and dancing to my new favorite song from Zanzibar. My head was reeling as I tried to fall asleep. Where would the next forty days be? I had planned to go to Iran, but my visa was in limbo. My other options were wide open, making decision-making all the more difficult.

Penny's husband Duncan suggested that I take the forty-day camel route from Sudan to Cairo. Apparently, there are renditions of this organized for adventure travelers as well as the real thing, in which camels are transported to the market in Cairo. But the season wasn't right.

Farid told of a Libyan oasis where everyone lives for music and dance. That would involve waiting around Cairo in hopes of obtaining a Libyan visa.

Sabriye told me about a women's shelter in Dubai called City of Hope, which was run by an American woman who had converted to Islam and donned the *hijab*. Dubai, I thought, was the last place I would want to spend forty days, but if I could volunteer in this woman's shelter, it might make an amazing segment for the book. I contacted the shelter numerous times and never received an answer.

Sitting at Abdu's with my computer once again, I overheard two American men talking. One from Redmond, Washington, a suburb of Seattle, worked for Microsoft. What a small world! I had moved to Redmond shortly before coming on this trip, and one of my housemates worked for Microsoft.

The other, Ariel, a young journalist from Mississippi, had gone to Burkina Fasso as a Baptist missionary but realized the folly of trying to convert Muslims to Christianity and resolved to merely live among the people, farm, and play soccer until his commitment was up. Both men were extremely well-traveled. Ariel was on a six-month journey from Poland through Eastern Europe and the Middle East. What were his thoughts on my next forty-day destination? Without hesitation, he piped, "Syria. You can't go wrong. The people are honest, sincere, and friendly. You'll love it!" Tourists I had met around the campfire also raved about Syria, and it turned out that Penny, Duncan, and their kids had met Ariel in Damascus. Unfortunately, an insensitive political cartoon depicting Mohammed PBUH with his turban made into a bomb inflamed sensitivities throughout the Muslim world. Islam doesn't even allow drawings of the prophet, so one can imagine the reaction to one that's offensive. Some travelers who had just been to Syria said tension was running high.

My mind wandered . . . Forty days in Zanzibar? Hmm. The unidentified song I danced to every night was wonderful. I had audio visions of what other music might await. An American University student leader staying at the Palm Trees Hotel assured me that Zanzibar would be a great choice. I read online that Zanzibar was tropical and had lots of beaches. Websites depicted it as a spa-like vacation spot. That would be great—if I could circumvent the luxury long enough to find local culture. A guidebook to Africa promised authentic culture and even mentioned that Nooruz, the Persian New Year, is celebrated in Zanzibar. I imagined myself dancing around palaces amid the scent of spices with rose petals floating overhead.

My last night in Siwa was the coldest yet. Malek, Frederic, and I holed up in one of Frederic's abodes, listening to old music from the 1920s, drinking hot chocolate, and making each other laugh. Pondering my last few hours in Siwa, we discussed the strange sense of time that made no sense. Frederic said he could never remember what day it was. I felt as if I'd arrived last year or the year before, but then it seemed like a huge hole had been cut out and suddenly I was leaving for Zanzibar. It was dreamlike and strange.

The several days it took to get to Zanzibar were serendipitous. First, I stopped in Alexandria, where my next door neighbors in the hotel turned out to be the same two Frenchmen who'd stayed next to my room in Siwa. When I arrived in Cairo, Malek rang and said, "Frederic just went to Cairo to fix his visa." We spent the day together. That night, I was standing by a railing at a music concert, and who walked up behind me but Dina, whom I'd roomed with briefly in Siwa.

I was supposed to fly to Dar es Salaam, and then take a boat to Zanzibar. The plane never showed up. A man at the Ethiopian Airlines office was handing out vouchers for us to take another flight in the morning. Just then, Malek rang again, "Duncan's in Cairo and he's staying at your hotel." Returning downtown by cab, I looked around for Penny's husband and found him in the lounge area typing on a laptop. He was working on a book about traveling to out-of-the-way places with his family of five—and how it all started with the tsunami.

Since leaving Siwa, I felt that Zanzibar was so far away. It wasn't the distance, rather it was the reality. I had never been in sub-Saharan Africa and, for the several days it took to get my visa and ticket in order, it felt like my time in Zanzibar was some time in the future, not anytime soon. The next morning, there was indeed an airplane waiting for us. Apparently, there hadn't been enough passengers on the initial flight, but this one consolidated the passengers and made stops in Sudan and Ethiopia. Eventually I arrived in what the locals refer to as "Dar."

ZANZIBAR, TANZANIA

KENYA

Mombasa ★

Pemba

Zanzibar

Dar es Salaam ★

TANZANIA

INDIAN OCEAN

100 Miles

"Where's the spa?" I wondered as I looked at the tumbledown market-place that had dust and blue trash bags blowing right and left. I thought about how this wasn't the exotic land of spices and grand palaces I'd imagined. My online research had shown the island promoted only as a luxurious tourist destination. Maybe I caught the wrong boat. Just then a giant shark fell from the sky onto the dirt in front of me. He had actually been atop a *daladala*, which are trucks used for public transport, but I wasn't accustomed to looking for sharks on top of trucks. Two men set about hastily chopping him into pieces to sell in the Darajani Market.

The sprinkle from the sky turned into a downpour. There was so much mud that my wide bell-bottom pants grew longer by the minute and my sneakers became invisible beneath a thick gooey coating. Last night's meal was starting to disagree with me.

Many guys hanging out around the shops tried to be my friend with calls of "Jambo" and "Mambo," Swahili greetings. *Jambo* is for foreigners; *mambo* is for locals. It dawned on me that the English term "mumbo jumbo" may have come from the greetings said to foreigners on the streets of Swahili speaking nations: "mambo . . . jambo." I made

133

friendly replies but didn't want any of the multitudes of hanger-outers to latch onto me. Taariq, a young man who looked like Will Smith but had deep black Arabic eyes, was more persistent, "Are you looking for something?" he asked. Yesterday's squid dinner decided to revolt, and I needed an emergency restroom. Seeing that I looked a bit green, he took me to his house and then asked, "Can I help you find anything else?"

He was polite, so after a brief pause, I blurted, "Music." I tried to explain about this Arabic-sounding song I liked. Taariq told me that the music I was looking for was called *taarab*, and he could show me where people who played it practiced.

We trudged down tiny waterlogged streets to an old house with a rickety wooden staircase. It looked abandoned. By the time we reached the top floor, I realized I must be out of my mind following this complete stranger into a place like this. We stood overlooking a forlorn rooftop with a sopping wet foam mattress in the middle.

"This is where they practice, but you have to come back in the night."

I thought I was in deep trouble and looked for an escape route. Just then a woman came out and said something in Swahili.

"They don't practice on Sundays, so you have to come tomorrow," Taariq translated.

The neighborhood was Malindi, and the house was where Ikhwani Safaa (Brothers of Love) practiced.

C☆ * . * . * . *

You can learn almost anything about Zanzibar's history and culture in House of Wonders, a former palace that is now a museum. Display after display was dedicated to taarab. In Arabic, the term means "to be moved or enchanted by song," or be "transported by music." Zanzibari taarab started around 1870 when Sultan Seyyid Barghash bin Said imported Egyptian ensembles to play at his palace. He was a lover of classical Egyptian music and sent a local musician named Mohammed Ibrahim to Egypt to learn how to play the *kanun*, called "ganun" in Swahili. This beautiful stringed instrument is something like a harp, played flat across one's lap or on a special table.

In Zanzibar music clubs aren't nightclubs. Rather, they are where lovers of great music join together to study, compose, and play. Ikhwani Safaa is a club that began in 1905, inspired by a group of visiting musicians from Turkey. The group can trace its roots back further than any other orchestra in Africa, and, at some point, every well-known performer in Zanzibar has been part of this group.

Knowing that Ikhwani Safaa is so important in the taarab world, I wanted to go right away and see them practice, but I had no idea which winding streets to navigate to get there.

Guidebooks and a sign in my hotel warned tourists not to walk in unlit alleys at night. Luckily, I ran into Taariq along the way, and he gave me his cell phone number for the second time. "You'll need it. Trust me." The winding passages on our way to Ikhwani Safaa were pitch black. I couldn't even see where I was stepping and knew if something were to go awry, there would be little I could do. Taariq sensed my discomfort and wasn't surprised. As I would soon learn, his answer to everything was "it's okay," in a tone one would use for a child with a scraped knee.

Up the tenuous staircase once again, three men who were turning a mattress over pointed us to a room. It looked like a classroom, with a blackboard, instruments, microphones, and rows of wooden benches. Sepia and hand-tinted photos of the group in days gone by hung in lopsided positions on the walls. The ceiling had the typical zebra-stripe pattern of mangrove, commonly used in older constructions.

Rough-hewn black-painted beams had white stucco packed between.

A ceiling fan converted the wet blanket of tropical humidity into a sultry breeze. This place looked like the Zanzibari version of Cuba's Buena Vista Social Club. But the musicians were having a meeting. "Come back tomorrow," they told us.

The name Zanzibar refers to two islands off the coast of Tanzania. The lesser known one is Pemba, and the other is Unguja, but people often simply call it Zanzibar. The capital and historic city, Mji Mkongwe, is also known as Stone Town because of the unique maze of stone buildings merging African, Persian, Arabic, and Indian styles. It was declared a World Heritage site by UNESCO in 2000.

A fertile island off the coast of East Africa, Zanzibar's location on major Indian Ocean trade routes contributed to its turbulent history of foreign domination. Persians ruled in 975 AD. The name *Zang I Bar* has Persian and Arabic roots, roughly meaning "coast of blacks." Persian intermarriage with Africans gave rise to the Swahili civilization, and these people became an important part of the trading network throughout the Indian Ocean.

After about 500 years, Portuguese navigator Vasco de Gama saw the island on his way back from India and decided to bring it under Portuguese rule. The foreign domination drained Zanzibar of its resources and contributed to an economic decline all along the east African coast.

Beginning in 1652, Omanis from the Arabian Peninsula came, taking control of Zanzibar. An increasingly brutal slave trade flourished as Africans on the mainland captured their enemies, and Arab traders organized caravans. In Zanzibar, slaves were brought to slave markets and sold to Arabia, Africa, Europe and America for a multitude of purposes, including laboring on sugar and spice plantations in European colonies.

Sultans built magnificent palaces throughout the island. Now well known for their elaborately carved wooden doors, mansions were built throughout Stone Town by wealthy Arab and Indian merchants.

In the 1870s, a cholera epidemic killed ten thousand people, and a cyclone wiped out all the ships in the harbor, save one, and decimated the clove plantations. Then slavery was abolished. Its economic power weakened, Zanzibar was left to the mercy of the British, who soon took over and declared it a British protectorate.

Zanzibar gained its independence from Britain in 1963 when it officially became the Sultanate of Zanzibar. Eighty percent of the population resented the fact that the other 20 percent—mostly of Arab and Indian descent—controlled all the wealth and power. So in January of 1964, four weeks after independence, a bloody revolution overthrew the government. Twelve thousand people were massacred and all but one percent of the elite classes fled the country, mostly to Oman. Suddenly, nobody that was left in Zanzibar knew how to run a country. The economy was devastated. Zanzibar united with nearby Tanganyika, and together they became Tanzania (as it remains today) which aligned itself with Eastern Europe and experimented for nearly thirty years with ill-fated socialism.

There are two political parties in present day Zanzibar: the CCM, which favors alliance with the mainland, and the CUF, which wants more independence. When I was in Zanzibar, local political issues were a favored topic of conversation, especially among young men in Malindi. The parts of town with colorful plastic flags strung between buildings were CUF strong holds, and posters of their leader graced the walls on each block.

Tourism is a major industry, but the tourist's lives are completely alien to those of the locals. There is little mixing, except for a few rich local businessmen and bureaucrats who can afford to eat at restaurants costing ten times the prevailing price for a meal, and men whose primary occupation is hanging out at trendy bars to pick up foreign women.

The infamous *papasi* (beach boys) are often heroin addicts. They roam the streets pestering people and offering their services as middlemen for tours, taxis, or hotels. Drugs are another source of income in Zanzibar and are widely available on the streets, even from some law enforcement officers.

My journey from Egypt had taken three days. Along the way, I'd made friends with an entire Nigerian television crew and taken a nine-year-old girl under my wing in Ethiopia. An Aussie pharmaceutical-company worker who was involved with an anti-AIDS NGO became my constant companion. We waited out all the delays together. Upon arriving in Dar es Salaam, Tanzania, he arranged for a car to take me to the boat dock and fought tooth and nail with the hustlers intercepting my ticket purchase with their scams. It took a lot of aggression to get rid of them and to convince the ticket sellers to sell me passage at the right price.

On the ferry ride, two young men stood singing. Shortly before arrival, one—a diminutive man named David—approached. I couldn't believe my luck when he said he was a dancer who made drums and sculptures. He started telling me about the regional dances of Tanzania. I asked him about taarab, the Arab-African music that I heard on the Zanzibar CD I got from Farid in Siwa. He offered to introduce me to a singer named Fatuma Binti Baraka, who I later learned was known as Bi Kidude, Zanzibar's most famous singer.

The Malindi Lodge was an adorable hotel on an ugly, trashy street near the port. My bags were huge, heavy with winter clothes I would not be using in Zanzibar. *Hakuna matata* ("no problem" in Swahili) was a phrase

I would hear constantly. One porter took the heavier one, and David took the other, carrying them all the way up the stairs to my room. I counted my blessings when I saw dozens of papasi hounding tourists with incessant calls of "spice tours," "change money," and the like. They got in people's faces and didn't let up. I was surrounded by three men—David, his friend, and the tiny porter who wasn't much bigger than my bag.

David showed me the skinny winding streets for which Old Stone Town was famous. In fact, Stone Town has the narrowest streets in the world. When I wanted to eat at Forodhani Gardens, the popular outdoor night market, he dissuaded me. "I'll show you a better place."

We stopped on a small street to choose a cooked cuttlefish, which the seller chopped in bite-sized pieces and put into a plastic bag. The "restaurant" was a small room run by a very large woman swathed in brightly printed African fabrics. It was a bring-your-own-cuttlefish kind of place. The owner served the accompaniments: *chapati* (Indian-style bread), *tambi* (spaghetti fried with sugar and cardamom), potatoes with spicy tomato sauce, *mchicha* (a bland green vegetable), and *chai* (a very sweet black tea spiced with cloves).

David also showed me a popular restaurant-bar with American prices and proceeded to order a beer, assuming I would pay for it—then he reached for my hair. I slapped his hand away and invented a nice "boyfriend" who would be arriving soon.

Every time I saw him after that, he was flanked by at least one foreign woman. That bar turned out to be a popular watering hole for foreigners, and local guys looking to latch onto female tourists.

Zahor, the front desk employee at the Malindi Lodge, told me about a famous retired taarab singer who had taken foreign students into his home. We found the singer, Mr. Chimbeni, dozing in the sun, seated on a sidewalk ledge with a line of cabbies.

His card said "TV actor, composer, and musician," but he also drove a taxi. I recognized his picture from a free magazine for tourists, *Swahili Coast*.

Later Zahor told me, "His wife just came from Mecca, and he can't have a woman in the house."

Mr. Chimbeni's story differed: "People don't trust Americans because during the last election, the American government got involved, claiming to make the process more honest, and messed things up. So if any American is doing more than a few days of tourism, they'll be looked at with suspicion."

Mr. Chimbeni was formerly a well-known singer for Culture Club, the other taarab group I read about besides Ikhwani Safaa. Culture Club was formed in 1958 as part of the Shirazi political party during Zanzibar's struggle for independence. This was a time of "Africanization," and after the revolution in 1964 they became the group most supported by the government. They gradually created a unique style of taarab with a more African, less Arabic flavor.

Mr. Chimbeni came on strong and insisted that I pay $100 for them to put on a private concert for me to film. Then he said I should promote the group in the U.S. After I turned the conversation around, we finally agreed that I would pay a dollar to see the group practice.

Musicians were filtering in. This place was simple and spacious, something out of the 1950s that hadn't changed. Plastic chairs were set up facing the musicians. Women sat on one side of the aisle and men on the other.

All the women wore headscarves, some made of brightly colored African print cotton and others black georgette with sequins. One woman at a time was called to take the microphone to sing solo. Each soloist removed her scarf, which I found unusual for Muslim women in mixed company. I asked Mr. Chimbeni why, and he responded, "They have to be expressive and move to the music. Scarves get in the way."

Their voices were high and nasally. A chorus of seated women echoed in unison. After each singer, the accordionist gave his comments and criticisms. The instrumentation was exquisite. I missed seeing a ganun, but there were violins, *ouds* (lutes), accordions, bongos, an upright bass, a *riqq* (Arabic tambourine), and a *dumbek* (Arabic drum). I introduced myself to a traveler watching from the men's side. A doctor from Brooklyn, he spent his vacation traveling throughout east Africa, staying with tribes on the mainland.

We invited Mr. Chimbeni to join us for a bite to eat and ended up at the Forodhani Gardens, the night market David had warned me about. Outdoor vendors sold fish kebabs, seafood, chunks of octopus and squid, boiled bananas, and grilled breadfruit.

The park, a ragged waterfront with dried grass, fills up with food vendors every night and is the most happening place in town for locals to gather. We had delicious Zanzibari pizza, a thin crepe on the griddle lined with a square piece of dough, onions, peppers, ground beef, mayonnaise and a raw egg. It cooked awhile then was folded into a square, cut to bite-size pieces, and topped by more salad plus tamarind sauce and ketchup.

Knowing I wanted a place to live, Mr. Chimbeni's brother, Yusef, introduced me to Yousri, the manager of a newly built cement triplex apartment house on the back streets of Malindi. It was pricier than I had in mind, so I said I'd think about it.

Another hotel worker knew of an apartment for rent at a slightly lower price, but it was dark and depressing. We happened upon David with an Irish girl on one arm and an Australian on the other. He said, "I know of two rooms where you could stay with families."

The owner of the rooms opened a gate and led the hotel worker, David and his entourage, and me up a series of shaky ladders to a smelly room furnished with prayer rugs and a television. It offered absolutely no security, and I thought it was likely that my computer and video camera would disappear, or that I'd have surprise visitors in the middle of the night, human or otherwise. He showed me another room in the same house with a vinyl floor and a filthy sagging bed. The communal bathroom was a cement hole boarded over with slabs of wood.

After a few no-shows, horrible rooms, and people telling me one price and later saying "for foreigners it's more," it was clear that I should just rent at Yousri's. Although the building was new, it was in a picturesque area full of narrow winding alleys and what looked like ancient ruins. I was happy to unpack my bags and set up a "home."

Groups of women sat on the downstairs steps. One woman breast-fed her baby, and another spent each day sealing plastic bags of spicy, crunchy *cassava* snacks by melting the edges together with the flame of a candle.

Every afternoon, across from the big mosque, lots of cats snoozed in the sun, sometimes rolling over to show their tummies. Old men napped on the steps, as well. There was an air of utmost relaxation and contentment in both the human and feline species.

Cries of *"mzungu"* (which means foreigner or white person) echoed in my wake as I tried to be inconspicuous. Desperate men with visions of dollars in their heads followed me constantly. Saying I was from Colombia instead of the U.S. got them off my back faster. After that, I heard "Colombia" ringing out from both sides of the street on a daily basis. Touts regularly tried to drag me into curio shops or tour agencies. Some acted tenaciously friendly. Others were in the market for foreign girlfriends. If they looked like druggies, I shook them off as fast as possible. Otherwise, I'd be polite but set limits to avoid their gluing to me. Sometimes saying "I live here" helped.

Claiming to be Colombian saved money too. Prices were inflated for tourists, but on a sliding scale depending on where you were from. It helped that Colombian pop singer Shakira was popular in Zanzibar. There was such a disparity between tourists, who might easily spend $500 a day, and the locals, who were lucky to make $3 a day. With the area's history of wealth being in the hands of very few, tourists now signified the rich "others." By comparison to most Zanzibaris, even a backpacker who spends $20 a day is rich.

The Swahili people inhabit nearly one thousand miles of east African coastline, from Somalia to Mozambique. Their language is spoken by over 50 million people. When writing in English, the word Swahili is used to describe their language, and when writing in Swahili, where *Ki* means language, they use the word *Kiswahili*. Hoping to learn a bit of the language, I headed to the University and met Faruk, a tiny bald man with few teeth. Fragments of teeth that remained barely hung on. His deep, clear skin and fine features were beautiful though. Every time I saw him, he wore an Islamic hat and an olive green safari suit. He agreed to be my teacher and left me each day with pages of homework.

The word Swahili comes from Arabic *sawahil*, meaning those who live on the coast. Over 1,000 years of interaction with the Middle East, India, Asia, and Europe has given Swahili a wide variety of words borrowed from other languages, especially Arabic. I could recognize some from having spent time in Egypt.

Tea is *chai* in many of the world's languages, Swahili included. "Later" is *badein* in Arabic, or *badaya* in Swahili. Water is *maia* in Arabic, *maji* in Swahili. And coffee is *gahwa* in Arabic or *kahawa* in Swahili. Some words are borrowed from other languages, but the context changes. For instance, restaurant is *hoteli*. There was a popular place in Malindi called the Passing Show Hotel. I always saw people eating but could never figure out where the rooms were—because it wasn't a hotel at all. *Piga picha* means "take a photo."

Spitting out sentences often took so long that, by the time I strung together all the words, I forgot what we were talking about. In turn, someone gave me an even bigger mouthful for an answer. Totally lost, I usually had to say *kidogo kidogo* (slow down).

Greetings required several layers of back and forth, which was refreshingly polite. I repeated these words so many times throughout the day that my tongue would get tied by the fiftieth time.

Greeting: "Hujambo."

Response: "Sijambo."

How is it going? "Habari?"

Very well: "Mzuri sana."

The interchange would often continue with, "How are your studies?" (or your family, or . . .).

There was more to learn than just language from Swahili class. When I asked Faruk if he leaned toward the CCM or CUF, he said "If we work at the university we are not allowed to take sides, but if it weren't for the revolution, I would not be working in a university or any professional capacity today. There was no social mobility before."

Regarding the significance of the number forty in Islamic culture, Faruk explained: "Forty days after the birth of a child, they shave the child's head, and the mother can go outside the home. Forty days after a person dies, they do special prayers and remembrances, and this is when the bones begin to disintegrate. On Fridays, the Islamic Sabbath, there must be at least forty people in the mosque at prayer time, which is why you see more people at the big mosque that day."

Another important concept, he explained, was "Swahili time." Sara, one of the women living downstairs, told me to come at 1:00. She meant 7:00 PM. Another day, I had an appointment at 2:00, and the person showed at 8:00. What was this all about? I'd be sitting like a dummy waiting all afternoon, and then people would come to meet me at night and think I was a flake because I'd given up and left.

Faruk drew me a clock and showed the difference between English time and Swahili time. After twelve o'clock, you add six hours to English time to have Swahili time. For example, one o'clock was seven in Swahili time. Three was nine, and six was twelve. At that point, the equation was reversed, and you subtracted six from each number. Seven o'clock English time was one o'clock Swahili time, nine was three, and twelve was six. I'm not talking about the time in England as opposed to the time in Zanzibar. Rather, English time was the official time, and Swahili time was what many people referred to.

When Taariq walked me to Ikhwani Safaa again I no longer watched my back. My new concern was tripping over missing cobblestones in the street or slipping on gravel, because it was pitch black and we walked blindly.

Eight musicians and five singers crammed into an area so small that whoever sang had to stand in the doorway. Several benches had room for an audience or chorus, but few people sat in them. Most of their over 1000 songs were written before the revolution, and had a sultry, old-fashioned sound, like vintage Havana meets Egypt's golden age. No one had sheet music. They relied on memory. Musicians practice six nights a week, year after year, and after awhile they become masters. This is a labor of love and respect for their art; it's not for the money.

One man, who sold bread by day, had an amazingly expressive way of singing. His style reminded me of an old Egyptian singer named Abdel Halim Hafez, but he sung in Swahili instead of Arabic. The music they made was so compelling that I felt some sort of magic and wished it would last all night.

Taariq explained that most songs are about love, containing symbolism, images, and proverbs. Now, the more modern, synthesized version of taarab called *rusha roho* breaks all the rules of subtlety that traditional taarab is noted for. "African life is about feelings. We don't have a plan for our days or our future, and what we love most is being together with our families. In Europe, people don't have time for their parents. When they are old, they go to nursing homes. That's not our life. It is our pleasure to care for our parents." He went on, "We sing about love, because that's all we have to sing about."

I asked what dance is done to taarab and got a look like I'd said a bad word. Later, I found out that "traditional taarab is not danceable." Audience members who feel inspired can approach the performers who inspired them and give a gift of money then return to their seats, but it is never considered proper to dance! It is like European classical music in that the audience sits and listens quietly for each nuance.

Taariq looked like a hip-hop teenager from New York. While women in Zanzibar dressed smashingly in tailor-made dresses of colorful African prints, silky black *bui bui* robes, or *kangas* (colorful cotton wrap skirts and headscarves), many men were not so stylish. Taariq was attached to wearing baggy trousers hung so low that he was in serious danger of losing them. A tall, lanky twenty-five-year-old, he seemed tender and childlike, yet intelligent with a gentle demeanor.

Taariq's house was around the corner from mine. I never knew if it was serendipity or the fact that he had a lot of time on his hands, but we bumped into each other every day, in all different parts of town. He helped me find all my daily needs at the local price, which was even lower than what they charged Colombians.

A female friend explained, "Young men in Zanzibar like to run errands and do things for women," so I stopped feeling guilty about soliciting his help. For most of my stay, Taariq was the only person willing to take me behind the scenes into Zanzibari life or give me advice that would keep me out of harm's way.

"Are you taking malaria pills?" he asked.

I'd just heard that one of the common strains from Zanzibar causes permanent brain damage. I trembled. "No."

Taariq took me straight to the pharmacy to buy a set of weekly pills with lots of side-effect warnings on the label. "These pills only lessen the severity of malaria. They don't prevent you from getting it," he said and added, "Most Zanzibaris have had malaria repeatedly and know what to do, but you're a mzungu so it will hit you stronger."

I often escaped to what I called "mzunguland" on the other side of town for a drink with an NGO worker or a nice dinner. Straddling two worlds, on many nights I ended up walking several blocks home, past ruins and benches full of sleeping men or feasting cats. Given the fact that Malindi was one of the major entry points for heroin, and desperate addicts were known to mug people, I always carried a video camera, I wasn't about to walk home alone. Taariq's cell phone number was one of my saving graces, and he was patient enough to come get me, even if I woke him up. Of course, he always got back at me by calling early in the morning with "I just thought of something you have to see." He got so enthusiastic about *40 Days & 1001 Nights* that he made a list of places I had to film and write about. I added a few ideas of my own.

One morning, we got up at 6:00 AM to see fishing boats arrive with the evening's catch. Hundreds of men waited by Malindi Port. Some bought fish for breakfast. Others were brokers, and quite a few laid small glistening fish on wooden hand carts or tarps on the sidewalk for sale to passersby.

Wooden *dhows* (sailing vessels that have plied the Indian Ocean for hundreds of years), dugout canoes, and other traditional boats were mobbed by people wading through the water to greet them. Pails for carrying fish were either thrown through the air or pulled from the boats on ropes. Ladies cooked porridge and traditional breads over charcoal fires to sell to the throngs of men.

Unaccustomed to seeing foreigners, people made comments like "What's mzungu doing here?" or "She's going to take our pictures and make money." Most activity happened around an abandoned clove oil factory. Taariq said, "Stay away from this building; they sell hard drugs inside."

We went to Tauro, a rustic, dirt-floored warehouse where traditional rice dishes *biryani* and *pilau* were cooked in giant pots for weddings and banquets. We entered as they were frying massive amounts of onions and soon left in tears.

For breakfast, we sat on a wooden bench watching dhows float by and eating *ugali*, a white corn meal mush that you make balls of with your fingers and use to scoop up green vegetables and bits of fried fish. On the side was a bowl of red beans cooked in coconut milk and some spiced tea.

Taariq led me through a maze of dreary alleys full of garbage, dust, and tiny cement houses. His maternal grandmother's home was dark. Some heavy-set women were sleeping on the cement floor. His grandmother made a living by cooking a snack called *vitimbua* (rice cakes made with coconut milk and crushed cardamom) and selling them from a small display case in front of her home. The process began by pouring rice batter into a mold. Into each round part of the pan, she melted a big spoonful of yellow shortening, dropped a ladle of batter and let it bubble until crisp around the edges, then turned it over with a long skewer. Fat was plopped in the middle of the mold, melting. The cakes were greasy but delicious. Two other ladies shared the porch, serving up croquettes made with fish or meat that were spicy, greasy, and good.

We headed past lots of garbage and graffiti to another house, where dozens of stray cats were waiting for lunch to be over. A woman was making *mkatwe waufuta* (sesame bread). She put the dough in a small frying pan over the coals, then turned it over and cooked the top. Surprisingly, the bread stuck to the upside-down pan and didn't fall into the fire during cooking.

Henry David Thoreau wrote in *Walden*, "It is not worthwhile to go around the world to count the cats in Zanzibar."

The human population of Stone Town is nearly matched by that of cats. A cat surprised me in my hotel room when I arrived. Cats roamed restaurants, shops, and even discos! Unlike the pitiful creatures seen in many countries, these kitties are fuzzy and content.

There is a lot of garbage to snack on, and the local human diet consists largely of fish. The cats have beautiful markings and languish contentedly in the sunshine or on *barazas* at night. Barazas are public meeting areas as well as the stone benches found in front of most houses in Stone Town. When I asked one of the ladies downstairs what to do with my garbage, she explained, "Put it on the baraza for someone to collect during the night." Hoards of cats attacked the bag as soon as it was set down, scattering debris all about.

Taariq told me about a program which vaccinated, spayed, and neutered street cats. He said a group used to capture the cats and bring them to trucks they set up in Forodhani Gardens, but he hadn't seen them for a while.

Curious about massive cat vaccinations in such a poor country, I kept bothering Taariq until he agreed to take me to "the farm." We rode out to a village called Bububu in a daladala. People crowded into the back and sat on benches. The contact-paper-covered roofs were so low that you had to sit hunched over for the entire journey.

A sign read "World Society for the Protection of Animals." The guard directed us to the back of a field with a few buildings, where cows lay all around. We sat with a man named Said.

"The cat program lasted one year," Said explained. "WSPA supports and guides government-run projects aiming to get rid of rabies and control stray populations in a humane way." In the year the program lasted, they spayed, neutered, and vaccinated ten thousand cats, nipping their ears as identification. There were still many kittens being born, but at least this program did something. Once in awhile amid the feline multitudes, I saw a fat cat with a nipped ear.

The organization had come to Zanzibar to work with donkeys, teaching villagers how to treat and take care of the animals. Their new project was to spay, neuter, and vaccinate stray dogs in several small towns.

I'd admired Zanzibari-style henna ever since I saw a woman with intricate orange and black flowers drawn on her hands and wrists. Taariq found a woman to do it for me. I went to her house, and she instructed me to buy "henna and pico."

The sky was often overcast in Zanzibar, but suddenly, the gray burst open, pouring sheets of water down the metal roofs. Rivers of dirty water flowed down tiny streets. I waded until I arrived at the designated kiosk, where a shopkeeper handed me a box. Pico turned out to be black hair dye, rumored to contain lead, so I decided to use only the henna. The design, painted using a triangle shaped tube ending in a ball point, was an elaborate cross between flowers and peacock plumes. Henna is a natural herb, but this stung my skin and smelled like ammonia. I asked what it was mixed with. She rattled off a list of ingredients in Swahili that I didn't understand. Oh well. It was already on my skin.

One day, we walked to Victoria Gardens, a park in the posh Vuga Road area. Taariq showed me a house they had lived in at one time, where his father had operated a travel agency. He explained that his father previously had a good government job in Dar es Salaam as well. He wanted me to see the hospital where his father had been treated. It was public, with a private wing. The lower area was a TB sanatorium. Taariq explained that the highest death rates in Africa are from TB, malaria, AIDS, and civil wars. The pretty buildings housing the hospital had been owned by a rich Indian man before the revolution. Then the government made them into a hospital. Only weathered wooden staircases connected the floors. Each large room had numerous beds full of sick and injured men, and little else. Rooms were bright and colorful and, although there was much pain, the colors, light, and wood gave it a feeling of more life than some dreary older hospitals in developed countries. Taariq pointed to a nearby building and said, "That's the VIP section, where my father stayed, but we can't go inside."

I kept reading about Spice Tours, but Taariq said, "Don't spend your money. I'll take you." He spent a day planning and called the following morning. "Are you ready for a spice tour?"

His plans usually included arduous detours through dusty roads and garbage, offering a view of Zanzibar most tourists don't experience.

We caught a daladala from the market, and it dropped us in a town lined with simple new cement-block houses. There were blue plastic bags and piles of garbage as far as the eye could see. It was an eyesore. I said, "The government should provide better trash pickup and educate the people on the value of their environment."

"There's no money," was his reply, then the usual consolation, "It's okay."

A young man from the village walked us up a very big hill through searing heat to the Spice Park. He showed us turmeric and ginger, pulling up the roots to have us taste. Then there were bright red peppercorns, and the cloves also had fruit. We saw cardamom, cinnamon bark, and lemon grass growing, and we ate tropical fruits. Another man wove a basket for me out of palm fronds and made a frog neck-lace and a hair-tie out of other plants.

A toothless man in ragged clothes approached, offering to get coco-nuts from a tree. He climbed a towering palm, singing and dancing all the way up. It was a professional quality show. His voice carried all the way across the fields. He tossed four coconuts to the ground, shinnied down the tree, and hacked them open so we could drink the juice and eat the flesh. He said, "I'm famous," and started rattling off documen-taries he had been in that aired around Europe, and magazines where his photo had appeared.

Taarab changed from an exclusively male enclave sung only in Ara-bic, when Siti Bint Saad, a potter, sang to announce her pots. She was discovered by musicians from Ikhwani Safaa long before women were admitted into the club, and she ended up making over 150 re-cords. Siti Bint Saad revolutionized the art form by singing songs with Swahili lyrics, thus making it accessible to the general popula-tion, not only the upper classes. Soon, her fame and the popularity of taarab swept the east coast of Africa.

Siti Bint Saad died in 1950 but left a protégé, Bi Fatuma Binti Baraka, who later became known as Bi Kidude, now the ninety-four-year-old grand dame of taarab song. She has won international music awards throughout Europe and Africa. I even saw a fancy restaurant bearing her name, and a film about her life entitled *As Old as My Tongue: The Myth and life of Bi Kidude* was released in February 2007.

Taariq knew where she lived and walked me there, winding around a maze of dirt streets through Ngambo, the old suburb of squat hous-es, then through some more winding backstreets, which were littered with piles of trash.

We found the living legend sitting on her porch. She led us inside to a mat by an old TV with bad reception, and lit a cigarette.

Taariq told me, "She loves to smoke and drink."

She looked healthy and was quoted as saying, "When I sing, I feel fourteen years old all over again."

When she asked what song I wanted her to sing, I requested "Ali Baba Pakistani Hindustani." I didn't know how it was supposed to sound, but the name stuck when I read about Siti Bint Saad at the museum, and how she had sung the song.

We looked through the previous day's *Weekender* magazine, which had Bi Kidude on the cover. It said that she had won the Lifetime Achievement Award in the past week's Buzz Zanzibar Music Awards. I'd read about her in magazines and seen her CDs for sale in tourist shops. Like many world music artists, although she had become internationally famous, at home she still lived a life of simplicity.

Weeks later, from the Busara Music Festival newsletter, I learned that Bi Kidude had gone into surgery. The story gave insight into her spirit: "Within weeks of returning from her eight-concert tour of Europe last month, Bi Kidude was rushed to Al Rahma hospital for an emergency hernia operation. Thankfully, within days she was up and about again and seemingly her usual cheery self. 'I shall cook for myself,' she said, 'I don't need anyone taking care of me.' However, she is now under doctors' orders to stay off the drum for the next six months, which she admits she will find hard, 'but at least I shall still be able to sing!'"

One of Zanzibar's famous attractions is the Jozani Forest, a wildlife refuge set aside as critical habitat for the rare red colubus monkeys. Taariq didn't see any sense in walking around a forest looking for monkeys, but I coaxed, "At least take me to the market so I can get on the right daladala."

None of the vehicles' numbers matched the routes I had written down, so I needed help. Normally, everyone sits on benches facing each other. The men sit on one side, women on the other. On this day, the daladalas were very crowded. The drivers squeezed in as many men, women, children, and plastic pails of merchandise as possible. Taariq saw me jostling to get in, squeezed between a big woman and an old man, and he decided at the last moment to join the melee.

We stopped at a large market outside town, where bicycles and giant bags of produce were loaded onto the roof of the daladala. They kept stuffing people in. Taariq was squished between me and another woman with big hips. I thought our hips would get smaller because we had to keep squeezing together to make room for more passengers. It reminded me of an old photo I'd seen of fifty-seven people in a VW

Inside the Grand Baiturrahman Mosque, Banda Aceh, Indonesia

Exterior, Grand Baiturrahman Mosque, Banda Aceh

Drinking water and people living in tents ten months after the tsunami, Aceh

Zakiah and Bustami eating lunch near the FBA, Banda Aceh

The oldest mosque in the Siwa Oasis

مخبز الجمهورية
أ.ب BRED

The Siwa Bakery

Married women wearing tarfotet in Siwa

Fishing dhow in Zanzibar

Bride and groom, Zanzibar

Zanzibar

Roman ampitheater in the heart of Amman, Jordan

Man dressed as a woman at a wedding in Ar Ramtha, Jordan

Atlas silk for sale in Hoten, Xinjiang

Man carrying dutars in Kashgar, Xinjiang

Street scene from the old section of Kashgar, Xinjiang

bug. Many people sat on plastic pails or directly on the floor. A money-collector hung outside the vehicle, holding onto a bar.

An hour later, the driver motioned for us to get off at an opening in the trees. On the nature trail, plant life was lush and bird life abundant. A wonderfully refreshing walk in the woods, it was worth the ride. Taariq, who had never been on a hiking trail in his life, soon got into the spirit of outdoor life. This forest was clean, garbage-free, and natural. We watched for monkeys, but they were so high up in the trees that only their movements could be detected. Later we saw several monkeys in a stand of trees. Some chased each other while others ate, dropping plant debris on our heads.

Taariq wanted to show me the secondary school he had attended as a kid, where he used to skip class, climb hand rails, and go swimming at the beach. The school was built over chambers where slaves had been kept while they waited to be put on boats and shipped out to sea. He didn't know the origin of this building, but it had a cross over the entrance. He said, "The British abolished slavery here and built Christian churches and schools where slaves were once traded. People think it was just the Arabs selling slaves and that Christians wouldn't do such a thing." I pointed out that the Americas had used a lot more slaves than the Middle East, and that the U.S. and South American and Caribbean countries are all predominantly Christian.

One of the former slave chambers was abandoned, while the other contained a rug and some clothes and was used as a prayer room.

I wondered about the safety of some broken floorboards in this three-story building with well-worn unpolished wood floors and staircases. It had beautiful sea views from the classrooms. There were separate staircases for the boys and girls, and another one for the teachers. They wouldn't allow a visit during school hours, but this was a Sunday so the school was empty. An employee let us walk around and film for a "donation" of five dollars. We both knew the money wouldn't go to the school. Taariq expressed disgust at the way foreigners get fleeced for every little thing. I was getting used to it.

I woke up after noon, still wanting to see Mangapwani Beach. Taariq protested, "No. It's getting late."

But I was determined to go. What a relief that he didn't let me go alone. It was a one-mile walk to the cave. We had to climb down some dark slippery mossy steps into a dank underground cave with a security guard and a self-styled teenage "guide." The path led almost another mile through the darkness to the beach. A small pool of fresh water contained giant black millipedes that looked like something out of a horror movie.

My flat shoes were broken, and the sneakers didn't go with long skirts, so I had worn the old sparkly shoes with four-inch heels that had gotten me around Indonesia. I had no idea we would be spelunking! I could barely scramble over the rocks.

Our guide gave the scoop on local cave lore: "Once there was a rich slave owner whose goat got lost. The goat herder went looking and found it in this cave. His boss said, 'This is a nice cave. I can do a lot here.' Although the trading of slaves had been abolished, he was able to do it illegally by hiding them in this cave and sending them through the passageway directly to the beach."

We walked down some stairs to the sea. It was high tide, so there was no beach at first, but walking through a bit of knee-deep water took us to a small beach with wooden fishing boats and fishermen preparing to go out for the evening. Taariq said, "We must hurry up because transport will be a problem." He was right. After all my stopping and photographing cows and such, we reached a dirt road lined with mud huts. There was nary a car, truck, or daladala in sight.

Sitting outside a hut eating cookies, we tried to come up with a plan of action. Loads of kids were curious about me, and one family offered to let me spend the night with them. Taariq said he would look for some distant relatives in a nearby village. He was upset about our predicament, but I liked the option of staying with the family, meeting people, and experiencing a bit of village life. Fortunately—or unfortunately—a daladala carrying a soccer team came by and gave us a lift back to town. By the time we got back to Malindi, Taariq was angry with himself, criticizing how he'd let me get into this bad situation. I assured him everything was fine, but his mood worsened, and he ended the evening sitting me on a baraza, saying, "I don't want to see you anymore."

It was really out of the blue. "Why?" I asked.

He didn't have an answer, just "I have a feeling things will end badly, very badly, so don't call me anymore." Then he left abruptly. I felt awful because I esteemed his friendship and didn't feel anything was wrong.

The next morning, he called to wake me up, and I never found out what had ailed him the night before. He just said, "I changed my mind," then changed the subject.

Taariq lived in a dark, depressing old house with threadbare furniture, and ladders instead of stairs connecting the three floors. His eighty-one-year-old father was stuck on the second floor, so severely disabled by diabetes and Parkinson's that he needed assistance with his every need. Most of the day, Mr. Ali sat in front of a snowy television set, staring straight ahead while colorful Bollywood movies danced before him. He rarely spoke but understood a lot, a man trapped inside an immobile body unable to say what he wanted.

Mr. Ali spoke three languages—Swahili, English, and Arabic. Rumor had it that he was once the richest man in Zanzibar. He married a total of eight times, sometimes to two women at once. His sixth wife, Feiruz, reputedly had been the most beautiful woman in Zanzibar. She bore Mr. Ali's first son, Taariq. Rich, handsome, and intelligent, he was the son with the bright future. Feiruz fled to London as a political refugee in the early 1990s.

The prodigal son, Taariq had been living in Mombasa, Kenya when his father came out of an eye operation unable to speak or care for himself and needed Taariq to come home and help care for him.

I sometimes sat with his dad, hoping he would understand something. He rarely spoke, but one day out of the blue he asked, "Where is mzungu?" (referring to me).

Taariq showed me some photos, including a framed one from when he was young. His father was heavy-set with a beard and hat, looking quite religious. They had an odd-shaped car that I'd never seen in any country. It was Taariq's job to crank start it from the front.

The first floor of the house had traditional mangrove beam ceilings and a couple of torn couches. The bathroom was a modern new squat-over-the-hole type. Two young servants, a boy and a girl, did cleaning, laundry, and other chores.

Taariq's younger sister Leila was tall and elegant. Even though it was a hot day and there was no air conditioning, she wore a long satin dress and plenty of solid gold jewelry. It was topped off with a traditional black bui bui and a flowing patterned headscarf. She looked like a runway model for Islamic fashion. Leila had a one-year-old boy. Her husband was in his forties, previously divorced, and had custody of three kids from his first marriage. Each day when she came to care for her father, she walked from the other side of town with all four kids in tow.

Leila lived in the family's other house, which was actually a spacious apartment in Michenzani inside one of the monolithic buildings designed by East German architects during the eastern block influenced era. To me, the development looked like an over-sized scar cutting across the land. In Zanzibar, where everything was on a small scale, and even ruins of palaces were little piles of rubble and stones, this never-ending complex wound around the city for kilometers like a boa constrictor.

I asked a few locals what they thought of the monstrosities, and they usually replied, "It's comfortable and gives people a place to live, so it's good." We outsiders are the ones who value history and want to preserve quaintness. This is a luxury because in poor countries reliable plumbing and walls that stay put are more pressing needs.

Taariq often said, "Leila wants to talk to you." A couple of times he left the room and an awkward silence ensued. Then, using the English word she knew best, she'd venture, "Hi."

Taariq would return and say, "How was the conversation?"

It was an awkward mystery and I paid little mind. One morning, he left me chomping on a chapati in Leila's dining room. I asked what she wanted to say, but instead of talking, Leila took out her collection of kangas, long pieces of brightly colored cotton that women wear in or near their houses. These days, they are made in India but still contain messages in Swahili. Leila explained how some kangas are for weddings, while others have profound sayings. Some are about love and can be bittersweet. She noted, "When a married couple fights, instead of the husband losing his temper, he buys his wife a kanga with the message he wants to say."

Every night, blackouts were scheduled throughout Zanzibar and areas of Tanzania. The mainland had an ongoing drought, and water levels were too low for the hydroelectric dam, so the blackouts saved electricity.

Between English time, Swahili time, and having to accommodate the blackout schedule, I could never figure out when Ikhwani Safaa's rehearsals were. Taariq called to let me know it was time to go hear the band.

Lights came on and the music began. I was overjoyed when they played my favorite song, to which I had been dancing since the days of Farid and the Siwa Oasis. I learned that the composition was created exclusively for the club by Ali Abdella Buaisha, the son of one of the founders of Ikhwani Safaa. This song, which I'd come to know as "Afkari" (Thoughts), was written in 1957, the first *bashraf* ever composed in Zanzibar. Bashraf is a classical style of music played throughout the Arab world and Turkey. Many scholars believe the style is originally Turkish. Half a century after the song's composition, I often heard it on the radio or emanating from old houses. Mr. Buaisha also composed Ikhwani Safaa's first Swahili song, "Shaba" (Bronze), in 1952. It was meant to caution the public against the love of worldly possessions. He fled to Dubai in 1964 upon being notified that he was on the new government's death squad list.

Sometimes we miscalculated the blackout and ended up at Ikhwani Safaa in the dark. One night, along with several musicians and singers, we sat on the roof of Ikhwani Safaa talking about djinns in the moonlight. Taariq translated. One man said, "Many people in Zanzibar believe there is a djinn called Muguwachuma who walks the streets at night. You can hear him because he has an iron leg."

Another explained the history of djinn magic. "There is a passage in the Koran that says it started in Iraq with two angels, Haruta and Maruta. They said, 'We will teach these things, though they are not good for you. If you want to go to hell or break up your marriage, practice this magic. If you want a good life, stay away from it.'"

I asked why angels would teach such a thing if it wasn't good for you, and he replied, "There has to always be an opposite: light and dark, good and bad, life and death. Humans are the most powerful creatures on earth because of our brains, but we can also be bad. That's why we have a choice between positive and negative, but we should always think and do positive things."

On the way home, Taariq told me about groups of women called *kibuki* who play music and do trance dances. Generally, no men are allowed in these dances, but an exception is made for gay men who want to join.

These women can be hired to ward off evil spirits in houses, and they also hold ceremonies of their own. Typically, they are led by a wizened old woman. Participants consume large quantities of liquor and strong nutmeg preparations but reportedly never experience hangovers. I asked how they could drink if they were Muslim. Taariq replied, "Maybe the spirits aren't."

During my next Swahili lesson, Faruk and I talked about Muguwachuma, djinns, and kibuki. Faruk said, "I used to hear something strange, so one night I slept by the door to make sure it was Muguwachuma. The following day, I went straight to the shaikh and asked for protection. Although this djinn never hurt anyone, I wanted to prevent djinns and spirits from coming around. The shaikh gave me four pages of Qur'anic writings, wrapped in plastic, to put in the four corners of the house. From that day on, Muguwachuma never returned."

Faruk hadn't looked out to see Muguwachuma. I later asked Taariq if he'd ever heard a visual description of the djinn. "No one ever mentioned anything but the sound."

As for the two angels starting the djinn magic in Iraq, Faruk had a different take. "Magic is our ancient inheritance. It comes from our culture, pre-dating Islam." Faruk told me that the shaikhs could help with many mystical and spiritual problems and that they could heal some sick people when doctors couldn't help them. He went on, "This happened with my wife who had excessive bleeding. She was given a paper with a verse written on it with saffron and instructed to put it in water and drink the saffron tinted water every morning and night for seven days."

More mysteries surfaced. "Any number that is not divisible by two, such as three, five, or seven, is lucky. When the shaikh tells you to pray or repeat something, it's always in an odd number. That gives you protection."

I asked about the kibuki, and he said, "It is very real. They go into trances and heal people as well."

Taariq took me to Biashura, a leader of kibuki, who looked about sixty, so I was floored to find out that she was ninety-three! Taariq suggested, "Maybe she's counting Islamic years. It's a different calendar." We tried to do the math. If the Islamic calendar has the same twelve months, but each month has only twenty-nine days, then we could take away six years. She would still be eighty-seven.

Her house was full of middle-aged women wearing kangas wrapped around their chests, showing bare shoulders. A young woman from Dubai was receiving a treatment for an undisclosed illness. Biashura gave me some lotion and a charm to tie around my leg for water retention then invited me to attend a kibuki initiation. Taariq had second thoughts and suggested, "Maybe you shouldn't go."

I thought, "How many foreigners get a chance to see kibuki? I'm going."

To get to Biashura's I had to navigate my way through Ng'ambo, otherwise known as the "other side." Stone Town was a historic area with winding roads amid carved doors and latticework overhead. Neighborhoods in Ng'ambo were similarly complicated mazes, but homes were diminutive, made of cinderblock, and there was no garbage collection at all. The only way to get rid of litter was to hope for a big wind.

It was proving difficult to find my way, so I called Taariq. Streets were neither paved nor lined with stones. A downpour came. We left Malindi and entered the dusty alleys of the outskirts. They were flooded with standing muddy water.

Being male, Taariq couldn't enter the kibuki; he was concerned because he didn't know whether I would freak out or get possessed once they started channeling spirits. He looked around doubtfully. "Call me in a few minutes."

Charcoal burners with incense sprinkled over the coals lined the dark entrance. An older woman in a trance led me to a room and sat me on the floor with some other women. They took away my black camera bag, which I was using as a purse, and said that "spirits don't like the color black." There went my telephone, so I wouldn't be checking in.

I felt conspicuous as the only foreigner in a room full of women who obviously knew the ropes. They danced to channel the spirits of soldiers who died long ago in a war in the Comoros Islands. These soldiers liked to drink brandy or cognac, so the women drank while possessed. I learned that if the spirits are attracted to someone they give them coins and offer them imported brandy. If you refuse, the brandy is thrown on your head.

A young woman who spoke good English introduced herself to me as Taiya. She worked for an NGO that restores historic buildings with funding from Sweden. I appreciated being able to communicate with someone, though it seemed incongruous to be having a casual conversation about historic preservation while people were falling into trance.

Two women swathed in stiff white fabric were escorted into the room, accompanied by spear-wielding elders. They were seated on two small woven stools. A woman in a trance danced before them. More women, wearing colorful kangas, stood up and danced. Those on my side of the room were uninitiated and had to remain seated. This was part of a four-day ceremony for the two women in white.

I had expected live drumming, but instead, recorded music came from large speakers playing a series of different songs and rhythms. A couple of songs had the same 6/8 rhythm I'd heard in Morocco. Some women shuffled their feet, others used hip movements, and one was tossing her head. The lady who escorted me into the room in the beginning brought a tea cup full of brandy, opened my mouth, and poured it down my throat by force. There was no way to say no. As more and more women fell into trance, the scene got wilder. I was getting more attention than I wanted from some women who were possessed by the spirits of men. I understood why Taariq was concerned.

One woman, whom they called Babu (grandfather), was obviously a chief of some sort. She was seated in a special studded leather chair, head wrapped in a turban, holding a staff. Others came to pay their respects. The room became more and more crowded. At one point the woman who was initiating the girls in white came over and poured more liquor down my throat, then tried to sit on my knees. An older woman came and reprimanded her. Sometimes they would toss water on other women, or rub fingers full of white powdered-limestone paste on their foreheads and behind each cheekbone. One woman took mouthfuls of brown liquid from a plate and spat it into a bowl.

Sometimes, they danced in front of each other, staring straight into one another's eyes. The old woman gave me a handful of coins. They later explained that it was a token of good luck, which would multiply into more money for my future. Some did cleansing motions on our faces and heads.

Although men usually aren't allowed, the accordion player from Ikhwani Safaa was there with the DJ; they were both male.

A teenage girl next to me started shaking and went into a trance. Those seated are not supposed to stand, so she stayed on one knee, tossing her head, just as we belly dancers do to theatrically depict an Egyptian trance ceremony called Zar. She tossed her head for a long time. People introduced each other as "father" or "my son." They often spoke a little English, recognizing that I would speak English. I wondered if there had been English speakers in the Comoros a hundred years ago.

When the event was over, water was tossed on the women in trances to revive them and bring them back to themselves. Then everyone was led down the hallway where the initiates changed clothes behind a white sheet and an elder poured water over each guest's head from a bucket. She then took buckets of plants and poured them over people's heads. I didn't get away without having my hairdo ruined. While I was looking for my lost shoes, the elder caught up and doused me with plant water.

Taariq was wet too, because he had been standing outside in the rain the whole time.

On the way back to Malindi, he got impatient with all my kibuki questions and wanted to change the subject. Finally, he took me to meet a woman who, along with her daughters, had the spirits of kibuki. Malika was a beautiful Arabic-looking lady in an elegant caftan, like one would expect a woman lounging in a palace to wear. She was making bread in an outdoor kitchen under a piece of corrugated metal. She lived in a simple, unfurnished room where her family gathered around an old black-and-white TV set.

I asked how they got involved, and Malika said, "I knew one of my daughters had the spirit because when someone came to rob the house she had the strength to fend them off like a man." The other daughter had swallowed a big needle when she was a child; the doctors didn't know what to do, so they went to Biashura who made the needle disappear without a trace. She told me, "You should go on Sunday, because they will wear the costumes of each spirit. But under no circumstances should you wear black."

Kibuki had been banned under the revolutionary government as un-Islamic. Now it was permitted again. It's African, similar to the Zar in Egypt and other forms of ceremony in other North African countries.

Most outsiders expect Islamic societies to be inflexible, unwilling to accept other influences. On the contrary, they often accommodate local rituals and traditions. I tried to learn more before returning to the kibuki.

In Zanzibar, spirits are perceived as beings created by God and not related to the devil. They can get into a person's body, but the host human is not held responsible for the spirit's actions. In kibuki, the spirits are Christian, and the practitioners maintain that they have to drink in order to make the spirits feel welcome.

The following Sunday, Taariq brought me back to kibuki, and this time he was allowed into the ceremony. I was taken straight to Biashura, who was seated on a chair that resembled a throne, holding a staff. Most of the women dancing wore red and white kangas. Some were dressed as men, all in white.

I was instructed to kneel before Biashura, who doused my legs and hands with brandy, then poured some down my throat. Some other women hit me on the back. She put spots of limestone powder on my ears and forehead. They tied a kanga on Taariq, who looked sheepish as he was brought in to kneel before Biashura. She dipped coins in the white powder and placed them in our hands for luck. Taariq gave me all his coins. Then one of the women said, "He will always have his hands open to give to others, so he'll always get more." The coins are supposed to go under one's pillow when sleeping. Biashura said, "You gave Tamalyn all of your luck." He wanted the coins back, but she wouldn't allow it. "It's too late."

Taariq left and I joined the seated women. Several women in trances danced up to me. Some danced with two long sticks. A girl in jeans was on her knees tossing her head. Another was completely covered in two kangas, kneeling on the floor in a trance. She finally collapsed. Sometimes the possessed women took people out to dance. I danced a couple of times. It was hazardous because everyone bumped into each other, and hands were flailing precariously close to my eyes. A little girl danced, and I was returned to Biashura, who made me drink from a bowl of water and white powder, then dumped the rest over my head and body.

I had a meeting scheduled afterward with a major mover and shaker from the arts scene, so I had to go home to change clothes. What kind of impression would I make, full of white paste and reeking of brandy? I got to the meeting with wet hair and mentioned that I'd been to a kibuki. One woman replied, "Which one? There are two this weekend and one of my coworkers is at a kibuki too." I then realized it wasn't so far out on the fringes.

After my last Swahili class, Faruk promised to take me to a village to meet Shaikh Mohammed. I understood this to be a mosque's religious leader, but when we got to the simple home of an old man, this shaikh turned out to be one who does magic by way of the Qur'an. I had expected to ask deep religious questions, but instead got my fortune told and promised a paper that would give luck and protection from African magic.

Shaikh Mohammed had been brought to many countries to do healings and remove spells. People had flown him to Oman several times, and he'd visited Dubai, Canada, and Guatemala. He was sixty-eight years old with ten kids and two wives. "I see a male spirit who is in love with you. Please return on Friday, as I will make a special charm to drive him away."

Back in town, we got off the bus at the market. Faruk took another daladala home and I walked alone. It was desolate and dark because the stalls all closed early. A man insisted on walking me. Then another came up behind me, and I knew he was too close for comfort. It became apparent that they knew each other, and when the first man reached for a door of a house, I bolted. My gut told me they were bad news. I wound around a couple of streets to lose the guys, then found a lady dressed in a black bui bui. She was pointing one way to get to Malindi. Two other guys came along and asked, "Where do you want to go?" and pointed the other direction, telling me to come with them. She gave me a "don't go" look and said, "I know who is who, and they are up to no good. Come with me." She walked me to a shop where two big ladies sat in kangas. One agreed to walk me home, but just then, Taariq came around the corner.

I didn't know why I was suddenly attracting such riffraff, but the weird energy continued. As Taariq said, "I have to protect you, because if anything happens, the police will come to me." We came upon a fight in the street, and I forgot to ask what he meant. Some boys led by a rough-looking teenager were beating a child of about nine with sticks, kicking him to the ground, then holding him upside down about to hit his head on the pavement. Taariq got in the middle and insisted they let him go. The boy was hurt and limping, holding onto his groin and lower back. Passers-by stopped, but no one had compassion for this child. The older kids kept trying to beat him again, but Taariq held them off. I thought they were a street gang. We took the boy home to a "poor house" where many families lived around a central courtyard. A line of children followed us. The boy's aunt was home but had no compassion either. She said, "He deserves to be beaten."

Taariq convinced him to go inside and get his religious clothes. We walked him to the madrassa. Madrassas are Islamic religious schools. The incident took place because the boy didn't want to go to madrassa. Taariq said, "Sometimes they take the kids by force and beat them if they don't want to attend." This child was hysterical and between sobs cried, "I'll get more beatings at the madrassa."

Taariq had his own issues with this because, when he was a boy, he had gone to a school where they beat the kids a lot. He'd been through this boy's pain many times as a child. I asked what this violence had to do with Islam. He replied, "In Islam, this is not acceptable. The madrassa I went to had the kids terrified into learning. It made them get top scores and win awards, but that isn't the way to do it. There is a Hadith, words of Mohammed that are not part of the Qur'an, where Mohammed held in his hand a type of stick that was used in that time to brush one's teeth. He reached the point that he could have hit a difficult child. Allah was watching, and he said, 'If I wasn't afraid of Allah, I might have used the stick.'"

In my next e-mail to Bambang, the Islamic lecturer in Indonesia, I told him what happened to this boy and asked if it was permissible to beat children in the madrassas.

He answered: "About the beating of boys in Zanzibar, you won't find it in the Qur'an. On the contrary, you will find verses like: *'La ikroha fi-din'*—There is no compulsion in religion. Or: *'Ud'u ila sabili robbika bil hikmah'*—You must call to the path of God with full wisdom. So it was against Islamic teaching. Maybe they misinterpreted one of Prophet Muhammad's sayings: 'Tell your children to pray when they're seven years old, and slap them at ten years old if they do not obey you.' It was purely an educational method on discipline. Nothing of the legalization on torture as the Western media thinks. Prophet Muhammad loved children. He frequently kissed his children and grandchildren. He let them ride his back as a horse. He'd carry them during his praying. When his friends commented about those behaviors, he said: 'Those who do not have love, will not be loved by Allah.' Madrassa is the equivalent of school. Madrassa means the place to study all knowledge, especially Islamic science. So the atmosphere should be of a sacred place, serene and full of love."

In contrast to the original houses made of palms and mud, in Stone Town the Arabs built houses out of stone. All of the stone houses were small palaces built between 100 and 150 years ago during a time when the region's power reached far into mainland Africa and across the Indian Ocean.

During the revolution, opulent homes of the ruling and merchant classes were confiscated by the government and converted to welfare housing, and several families were moved into each dwelling. No funding was allotted for upkeep, so the city deteriorated.

By the mid 1980s, authorities realized that this historic area was in danger of being lost. The Aga Khan Trust for Culture joined forces with Stone Town's Conservation and Development Authority to try to save the buildings. Many had already collapsed, sometimes killing their inhabitants. I used to think there were a lot of construction sites and ancient ruins in my neighborhood, but time opened my eyes to the fact that I was living amid the rubble of homes that had fallen not so long ago. I understood why my apartment building was new; it was on the site of a collapsed home. My balcony overlooked more destruction. One last family lived in the ruins, hanging their laundry over a pile of stones and keeping a refrigerator wired to someone else's electricity.

One day Taariq, who loved to talk politics, took me on a walking tour of Malindi to see how many posters of the CUF party leader hung on walls and doorways. I was tired and hungry, but he wanted to show me "just one more thing." Behind a huge set of carved double doors adorned with brass spikes was an old mansion called Jumba La Buri, or Free House. It was full of families. Each family lived in one room of this home that had once belonged to a wealthy Indian family. More than fifty people shared two bathrooms. Part of the place had already collapsed. The staircase leading up several floors had planks of wood missing, requiring huge jumps so as not to fall into oblivion.

All that remained of the kitchen was a gaping hole in the second floor. A woman bathed her toddler in a large plastic bowl, perilously close to the orifice.

Behind her was an unusual-looking bed made of woven ropes propped up against a wall. Taariq explained that it was for washing dead bodies.

I asked, "Why do they have that in the house?"

He replied, "With so many living in one place, people are bound to die every so often."

Women cooked on gas burners and sat on plastic buckets to eat.

Hanging laundry surrounded the passageways and courtyard. One man pleaded, "Someone needs to help us. The Aga Khan owns this house, but he wants us to leave, so nothing gets fixed."

This was contrary to what I'd read at the House of Wonders about the Aga Khan Foundation's generosity and benevolence. Taariq said, "The Aga Khan had many houses before the revolution. Then the government took them, but the foundation has the deeds, so he can take them and do what he wants." I was confused. Is the Aga Khan a philanthropist or a slumlord? Folks in the neighborhood saw him as the eternal rich oppressor, paying no mind to the fact that there have been a succession of people called "Aga Khan," a title which indicates that he is the spiritual leader of the group. The projects and holdings are part of a worldwide organization run like a corporation. The present Aga Khan had merely inherited the helm.

Inside the building, I was allowed to film. Residents said, "We want the world to see how we live. Then maybe someone can help us."

Followers of the Aga Khan are Ismailies. Taariq said, "Ismailies aren't real Muslims. The three sects of Muslims in Zanzibar are Ibadhi (from Oman) who are about half the people; the rest are Sunnis and Shiites." I asked him why he didn't consider Ismailies real Muslims. He said, "They don't pray five times a day. To be a Muslim, you have to follow the rules of the religion."

I met Amin, head of Aga Khan's offices in Zanzibar, through his girlfriend, who was taking my belly-dance class. He explained a little about the organization as we sat around listening to taarab by the seashore. The next day I went to his office for more comprehensive information.

"The Ismailies are open toward all faiths and believe that the world should be plural. Not everyone the same. The Ismaili sect of Muslims believes that Islam is ever changing."

Amin explained how the Aga Khan Foundation works: "It's a multifaceted philanthropic organization with projects throughout the world. The Aga Khan is head of the Ismailies, their holdings, and the charitable organizations, which encompass education, health, arts, and architecture. The organization is nonreligious, and the people they help are usually not Ismailies."

Amin continued: "Buildings in Zanzibar don't belong to the Aga Khan. We collaborate between the government, private owners, and tenants in finding solutions that are holistic, not just patching up buildings and making them better for cosmetic purposes. Tenants are moved into temporary 'halfway houses' for six months while the buildings are restored.

"Then whoever pays the back rent they owe can move back in. That rent goes into a maintenance fund, which keeps the building from falling apart again. The only people who have a right to live in the buildings are those residing legally. There are many illegal sublets, which crowd the buildings more. Tenants moving back in must be the families who were originally given the sections of the houses by the government, usually for three dollars a month. If they divided them and rented rooms to others, these people cannot return."

Stone Town was declared a World Heritage Site in 2000. From 1982 to 1992, eighty-five historic buildings crumbled, and fifteen partially disintegrated. Every year more buildings collapse.

Several blocks from my apartment was a showpiece of restoration called the Old Dispensary, a beautiful green and white building with elaborate latticework on the outside. Now a cultural center, it was restored by the Aga Khan Trust for Culture.

The luxurious Serena Inn hotel was another Aga Khan project, which was made from the remains of an old building. Youssef, the door man, dashingly decked out in the hotel's old Omani-style uniform, gave me some spiced coffee, like the brew old men sell at the barazas after sunset.

I asked, "Which way is Tippu Tip's house?"

Born Hamed Bin Mohammed El Magrebi, Tippu Tip got his nickname because his red-rimmed eyes resembled those of a tippu tip bird. He had been the most infamous slave trader in Zanzibar. Today, his former mansion houses several families. Nothing has been restored. The government simply gave them the house. One man, who Youssef said is "a drunk and cannot be trusted," let me enter his part of the home, gave a guided tour, then tried to sell me some paintings. Youssef stayed with me the entire time.

It was a beautiful, spacious area with several loft-sized rooms and very few things to fill the space. The oceanfront views were fabulous, as was the tattered latticework surrounding each room.

☾☆ ⁎ ⁎ ⁎ ⁎

I told Youssef I had seen a listing for "Yoga Classes at the Serena Inn," and that I'm a belly-dance teacher. He introduced me to the hotel manager who introduced me to the yoga teacher, and we agreed that I would teach belly dance right after the yoga class twice a week.

My Swahili teacher, Faruk, couldn't understand when I tried to describe yoga. "Why would anyone want to stretch?" Taariq echoed his befuddlement and they both asked, "Are you sure you want to do this?"

The instructor, Tanya, was from Seattle. She was writing a book about the parallels between Vedic yoga and Masaii healing methods. (Masaii are traditional pastoral people in parts of Kenya and Tanzania.)

Executing Ashtanga twists under the palm trees with the sound of waves in the background was an incredible sensory escape. Each yoga student was atypical of Zanzibar. I would have expected to see such an array of slender blond women and an occasional Asian in a yoga class in California or Hawaii.

Through yoga and belly dancing, I met Emma, a British expatriate who spoke fluent Swahili and had lived on the island for fifteen years. We agreed to have a "girls' night out" when the classes finished. One of the women told me, "Zanzibar is a small place where everyone knows each other." That's what Taariq said too, but somehow I doubted the yoga students knew my neighbors in Malindi or vice versa.

On one of our nights on the town, at the Serena's elegant lounge, we met Amin's eighty-year-old uncle visiting from Vancouver B.C. He'd lived in Zanzibar in the 1930s. Now he was back to visit and to search for the house he'd lived in as a child. I asked, "How do you see Zanzibar now?" He was silent. I asked what it was like when he was a boy, and he replied, "You had to see it." His lack of words spoke volumes.

Sahar, my landlord's wife, told me, "The women in my family want to see you dance." Her sister Amina, who tutored computer science at the university and had visited my website, added, "Now we want classes."

Shortly after sunset, I brought my miniature laptop onto the roof, plugged in another speaker, and tied hip scarves on Amina and the little girls, Amar and Jamila. During our first rooftop belly-dance class, Sahar's adorable fifteen-month-old son, Saladin, stretched along with us. He wore a white Arabic robe and an Islamic hat that fell off as he bent forward. Jamila slid her head, Amina could move her ribcage, and Amar was the princess of hip shimmies. Amina told me that she walked around at her work doing head slides all the next day.

We danced with veils, and then Sahar asked me to demonstrate floor work, which she had seen in an old Arabic film. Things like dancing on your knees and doing backbends from a sitting to a laying position are athletic and take a lot of practice. I hadn't done them since starting to travel but got on my knees on the mat laid over the bumpy cement roof and gave it my best, surviving a backbend, knee walks, and touching my foot to my head. Having spent time in Egypt, my dancing had improved. It had become more sensitive, earthy, and authentic, but I hadn't had any need for the more showy aspects such as floor work, so

I hadn't done them. In the Arab world, a dancer doesn't jump through hoops or do contortions. Audiences are more interested in how you interpret the music.

Blackouts began and Amina started working late hours, so our classes became infrequent. Darkness wasn't the only consequence of a blackout. Fans and air conditioners didn't work either, so cement buildings became like boiler rooms. During a blackout, I fetched my computer, and Sahar, her kids, and I sat on the baraza watching a film I'd made about Indonesia. It attracted quite a crowd. In Zanzibar there were public televisions on the street for people to stand around and watch. My computer was serving as one of these.

When Amina came, we brought a camping lantern onto the roof to do class. The most treacherous part was navigating the pitch-black stairwell made of slippery tiles, which had no railings. One false step and a child could tumble down three flights of stairs.

Later, I went downstairs to go out and found the homeless man who usually slept next to my apartment building zonked out on my doorstep. I'd had to step over him before, but this time I was in a quandary because his foot was in the way of my closing the door, and I couldn't wake him. A man passing by laughed at my predicament but finally came over and roused my embarrassed neighbor, who slept on the baraza from then on.

Amina, Amar, and the family's domestic helper named Shams invited me to go swimming. They wore bui buis or kangas, workout pants, and T-shirts. We stopped at Sahar's mother's home, picked up some teenage girls of the family, left our belongings, and walked to the beach. Amina said, "We can't leave anything except our shoes and head coverings in the sand because of thieves." Only men and boys swim in Malindi or at the downtown beaches, so we went behind the Serena Inn. Men were playing soccer on the main beach, so we went down a ways to swim fully clothed as wooden dhows with huge sails bobbed by. It felt as if nothing had changed here in over a hundred years, until a huge slab of packing foam floated by.

Groups of young men hovered around to look at us. A policeman came to warn us about a woman swathed in black who was a known thief. "If you see her, don't leave your belongings." A young male cousin came to stand guard over headscarves and bui buis as we swam until sunset. High tide soon reached the side of the hotel, erasing the beach. By the time we got out, the little boy had already hung our things on a pipe.

When I asked about her brothers and sisters, Amina paused. She explained, "My mother and father had me, then they got a divorce and each remarried. Each of my parents had nine children, so I have two brothers and fifteen sisters."

Emma led me to "Jaws Corner," a baraza. I was introduced to Saida, a tiny rotund woman swathed in a black bui bui and headscarf. She sat on a baraza in this crowded plaza, which came alive at dusk when dozens of people from the neighborhood socialized, drinking bitter black coffee from tiny cups. Saida explained, "People need to be with each other. It is good for the health, so we sit together and drink coffee in the morning and again in the evening."

Another day, as I plied the winding alleys looking for Jaws Corner, a tiny girl in a black bui bui stopped me. My first thought was that she must want a pen or money, as often happened with the children in the Siwa Oasis. She looked up at me, caught my eye, then took my hand and gave it a tender kiss; gently reminding me not to project my past experiences onto others.

When I found the lively corner, I was the only woman and didn't know anyone, so I spoke with a retired German man and a guy named Nasser. When I asked about Saida, Nasser promptly dialed her on his cell phone.

I protested, "Don't worry. Let her take her time."

He insisted on calling.

Later Saida told us, "Someone named Kamal was looking for me. I still don't know who he is."

I said, "It was me, Tamalyn." We laughed.

Beneath her black robe and head covering, Saida was surprisingly racy. Once, a man fell off a motorcycle and she asked, "Are you okay?"

He brushed himself off. "I'm fine."

She went on, "I don't know. I think I'll have to inspect." Her suggestive tone was not in keeping with the Western image of covered women. She jokingly kept up the bawdy banter, and none of the men seemed uncomfortable or disrespectful because of it.

Taariq talked a lot about Bwawani, a popular disco complex. The government owned a big hotel that had been elegant in its heyday, around the beginning of the revolution. Now it was in such a state of neglect that nothing functioned. They leased out one of its banquet halls and two popular bars. Rusty tables and plastic chairs surrounded a cement dance floor. A huge empty pool loomed in the middle.

Taariq said the pool used to be full when the place was much nicer, but because the pool belonged to the empty hotel, it was empty too. I commented on the danger of someone getting drunk and falling in. Taariq agreed, "They'd die." There was no warning or fence around it. I couldn't believe people even came to this decrepit place. They were so used to it that the gradual emptying of the pool had gone unnoticed.

Much as I tried to avoid it, I let Taariq rope me into going to the "pool party" again, promising to give the Bwawani another chance. This time, the pool was half filled with water, and the dance floor was packed, mostly with men. Twenty-something-year-old guys danced together and in groups, moving very little to the American hip-hop songs and the Swahili rap, which is called *bongo flava*. Giant speakers made my eardrums quiver. There were a few girls, dressed in sleeveless tops and tight pants. Some came with their husbands; others were prostitutes.

We met the organizer of the Opposition Party demonstrations who explained, "There are heavy resentments and political divisions here. The opposition party wants Zanzibar to be more independent, to have its own flag, to make all mainlanders bring their passports and go through immigration in order to come."

Apparently, there had been an election that was rigged. The Opposition should have won—but didn't. They asked the U.S. government to monitor the voting process, but its representatives didn't go into the villages where most of the votes were stolen. He said, "Zanzibaris want the country to be more Islamic." I asked about the future, but he said, "People aren't ready to die yet. Maybe in fifteen years they'll rise up and things will change."

Another night, I was home sewing and working on the computer when Taariq called, "I have to come over and talk to you." I went downstairs and around the corner to sit on a baraza. "There's taarab tonight at Bwawani. It will be really good!" I didn't want to go out, but he kept insisting until I succumbed.

Bwawani was the same as other nights. The poolside looked listless, but Taariq was feeling flush and brought me downstairs to the real disco. A song by Shakira blasted through the room. He said, "The taarab is coming."

This disco was painted pitch black and there were blinding flashing neon lights that never ceased. There wasn't any taarab. He said, "Now, you'll see what Africans really like." The music was mainstream American and a bit out-of-date. I couldn't get mad at him because he was so earnest, and it was clear that he really wanted to go dancing. After a bit, they played some bongo flava and a set of songs from different places in Africa—Uganda, Kenya, the Tanzanian mainland, and South Africa.

I had read about a famous African music aficionado, DJ Yusef, who organizes the annual Busara Music Festival. I mentioned his name to Emma, and she replied, "It's best to go to his house. I'll take you there."

He told us about a full moon celebration he was organizing in a beach village. The party was in a distant village of Kendwa. Since Emma was well connected, we ended up traveling to the other end of the island in a fancy car with Anwar, one of the head honchos at the airport.

We drove past some villages of thatch-roofed huts and some with small houses made of mud bricks and saw carts pulled by cows, as well as lots of animals running in the streets. Cars were a minority among the carts, pedestrians, animals, and bicycles.

We stopped first at a beach with a complex of tourist bungalows nearby. A sudden cry pierced the air. *Zumari* is a shrill-sounding horn that, when blown, sounds like the Egyptian *mizmar*. Anwar said that it originally came from Egypt. Several drums started to beat as a show commenced. A dozen men and women wielded sticks and pieces of fabric, dancing with legs open and hips moving in fluid circles and sways.

We drove to Kendwa down what was more like a bumpy trail than a road. It was dark; the red earthen path ahead of us was all I could see in the headlights. Parking by an expansive hotel complex called "Sunset," we traipsed through a large outdoor patio restaurant full of Westerners, greeting people both Emma and Anwar knew.

Then we moved on to another hotel that had a large outdoor disco-bar where DJ Yusef was spinning. It looked like a typical touristy place where dreadlocked guys and mzungu women congregate. European women wore casual tank tops and skirts—kind of a "hippy while on vacation" look.

I was thinking we'd come too far for something so bland, but then a group of acrobats took to the dance floor. These young men did dangerous flips and a balancing act that involved perching Coca-Cola bottles on sticks in performer's mouths while they rode seven-foot-tall unicycles.

Afterward, one of the performers showed Emma his collarbone which he said had been broken eight times. She asked how they got paid. He replied, "We pass the hat."

Off to the side, one skinny guy in a Bob Marley T-shirt stole the show with his wild dancing, going into a snakelike trance and winding up writhing in the sand on his belly.

After the show, audience turnover was complete, and the dance floor filled with African guys. Very few Westerners remained. Men took over, dancing their hearts out with utter sensuality and elasticity. The music ranged from bongo flava to clubby-sounding Afro, salsa, house, and such. I'd been hoping for something more ethnic and less hip.

When I walked to the beach, it was idyllic. The full moon had been two days before; there was still plenty of moonlight. The tide was low, so the moon reflected on the turquoise water and a wide stretch of white sand.

Emma took me to the Old Fort to hear one of her coworkers sing. I expected one guy to be crooning in a concert. Instead, a huge hand-painted banner dominated the stage, along with a pair of gigantic speakers. Bleachers were packed with young people, each of whom had paid $2 to get in. It was like the *Gong Show* in a picturesque amphitheater of the Old Fort, also known as Ngome Kongue, which had been built by Omanis in 1701. The crowd was mostly eighteen- to twenty-five-year-old males in droopy pants. Canned music played as each participant sang and danced to his own composition. They ranged from good to okay to terrible.

The most amazing by far was Emma's friend Dotcom, who had an all-male group of teenagers behind him doing incredible break dancing with an African flair. He'd organized this group of boys to get them off the streets, away from drugs.

Collective voices became a roar when a young woman in jeans and a one-shouldered top did an extremely sexual dance on her hands and knees. Young men rushed to the stage to give her tips. I found it strange to see this overtly sexual dancing embraced in a town where women on the street wore veils. She was the hit of the show, and even women were putting tips in her pockets.

Twice a week, I passed a handwritten sign advertising "Tourist Show at the Old Fort." It didn't sound promising, but tourist shows often give an overview of cultural dances, even if they aren't of the highest quality.

I was one of three audience members. A conga drummer and a man with a long piece of curved metal played percussion. Four people sang and danced. Men wore long cotton pants and no shirts, while women wore caftans and scarves at the hips. They did two dances: the first, called *chidocha*, from mainland Tanzania, had simple steps with some hip movements and was danced in celebration of marriage and good harvests; the second, called *conga*, was for Zanzibari women to demonstrate to young brides what to expect in marriage. Actually, the men and women both danced, using a long tube laid on the ground with two people holding the ends as two more danced over the center, doing small hip circles very close together, facing one another.

After that it was blackout time, so the show was suspended for an hour. Muhidini, a small man who worked at the Old Fort, sat with me and told about a group of prison guards who practice dance and drumming every day. He offered to take me to the prison to watch them. I thought that sounded interesting, but the head drummer said practice was temporarily suspended. I asked if he knew of any traditional dance classes around town. He said, "You haven't seen anything. We can put on a whole show for you complete with regional costumes."

The drummer came on wheeling and dealing in full force. "How much are you willing to pay?"

I had been through this before with Mr. Chimbeni, so I said, "I'm only interested in taking a dance class or maybe seeing a rehearsal."

Something had gotten lost in the translation, and it was also a case of seeing me as the rich foreign money tree. He finally gave up, and Muhidini invited me to a wedding later in the month.

Lights came back on and the show resumed. This final dance lasted half an hour. *Sindhimba* was a mating dance from the mainland, in which partners chase one another, bumping pelvises. Charging with provocative hip movements, they push with the private areas and then run away. Two Norwegian men who had come in during the blackout were puzzled. "This is not a Muslim dance!"

"No," I assured them, "it is a dance from the mainland. Dances can represent anything in life. Traditional dance often shows a part of life that's cause for celebration."

Wedding day came, but I didn't have much confidence in Muhidini's plans. After a series of missed encounters and confused communications, he said, "Meet me at the post office," but sent me to the wrong one. Really doubtful by then, I was prepared to extract myself from a sticky situation at any moment.

I judged wrong. His entire family had rented a daladala, which was waiting for me. Not expecting much, I was still wearing jeans. But the vehicle was full of elegantly dressed women in silky dresses and bright flowing head scarves. We went to a nearby village, where Muhidini said, "Follow my mother." He encouraged me to film. I sat on a mat with a group of women, drinking coffee and eating sweet *haloua*. I felt like they merely tolerated my presence and looked at me like a creature fallen from outer space who was best ignored.

A group of young girls dressed like nuns, in black frocks and purple headscarves, approached and sat on another mat. Several men with frame drums sat across from them. One in the middle sang with a loud scratchy microphone. Women got up to dance, waving headscarves with mild hip movements to the religious songs. I was ushered inside and encouraged to film Muhidini's thirty-year-old brother and his thirty-two-year-old bride taking their wedding vows in a bedroom. She looked extremely hot and uncomfortable in a fancy mint green dress and loads of gold jewelry. The bride was divorced with two kids, and Muhidini's brother had divorced four months earlier.

The Zanzibar International Film Festival, or ZIFF, is of such a scope that it takes all year to organize. With offices located in the Old Fort, it is one of only five major film festivals in Africa. It also includes dance and other cultural performances, panels, and book readings.

Furaha, the ZIFF communications coordinator, showed me around. When I asked how the local people reacted to this festival, he explained, "At times, they weren't very open, because some dance performances and film content upset conservative Muslims. We're careful of the films we show publicly. If one includes kissing or is too sensual, we screen it in a more private area."

The festival performances, workshops, and lectures have outreach programs aimed at involving women and featuring female artists. Furaha said, "During ZIFF, Zanzibar comes alive with people from all over the world."

Emma, who knew everyone at ZIFF, told me "One of the founders, Emerson, has a house with a golf course right in the middle of Stone Town." I couldn't imagine that. Then she called him and told him a belly dancer was in town.

Emerson is one of the biggest creative forces in Zanzibar. A fifty-seven-year-old New Yorker, he was instrumental in starting not only ZIFF but also the Busara Music Festival and the Dhow Music Academy. He showed me a newspaper article about his latest project, Zanzibar's first opera, which is about Salme, a renegade princess who eloped with a German.

We had sodas on a tiny rooftop that took several flights of steps to reach. His house was tall and thin. Each of its several floors had a plain room, a kitchen, or a bathroom. I forgot to look for the golf course but saw the sunset over miles of tin roofs.

The Dhow Academy's director, Hilda, was a German woman who had come to Zanzibar five years earlier as a volunteer for the film festival. She ended up running the music school, which had been set up to teach and preserve Zanzibari music. Located in one of the historic buildings along the waterfront at the top of an uneven staircase made of giant stone steps, the school had a lot of written information about the history of taarab.

Hilda was puzzled by my project, as people often are, and wanted to know my motivations. I explained that I didn't have a specific point of view or goal in mind, other than to put a human face on the Islamic world and go places, poking around for forty days and reporting my experiences with no agenda or control over the outcome.

From Hilda, I learned that the other traditional musical form of Zanzibar besides taarab is *kidumbak*. Kidumbak is related to taarab but is more rhythm-based. Many musicians hone their skills in kidumbak groups before being admitted into a taarab club. She explained, "There's a dance associated with it in which the women do a lot of hip shimmies."

Brass bands called *beni*, which originated around the turn of the twentieth century as a mockery of colonial-style military bands, are now popular as wedding entertainment. Women in the audience join as chorus singers or dancers.

Hilda went on to explain that each of the two main taarab clubs has its own style. "Culture Music Club is more African, and Ikhwani Safaa keeps the Arabic roots."

I asked about changes in taarab over the years.

She replied, "At times they had to use political themes in the songs, and for a while groups consisting of only women flourished, but none remain."

In the music library, I listened to a Siti Bint Saad 78 rpm recording. Though scratchy, it was a real treat. Her orchestra sounded much smaller than what I had heard recently. The only instruments I could hear were an oud and a violin. I bought a CD of Ikhwani Safaa that was produced in France. The cover had a booklet with photos of the artists, several of whom I recognized from rehearsals, and many of the pictures had been taken in the same room where I'd seen them practice.

Ikhwani Safaa agreed to let me videotape their rehearsals for my film. After a week I was finally able to capture the two bashrafs (Ottoman inspired instrumentals) I had been waiting for, including "Afkari," my favorite belly-dance song. I went home and played back the last rehearsal on my video camera. I couldn't stop dancing! I wanted to dance all over the apartment, but that meant carrying the camera from room to room, which would interfere with my arm movements.

Bing! An idea hit me like a rock on the head—a new CD called *40 Days & 1001 Nights, Bellydance Music for Tamalyn Dallal* by the Ikhwani Safaa Musical Club of Zanzibar. They were such traditionalists that they might nix the idea once I said it was for belly dancing, but I wanted to try. I had to gather information and put my ducks in a row before approaching the committee.

Unable to contain myself, I spilled my idea to Furaha during what was supposed to be my interview with him about the film festival. He recommended talking to Hassan, who owned a recording studio. The next morning, Hassan and I met, and he explained that he charges by the song. I figured that Ikhwani Safaa songs tend to be long, so that could help economize. He laughed and let me get away with making each track nearly ten minutes long.

In his forties, he was a tall man with a strong presence. He didn't smile a lot but seemed calm and collected, with a deep, booming voice that made me feel at ease. I asked him to translate my idea and help negotiate with the musicians.

On the way to Ikhwani Safaa that night, I told Taariq of my plan, voicing my concern about whether such a traditional group, which plays non-danceable music, would be willing to collaborate on a belly-dance CD. My second trepidation was telling Taariq that someone else was going to handle the negotiations. I felt more comfortable being represented by an older man who was in the music business. Taariq's face fell when I told him. Regaining his composure, he said, "Be careful. People say that Hassan is a rapist."

I'd never heard him talk bad about anyone and was taken aback!

"What?" I asked.

"I heard from a reliable source that he took a singer home and held her hostage, forcing her to do every sex act imaginable until she escaped a week later." I told him it was probably a rumor, but he warned, "Be very careful dealing with Hassan." I asked why he wasn't in jail. He explained, "His family is connected to an important member of the government. Besides, the police won't do anything. If she was the type of girl like my sister Leila, they would arrest him, but this was a singer. They're not going to do anything."

I'd been hearing about the triple standard: a woman with money or family was treated with respect, but lower-class women, especially those without anyone to defend them, were often used for sex. They might be house maids or women with tarnished reputations. If one of these women was raped, it was often assumed that she did something to bring it on, and the law looked the other way.

My mind was in a state of confusion. Hassan was the most reasonable, sensible, and businesslike person I had met in months. He was even the type of guy I would date, except that he'd already mentioned a girlfriend in the U.S. Could there actually be a monster lurking behind this facade of normality? I decided to be wary but not to change my course of action over something that could be unfounded.

The day came for us to go to Ikhwani Safaa, but when I called Hassan, he said, "I'm in the hospital. I had a hernia operation this morning."

"Would you like me to come visit?" I asked.

"Sure. Meet me in the VIP ward and we'll discuss a new plan of action."

I told Emma "Hassan's sick, so I want to visit him."

She countered, "He's full of it!"

"No. He's in the hospital."

Then she got concerned and went along.

I expected such a dignified man to be in a posh hospital room with flowers by the bedside and nurses hovering about. Instead, the "VIP section" was a long dark walk from the hospital. If any place in Zanzibar was haunted, this had to be it. Hassan's dismal room was big and empty, with sheets over the windows. It would have been an excellent location for filming a scary movie. There was no one around. I told Emma that I would be terrified to spend the night there. I would have worried about who—alive or otherwise—might walk in during my sleep.

How strange to see a prominent man who seemed so strong lying on a crooked metal cot with an empty IV bottle dangling from his arm. He assured me that people came by to check on him, and said he would stay for two days, then rest a few more at home.

Cell phone in hand, he called Soud, the chairman of Ikhwani Safaa, who spoke fluent English and lived most of the time on the mainland. We agreed to have Furaha from the film festival office help negotiate and communicate with the musicians. On our way out, I made a pact with Emma. "If I get sick from malaria or something, please make sure I go where the common people all suffer together."

The next day, Furaha informed me that he had to make an emergency trip to his village near Arusha. Now it would have to be Taariq's job to explain my vision to Ikhwani Safaa. I brought my computer and a DVD of me dancing. Taariq was full of ideas and smart enough to help me. Unfortunately, he flatly refused to wear anything but his dangling baggy pants. I was concerned that the club's elderly committee might not take me seriously with him doing the talking.

Fortunately, all went well. We negotiated a deal that was good for all parties. The only hitch was that they refused to record in Hassan's studio. I couldn't squeeze a reason out of them. They just said, "You'll need to find another studio."

Zanzibar is a small, poor island, not a hot spot for music production. In fact, the only music store I could find survived by bootlegging copies of copies of homemade recordings on an old computer.

Taariq tried to find Baah, who ran the Bwawani Disco and supposedly was Hassan's competition in the recording business. He was out of town for a few days, and I didn't want to wait. One of the musicians tried to make a deal with the music school—at twice the price. I decided to insist on working with Hassan or scrap the idea. Taariq suggested that if Ikhwani Safaa didn't budge, we should give them the option of finding a studio that matched Hassan's prices.

Turning into an insomniac over this project, I lay awake waiting for a reasonable hour to call Chairman Soud. He said, "No problem," and promised to speak to the musical director.

That night, I had my hands full with the band's musical director, Jamal. He was a prim, tiny man with a sour expression on his face. He refused to work with Hassan, and then stood on the corner of the roof and sulked inconsolably, insisting that Hassan would pirate the music and nobody would get any money. Taariq tried reason, explaining that this was my project. I was the one producing it, so if Hassan bootlegged the music, I would be the loser because I was the one who paid for it. We finally got a call through to Soud on the mainland with a plea for help. It appeared that working with Jamal was going to be a challenge.

Taariq was a great help, listing names for the CD cover and planning the logistics of the recording session. He explained that Hassan's studio was in another town. We would have to rent a daladala and cater lunch for the musicians. I would never have been able to handle all that in Swahili, and if I had, it would have been at the mzungu price. Luckily, Taariq knew what to do. For the photo shoot, I said they should dress the way they wanted to be represented, but Taariq countered, "I'm going to tell them to all dress up in their uniforms. Trust me. If they wear what they want, they will come in anything." He told them to bring black and white suits. Some of the musicians didn't want to be photographed, but some who weren't on the CD volunteered for the photo session. I had to keep insisting that the people in the photo be the same as the ones in the credits and the same ones who would actually play in the recording session.

The next day, I kept getting missed calls from Taariq using a variety of different numbers. That's what people do when they have no phone credit. I had a lot to do and was on my way to the ZIFF office, where the only graphic designer in town worked. Matt, who was from Australia, agreed to create the CD cover and label. I planned to send the music and graphics to a distribution company in the U.S., so the CD would be done on time for my workshops and shows when I got home.

"Please come over. I have to talk to you," Taariq pleaded. He seemed nervous about setting up the food and daladala. "They'll need a deposit."

I said, "Find out the prices first."

His behavior was strange. I had noticed that he'd lost a lot of weight in the past couple of weeks and harbored suspicions I hadn't wanted to face. I wondered if he did drugs and even asked him one day. He had said, "I used to smoke 'mari-ju-ana'" (that's how they pronounce it in Zanzibar). Another time, he admitted, "Sometimes I still smoke."

I needed film for my video camera, and if he bought it I would save several dollars. I reasoned that this could be a test. If he was desperate for drugs, he might take the money and not show up with the tapes, but that would be better than something worse happening later. I had a bad feeling. I was concerned about him, because he was truly a nice person, but also worried because I would need to fork out a lot of cash for the recording and studio. If he was doing drugs, this could be dangerous and jeopardize the project for everyone. I gave him the exact amount of cash for the tapes, and we parted ways.

Throughout the day, my mind flip-flopped between sadness and anger. He was a beautiful person with so much potential. Was he wasting his young life? Could he have been helping me in order to get kickbacks from my purchases? Why hadn't he taken my video camera or computer when we were alone on the dark streets? He knew all the money I was paying the band and when. No matter how nice a person, if he were desperate for drugs, he might do anything.

A whirlwind went through my mind as I tried to focus on Matt's computer and the wording of the text. I prayed that if Taariq was doing drugs, it would be revealed immediately. I didn't want to exclude him unfairly, but I wasn't willing to put the recording project at risk.

Over cappuccino in a posh café, I rang Emma to ask about a party I had missed. She said, "I met someone who knows Taariq. He said to warn you that he's doing drugs and to be very careful."

I called her repeatedly, asking a more local perspective on what to do.

Emma said, "Don't confront him. Things can escalate fast in Zanzibar. Just play along like you don't know anything, and gradually get rid of him."

That isn't my nature.

I was on my way to Ikhwani Safaa, lost as usual, when Taariq came along with my film in hand, acting completely normal with the exact number of tapes I asked for. My first words were, "I know you're doing drugs."

He quickly admitted that he had been in a drug program and relapsed. "That's why I was in Kenya. They don't have any programs here."

After returning to Zanzibar, he'd been clean for several months. His relapse started with a beer, followed by a joint, then a joint laced with heroin. He thought he could stop at that, but he was back to being addicted after just one smoke. Now he needed more every day. It only costs about one dollar for a hit of heroin in Zanzibar. He had injected in the past. Since rehab, he didn't do that, but feared he would. He told me that his family knew about his drug use. They were very upset, but gave him money to buy heroin until he could return to Kenya. I later learned that most families have at least one addict and have no choice but to pay for their drugs. Otherwise, they were likely to do something illegal, getting arrested and bringing on another set of problems. In Zanzibar, the drug problem is seen as the responsibility of the family and there aren't rehabilitation programs or a support system.

He walked beside me to Ikhwani Safaa and wanted to go inside to help with the photo shoot. I was upset on many levels—sorrow, fear, and anger at being deceived, then anger at myself for not catching on sooner. Then I was upset at everyone in the entire neighborhood, who surely knew that I was hanging out with an addict and never uttered a word. I needed to concentrate on this CD project, and even looking at him sent all the mixed feelings swirling through my brain. He was offended when I told him not to come up to the club. I finally agreed to stop by his house to continue the conversation later.

The musicians wore short-sleeved white shirts in need of ironing, black pants, and red bow ties. Two guys didn't show up for photos because they didn't want to be in a picture. Finally, the bass player put on his wrinkled shirt and I had to keep coaxing, "Tuck it in." The other guys tried to get his collar and tie straightened out. After a couple of "piga picha's," he was happy to return to his comfy old T-shirt and well-worn hat.

After rehearsal, I asked the percussionists to stay and work on the drum solo. It turned into a party. To my surprise, Bashir the flute player started belly dancing!

Taariq's name wasn't mentioned, but Bashir and the main drummer, Abdel, offered to walk me home. I didn't want to ask them to take me to Taariq's because visiting him at such an hour would surely arouse curiosity. I also didn't want to walk the dark streets alone, so I didn't visit Taariq that night.

As I went downstairs to set a bag of garbage on the baraza for the nightly cat attack, I heard a whistle. Right behind me was Taariq, looking totally pathetic and dejected, holding my pile of laundry. I had given it to him so his maid could wash it.

On the verge of tears, he said he'd been waiting a long time and had many things to show me, but that I didn't care, and "You probably just wanted my story for your book." He was in pain and never wanted to see me again, but I felt we needed a better closure than this. I insisted on fulfilling my promise to go to his house.

There, he showed me a file of his writings about what it is like to be an addict. He said, "When you read this, you won't like me anymore." The previous week, he'd told me about his difficult childhood and how badly his parents' breakup had affected him. He had wanted to show me a file of writing about his life. This was the file I never got around to looking at. It was graphic about shooting up, stealing, and feeling bad about himself for hurting his family. He was reaching out for help, so I told him "I can't be around you if you're doing drugs, but I'll be there to give support if you quit."

He already had a plan, and had even written it out point by point, suggesting that he could either enter a hospital or go to his cousin's house outside of town and have her lock him in a room for a few days. The hospital sounded like a better option. He wouldn't be strong enough to detox in Malindi, because people deal all around the area. He said, "You feel really horrible and sick during withdrawals, and I know I'll give up."

He planned to talk to Leila about her taking care of his father. I said, "She loves you and will stay here a few days so you can go to the hospital." With a husband, three stepkids, and a one-year-old baby her hands were full, but surely, she would comply. He said an uncle was coming around 11:00 AM, and he would talk to him about paying the hospital bill. It wasn't very much and I could have paid it, but if I did, it would have been too easy for him to relapse again because he would not have to be accountable to his relatives. He already had everything worked out in his mind but needed someone to stand by and not let him renege.

I called Soud and pleaded, "I don't speak Swahili and can't set up the food and transport. I'll pay what's reasonable, but don't expect me to do the organizing." There were never any questions asked, but every detail was taken care of by Jamal.

In the morning, I checked on Taariq before leaving to make sure his resolve hadn't wavered. His uncle, who had been a politician, and some cousins were upstairs, sitting with Taariq's father. I stuck around as a visual reminder. Taariq called his uncle downstairs.

The uncle responded, "Why do you have to detox now? You need to take care of your father. You can go back to Kenya as soon as your stepmother gets to town."

It didn't take long to convince the uncle to change his mind.

We waited for Leila to arrive with lunch for her father. She was disgusted and said, "How many times are you going to detox?"

I asked how many times it had been, and she explained that before the Kenyan rehab, he was always quitting and starting again. "He has been doing drugs since the age of seventeen, for eight years," she said, adding, "It is so common here, and as long as he is in Zanzibar, he will always do drugs. You walk out the door, and there they are. People offer them and he can't say no. That is the problem in this country."

Leila agreed to take care of her father day and night. She said, "I was so sad when I smelled drugs on him again," and asked if I hadn't noticed the smell. I felt naïve. I wouldn't have recognized the smell of heroin.

I went with Taariq to Al Rahma, a private hospital on the edge of town. It looked like a white stucco apartment building with little arches. The receptionist was indifferent when Taariq asked to go in for detox. She gave him a blank file and said to wait in a chair. He met the doctor and was admitted. When they offered him a private room, he said he wanted to be with other people. So he was given a cot in a room full of similar cots with only one other patient, who was in no condition to provide company.

The sky was closing in with eerie shades of yellow and grey, and the humidity was so thick that I knew a storm was coming. Walking along the beach, I noticed that even the old wooden dhows were suspiciously absent. Sunset was moody and beautiful with far off flashes of lightening.

Bashir invited me to hear him and several other Ikhwani Safaa members play at the Serena Inn. The lightning came almost upon us. Sudden gusts of wind brought a torrential rainstorm that blew the tablecloths off. The musicians grabbed their instruments, and we all ran inside to sit out the storm.

When the rain subsided, everyone left. The street was absolutely silent: no cars, not a soul walking, just the sound of soft rain. I didn't want to pass "Suicide Alley" on my way home. It was a street in the middle of the tourist area, infamous for muggings and street crime. Everyone was warned not to walk there alone unless they saw people around. Youssef arranged a ride for me on the back of a tiny scooter driven by a handsome midget. The driver was a music teacher at the Dhow Academy and had been playing accordion that night.

I was delicately perched sidesaddle, holding my long parachute skirt and trying not to slide off the back. We were the only life on the ancient little streets as the sky flashed in the distance. It was one of those fleeting magical moments, like being in a strange foreign film.

Just as I started having fun, my phone rang. I didn't answer, but it rang again and again. When I finally answered, it was Taariq. "I can't reach Leila. She needs to send me some food." It turned out that the hospitals in Zanzibar didn't give meals. They didn't give him any drugs for detox either, just some vitamin-B complex, glucose, and rehydration.

Rafiq, the man with the scooter, drove me straight to Ikhwani Safaa for our last rehearsal. Abdel wanted to see my finger cymbals. He was muscular and weathered like a seaman, but the cymbals seemed to cast a spell over him as he put them on the wrong fingers. He started playing and belly dancing around the room. I wondered if there was some ancient memory of belly dancing that bubbled up periodically, indiscriminate in whom the moment chose.

Leila called to see if I was going to visit Taariq. The next day, we went together to bring his lunch. He had an IV in his arm and was bored. This time, at least, there were more patients filling the beds in the room. He said he felt sick, "But it comes and goes. I can handle it." He looked good, but his mood was noticeably dark. I tried to be cheerful and tell him how thankful I was for all of his kindness and help. He said, "You can see it that way, but I don't think so."

He lightened up when a large family came in to visit another patient. Taariq pointed out a man in the group, "That's Abdellah Issa, the famous singer." I loved one of his songs that I had heard in a grocery store so much that I had bought a bootleg tape. He recognized Taariq and came over to greet him affectionately. This famous singer acted totally natural finding him detoxing in the hospital. It was as if we all just met on the street. We talked about music and our projects and exchanged phone numbers.

Jamal got nicer by the day, and we soon became friends. He would send me text messages in Swahili simply to wish me a nice day. One morning I was shopping across town when he called to invite me to a wedding. He was downstairs at my place, so I rushed home. Jamal seemed straight laced, proper, and gentlemanly, carrying an old fashioned umbrella and his violin case.

We rode to a village and found crowds of spectators, from children to adults, wearing everything from tattered rags to elegant dresses. I never saw a bride or groom, but the party was in full swing.

Behind a house, where the dirt alleys converged into a small open area, women danced in a circle around several musicians who were playing a variety of horns. They walked with sensual hip circles and shimmies. The *beni* music sounded like a cross between a military brass band and African drumming, both strong and compelling. Women took turns standing on chairs and doing incredibly flexible and pronounced hip isolations. Later it was two women at a time, or a woman and a man.

The beni band stopped, and everyone rushed behind another house, where several percussionists played kidumbak. A man sat with his foot on a handpainted wooden box, holding up a stick that created tension on a thick string. The sound was rich and bass-like. Jamal took out his violin and joined them. This combination of violins and deep percussion sounded frantic. The dancing was similar, but the music lost its grandeur and dignity, veering toward wild and crazy. Dancing became suggestive, especially when two people stood on a bench together and got close, sometimes bumping one's crotch into the other's behind.

Once again, hundreds of people rushed over to the beni band, where the women resumed their circles. One lady got me up on the bench to dance, and everyone screamed as I imitated her hip circles. They may not have thought that mzungus could move. I had never seen anyone dance with the sharpness and fluidity that they had, though.

Rushing with the crowd back to kidumbak, I sat on a bench surrounded by children. The dancing became increasingly sexual, between members of the same sex. My guess is that it was instructional for the bride, then for the groom. But where was the newlywed couple? At some points, three or four women would be bumping pelvises and lifting legs together. Two men mimicked sex acts in a way that still looked like dancing, but then one opened his mouth and stuck his tongue out, simulating oral sex on the other. They never actually touched, and all clothing remained in place. It was hot and steamy.

The hostess kept making sure the children stayed out of the way of my camera, which surprised me. People didn't like to be filmed on the street, and these dances were definitely not for primetime, but they wanted to be filmed.

On the way back to Malindi, Jamal asked, "Sawa?" (was it good?)

I wondered if this was the same dance Hilda had told me about at Dhow Academy. Did it get polished up for school concerts, or was this just a wild crowd, adding its own touches to an already sensual dance style? A couple of my neighbors said, "What you saw was normal."

When I came home, a lady was standing on the doorstep. I'd seen her hanging around with the vendors and other neighbors. She said "Hello, Tamalyn," and waited for me to open the door. Instead, I knocked on Sahar's door, and the woman went inside first. We were both given chairs. After that, I didn't even notice her. I just assumed that she was a friend of the family who didn't talk much. After Sahar, Amina, and I spoke awhile, the woman got up and said goodbye.

Sahar asked, "Do you know her?"

"No."

Amina said, "Neither do we."

That raised questions. Did she simply want to be my friend—or was she trying to get into my apartment?

☪ ✩ ⋆ ✩ ∘

The night before recording day was like the night before Christmas when I was a child. It was hard to sleep. If all went well, I knew the project would be a success and we could all benefit. I was taking a big risk, depending on the recording studio to follow through, do a good job, and not have any technical difficulties. There were ten musicians to count on. I hoped everyone would show up. Attendance had been inconsistent during rehearsals, and I don't think there was a day when everyone on the project was present. It was like herding cats. When one came, the other went.

Recording day was an exception. Jamal waited for me on the corner and we walked to Ikhwani Safaa, where the daladala was waiting. Two guys were missing, but after picking up the food we tracked them down. I noticed discrepancies between the people who showed up and the names on the list. All were great musicians, but I needed to have the right people on the list of credits and would have liked the names to match up with the people in the photo. I made some last-minute changes to the list and would go over the changes with Matt the next morning. We rode out to a village full of affluent Miami-style homes. This was the first time I'd seen such big houses in Zanzibar.

"Where is Hassan?" I wondered as the men tuned up their instruments on his patio in the oppressive heat. Abdel took a nap on the pool table. I seized the opportunity to have everyone sign the final contract, which we had been tweaking all week. No one could read it save Rami, who came along as a security guard. I think he was part of the club, but I'd never seen him play an instrument. I thought, "Hassan must be here, since the door's open." So I called him. He came out in his pajamas, Arabic-style—a long robe and PJ pants.

We recorded for seven hours straight in a hot, stuffy, soundproof room. The air conditioner was noisy, so it was turned off. The studio was like a sauna and steam room in one!

The first two songs—the most important—went beautifully.

Although he took a lot of breaks to go back to bed, Hassan was helpful, having them repeat each song until it was right. The problem was that, although this was the most state-of-the-art recording studio in Zanzibar, it only had two tracks. That meant five guys for each microphone, strategically placed so everyone could be balanced and heard. There was minimal possibility for mixing, so they couldn't just redo one section. If a note went sour, they'd have to repeat the whole song.

The last two songs went without a hitch, but the one in the middle was a problem. A note kept going down when it would have sounded better up. I insisted it be changed, and Hassan backed me up, which caused tension. I was afraid Jamal would walk out. Luckily, he stood and took a deep breath, and they played the entire nine-minute song for the fifth time, successfully.

In rehearsals, I usually avoided Rami, because he kept pestering me to give him a camera. I decided to be friendly on recording day, so when he asked me to sit outside with him, I did so out of politeness. He invited me to his home, so I asked about his wife and kids. He said, "I have five children, and my wife is a teacher. When you come to Zanzibar again, you should stay in my home." He wrote down their names and ages, then I thought I heard wrong when he said, "You choose one of my children to take back to America. When you meet them, you will decide which one you like."

I explained, "I'm a traveling belly dancer. I can't be carting around other people's kids!"

I didn't elaborate on the absurdity of the suggestion, but he kept insisting. Finally, he said, "There was an American man who was going to take one of my children. He was supposed to send me $2000 for the visas and paperwork, but never did. The money is only for the visa. The child is free." He wasn't hearing my refusals, so I went back inside where it was steamy.

A long day of recording was over, mission accomplished, and we were all happily exhausted. Some of the musicians told me that they also lost sleep worrying about doing a good job.

I took a short nap, and then Taariq called me from the hospital and said, "I'm bored. Give me my cousin's number."

"Why?"

He was impatient. "I can't get out until the bill's paid."

"A lot of people made sacrifices so you could detox. You're not supposed to leave yet."

He insisted, but fortunately, I didn't have the number anyway.

I couldn't open my door because something was in the way. It was Saladin, my little one-year-old neighbor, sitting alone on my doorstep. I took him inside to his mother.

Sahar said, "People are strange. We let one of my husband's friends take him, and instead of bringing him back, he just left him." She didn't seem alarmed or upset. If this happened in the U.S., the situation would be seen as child endangerment.

She agreed, "He shouldn't do that."

This brought up the topic of strange behavior. Amina came, and I talked about Rami wanting to give me one of his children.

Amina said, "He must be from the mainland. They have no problem giving their children away. A Zanzibari would never do that."

Maybe he thought that by having a child grow up in the U.S., other family members would be able to emigrate.

This thinking makes children a commodity, which can easily happen in a poor place where survival is more important than concern for a child's future emotional baggage. It was also possible that he wanted me to wire him $2000 and never intended to give up his child.

The topic switched to Taariq. Amina said, "Drug addicts in Zanzibar are such expert thieves that they can steal your phone from right next to you, and you won't even know it."

She added, "Taariq's the most famous thief of all."

I said, "He's never asked me for anything."

"He might be waiting for the big haul, right before you leave." She suggested that I announce that my departure would be one date, but actually leave earlier. I pondered the possibilities.

He'd had plenty of chances already and had not taken them. But, just in case, I was relieved that he was in the hospital when it came time to pay the band.

Sahar countered, "He respects you a lot and cares about you. Try to be supportive so he can change."

This story was starting to sound like a modern-day *Thief of Baghdad*.

No wonder I sometimes had a scary feeling of foreboding. For all I knew, he might have drug debts to pay. Or someone else might have been watching us and planned to do the stealing, knowing that he would end up taking the blame. Or he might have known something I didn't and stuck around, appearing around every corner to protect me from drug people who saw me as an easy target.

What I couldn't believe was that the only person who clued me in on the fact that he did drugs or stole was Taariq himself. Everyone knew, and most of my neighbors were aware that he was showing me around. Yet they said nothing, at least until Emma got wind of the situation.

☾ ✦ ✶ ✦ ✶

Another busy day followed, as I returned to Hassan's place for editing. I seriously doubted the rape story, but after Ikhwani Safaa's reaction to Hassan and all the weirdness I'd experienced lately, I still harbored mild trepidation. With Taariq out of commission, who would I bring along as a bodyguard? Should I hire the homeless man who sleeps on my steps, or ask Bashir? I didn't think either of them would be a deterrent if the stories were true. I considered telling Matt, with whom I had an appointment first thing in the morning, to expect a call from me by a certain time. Then if he didn't hear from me and I didn't pick up the phone, he could come to the studio with the police.

ZIFF did business with Hassan, and I would feel silly saying I needed them to protect me in case he was a rapist. If it wasn't true, it would be terribly slanderous to perpetuate this rumor. I'd have to tread carefully.

Tweaks on the CD cover took awhile, so I brought up the subject of Hassan. Matt assured me, "he's not a rapist."

It was raining when a tall skinny papasi got me a cab and sat in the front seat. I said, "We're not taking him."

The driver said, "Don't worry. He's my brother. I wouldn't leave him out in the rain."

I put the driver on the phone with Hassan, thinking he was getting directions to the studio, but we ended up back at the hospital. Hassan met us there and gave instructions on getting to his house. He said, "The music's edited and ready. Just wait ten minutes while my technician burns the masters. Tell the cab to wait and take you back." The driver commented, "That area is so posh that people like the president's family live there."

I pointed out his house. "Stop here."

I expected them to wait outside, but the maid let the skinny papasi in. He immediately started casing the place, rushing from room to room with jerky movements. It took a lot of effort for me to get him out the door. All the while, I studied his posture, the slouch and concave chest Amina told me was typical of heroin addicts. After I got him onto the porch, the maid approached, cell phone in hand. Hassan was on the line warning her not to let him in. She closed the gate and locked it. The dubious pair made a scene, screaming and yelling, trying to charge me some outrageous amount. I gave them the amount I thought was correct for the ride and that was all. The papasi persisted, but the nervous driver said, "Okay. Let's go."

Later, I asked Hassan, "What about me?" Wouldn't he want to warn me not to ride in the cab with these shady characters? I finally learned to watch my own back in Zanzibar—because nobody else was going to.

The amiable technician named Hababu and I had to re-edit and mix for several hours. It got as good as it could get for recording a ten-piece orchestra in a two-track bongo flava studio. One speaker was out, and we could only hear the music on a computer, so there was some guess-work as to what the CD actually sounded like. Hababu didn't speak any more English than I spoke Swahili, yet with a little patience we understood one another perfectly. Sometimes I just pointed to the lines on the computer and made a scratching noise.

Hassan called me and said, "Hababu has to travel in a little over an hour, so take care of any details before then." There was a lot more work to be done, so I ignored that and got him to fix everything, which took several hours. Hababu was good natured, and it was a miracle that we successfully fine tuned the minute details without a translator.

I fell asleep on the couch while he burned the masters, then awoke with a start when I saw Hassan sitting in front of me. Pleasantly busi-nesslike and friendly, we shared other assorted small talk. Then he called a cab.

I called the Dhow Academy to arrange to hear the CD on a better sound system and get expert opinions about whether anything needed to be done with another round of mixing and fixing in the U.S. Jamal, Bashir, and the music department staff gave their input. On a stereo it sounded really beautiful, but we agreed on a couple of adjustments. Though just a good boom box, it may have been the best sound system in Zanzibar.

I was starving when I ran into Hassan on the street. Since the rainy season was in full force, many restaurants were closed for renovations. Hassan was starving as well, so I suggested finding a place to eat. I couldn't imagine Chinese food in Zanzibar, especially after spending so much time in Hong Kong, but his favorite place was a Chinese res-taurant where everyone knew and welcomed him. The food was good, and I asked him questions and learned a lot about him.

"During the socialist times, I finished school and had to get out of Zanzibar, so I went to Greece and joined the Merchant Marines," he recounted. "I traveled the world for eight years, having all sorts of new experiences, but finally realized that Zanzibar is the best place to live, at least if you have money." His focus shifted to getting financial stability and earning enough money abroad to build his house in Zanzibar. Later he left again and returned with enough for the recording studio. He said it was the first studio in Zanzibar.

He continued, "Everyone thought I was crazy and said, 'No one wants to record at your studio.' I became successful and created a new form of bongo flava with a distinctly Zanzibari flavor called 'Zanzi Flava.' People think I'm the devil himself and worry that I'm taking the boys away from Islam. I actually give them something constructive to do and a way to earn money with music. Now some families see the money, and their ideas are changing." I asked if any of these kids fall into drugs. "On the contrary," he said, "this gives them something to do instead of drugs."

He had a lot of advice for young people, many of whom were looking for a way out of Zanzibar, especially through marrying a Westerner. He said, "I've watched Zanzibaris get caught up with materialism in the U.S. and become slaves to the latest consumer items instead of sending their money home to build something in Zanzibar. I tell everyone to build a small home, so if they come back they won't have to stay with their parents in a crumbling house, especially if they come back with a wife and kids. A lot of young men think they can get a woman to take them away, but I tell them 'finish your education,' and I try to discourage them from having too many illusions about life in other countries. Some think they don't need to study because they'll go out of Zanzibar, but if they don't study, they'll be worth nothing in other countries and the woman will get tired of seeing them sitting around. In a few months, she'll send them home."

With only a few days left in Zanzibar, I decided to take a break from Malindi and get some fresh air. A lone cab driver said, "Taxi?" I responded, "How much to Jambiani?" That was a small village on the other side of the island.

The tourist season had come to a close, so most little clusters of bungalows sat empty. I stayed in a place called the Oasis, where a dreadlocked young man named Fido attended.

In Jambiani, the local industry was seaweed farming. Seaweed extract is used in everything from toothpaste to medicines. Apparently, two Chinese companies buy most of their harvests—at four cents per kilo of dried seaweed. One kind that's harder to grow commands eighteen cents a kilo. Imagine how much wet seaweed they have to harvest to make up a kilo once it dries!

The tide went out so far that the women harvesting the seaweed were barely visible. Fido took me walking among the farms. There were sea urchins everywhere. I was afraid of stepping on one. Sometimes they were beneath the seaweed where you couldn't see them. We walked barefoot far out into the tide pools.

Each woman's harvest was carefully tied into rows on strings, and the workers tended the crops with tender-loving care. Some picked their crops and brought them back to the village in big bags balanced atop their heads, then spread the seaweed onto the earth to dry. Each plot was small, and when I added the numbers in my head it was clear that this labor-intensive crop earned very little income.

I tried to catch the 2:00 PM daladala back to Stone Town, but since they aren't on a fixed schedule, none came until 3:00 PM. The sun was scorching as a truck barreled through town, didn't let me on, and then turned back again. I was worried about getting back on time to teach my last belly-dance class.

The only thing that saved me from getting grumpy was the sound of little voices squealing in unison "piga picha!" A dozen kids gathered around, jumping up and down. Some had ripped clothes and hopelessly snotty noses, but they were thrilled to have their pictures taken. I would take a shot and then show it on my little video screen. They were screaming with delight and trying to reach for the camera. I got concerned about so many hands grabbing the screen at once and tried a diversionary tactic. I took both of a little boy's hands and swung him around. Then all the kids competed to be swung in circles, giving me quite a workout.

Finally, a daladala came. All the passengers were men. Many carried fish but had to leave them by the entrance so as not to stink up the whole daladala. I barely made it back for class.

☪ ⋆ ⋆ ⋆ ⋆

Every day since I had arrived in Zanzibar, until I confronted him about his drug problem, I'd run into Taariq in the street. I would be walking and, rest assured, there he was, behind me or around the corner. Since that fateful phone call, I'd never seen him on the street, and I doubted we would ever meet again. I was walking the dark backstreets to Ikhwani Safaa, to hear them one last time and say goodbye. Coming around the corner was someone vaguely familiar. Could it be Taariq? If so, his clothes looked better and he'd gained weight. I didn't recognize him, so I ignored his approach and kept walking. He was waiting beneath the club when I came out.

It was like old times, sitting on a baraza with him telling me "one more thing" about spending his days with Leila, keeping off of drugs. Then I got up to leave, and he said, "By the way, I forgot to tell you, my father's doing good," then, simply, "My stepmother came home, so I'm going back to Kenya on Monday."

I caught up with Emma at an elegant restaurant called Livingston's.

She said, "You just missed the taarab."

I looked back and saw several musicians, including Abdel, the drummer from Ikhwani Safaa. When I went to say hi, he introduced me to Matona, who I'd heard was the best musician in Zanzibar. I'd wanted to meet him but hadn't known how to. Abdel told him about my dancing, and Matona opened an instrument case. He played violin and oud, and Abdel drummed. They played old Arabic songs, each man showing off his virtuosity. I enjoyed dancing for myself, although this impromptu party drew the crowds out of nearby restaurants and bars into the window to watch. We kept going for a long time as if it were some sort of reunion.

Emma organized a going-away party for me after yoga class. Matona came to play, along with Abdel and an oud player who was Matona's student. There were a lot of people, many of whom I didn't know, but the guests included Soud (Ikhwani Safaa's chairman from the mainland), Nassor Amour (the ganun player), and even Taariq. There was the owner of a local restaurant, his wife and child, the lady who sells sodas and cassava chips downstairs, with her little girl and Sahar's daughter, Amar, plus all the yoga students. We celebrated on the balcony of Dhow Academy, above the street and overlooking the sea. I was still in my yoga clothes, with a belly-dance hip scarf stashed in my bag.

The sun set as the musicians tuned up. They played and I danced. Emma's neighbor, a Palestinian lady, couldn't imagine an American having an ear for Arabic music. I got her up, and we danced together. She wore a caftan and tied one of my veils around her hips. I liked her homespun Arabic style and hoped she would take over teaching belly dance in Zanzibar.

We took pictures. Then Emma, Taariq, and I went to Forodhani Gardens to eat Zanzibari Pizza. It had been weeks since I'd been to that familiar gathering place that was so representative of Zanzibar.

I went upstairs to pack and put my new CD in my computer. Out came the softly melancholic song "40 Days." A wave of sorrow came over me. I have a lot to be excited and enthusiastic about in life, but that's not the case for many people in Africa. For me, there's always something new and someone interesting on the horizon, and my options are wide open. Many people I know in more prosperous parts of the world have good prospects in their lives and the freedom to fulfill their dreams.

I played "40 Days" over and over, feeling sad because my friend, who I believe was a true friend, should be young and full of potential but has to struggle to stay clean—a product of the corruption, the semiofficially sanctioned poisoning of young men, and the greed that destroys lives and undermines society. I felt sad, thinking of this island with generations of pain permeating its soil: the slavery, the massacres, and the present decay. I thought about Taariq, a mere reflection of all that has happened to his country. How hope was not lost, but what a struggle it was to keep that flame from going out. "40 Days" played again, and I was thankful that I had found my song, "Afkari," which means dreams. And I was thankful that I had the luxury to search for something as elusive as dreams.

JORDAN

SYRIA

IRAQ

ISRAEL

Ar Ramtha

★ Amman

●Madaba

Dead
Sea

JORDAN

SAUDI
ARABIA

⊗ Petra

100 Miles

THE BIGGEST STARBUCKS I'VE EVER SEEN is surrounded by scarred earth, vacant lots, and stone mansions. Much of the city looks like a construction site with glaring Americanisms; it's a place where Burger King, KFC, and Pizza Hut are considered classy. Safeway is an all-purpose megastore selling everything from garbanzo beans to flat-screen televisions. In contrast to the brightly lit plastic signs of foreign fast-food giants and the oversized neon buckets with Colonel Saunders's image overhead, all of Amman is cut from the same kind of unpainted stone. Whatever isn't plastic or neon is monochromatic, from the ancient Roman ruins to the historic old houses that date back to the 1950s, when Amman began to emerge as a desert city. When the sun hits during certain times of day, the city glows in shades of pink and gold.

At first impression, Amman was ugly and bland. But, so often, people would blurt out, "I love Amman."

"Why?" I would query.

The response was often, "It's peaceful." Peace isn't taken for granted in this region of the world.

Arriving at 1:30 in the morning, I found that the Jordanian dinar was worth 50 percent more than the dollar, a sure indication that living wouldn't be cheap. Five star hotels were abundant, but I had heard from other travelers that "the only affordable place to stay whose conditions wouldn't disgust the heartiest of travelers is the Palace Hotel." That statement sounded extreme.

Absent was the battle I usually have upon exiting airports in exotic locales: bargaining for a ride in a rattletrap taxi and having several drivers grapple to put my bags in their cab. Instead, an orderly line of Mercedes taxis waited. Each arriving passenger bought a fixed-price ticket, and porters wheeled our bags for free. The thirty-kilometer road to Amman was smooth and spacious. At once, I found myself alone with the driver in the middle of darkness, making small talk, when suddenly he changed the subject, "You must marry a Bedouin."

I responded, "Aren't most Jordanians descended from Bedouins?"

He replied, "Yes. I am a Bedouin . . . welcome to Jordan."

At 3:30 AM, I wound up at the "Amman Palace." Not a soul stirred on the street. Its spacious lobby was decked out with marble and mirrors. I took a room, sight unseen. When I exited the elevator, the façade faded. This was a monolithic dump with many a long, gloomy corridor. The bellboy led me past dozens of empty rooms and opened the door to a drab, olive green room with a stench of mothballs so strong it stung my eyes. It looked spooky, like something from the Soviet era. I got someone to open the window and tried to sleep on one of the beds, which had no sheets, only tattered blankets. The next morning, I learned that The Palace, not the Amman Palace, was where I wanted to be.

There are two sides of Amman: the East (old) and the West (new). The East Side, where I stayed, was built from the 1920s to the 1950s. Streets and alleys are lined with caftan shops. Covered in cross-stitches, the caftans are painstakingly hand embroidered in nearby villages. The area is a mishmash of old and new structures jumbled atop one another, with the King Hussein Mosque and a big Roman amphitheater in the middle. Natural-juice bars, sweetshops, and falafel and *shawarma* stands dotted the sidewalks.

A banner on one of the only houses downtown read "The Duke's Diwan." I climbed a set of stairs leading into a house built in 1924 that served as "The Emirate of Transjordan's" central post office for many years. It was leased to Mamduh Bisharat, known as "The Duke." I met this eighty-something-year-old man, who gave me a Xeroxed flyer and said: "This house is an example of keeping the ancient Greco-Roman city of Philadelphia, upon which Amman was built. Its authenticity and character are alive. I want this house to host artistic and literary discussions and to take a stand against the onslaught of modern architecture that is enveloping the city." No activities were on the agenda, but there were a smattering of paintings by local artists on the walls.

My original plan had been to stay forty days in Syria, but a war broke out. Israel was bombing Lebanon and there was serious conjecture that Syria might be next. It was easy to switch my ticket to neighboring Jordan. Although I knew I wouldn't find the same architectural charms, it is a peaceful kingdom that has welcomed many refugees with open arms. Jordan has only been a country since 1921. Before that, it was a land of nomadic Bedouins, a backwater of the Ottoman Empire, where the first king, Abdullah I, ruled from a train car.

The East Side had some local color and people were friendly, but there seemed to be a conspiracy to fatten me up. Mustafa, the cookie man, called me into his bakery, plied me with diet Pepsi, and didn't let me out until I'd sampled at least a dozen cookies. The smell of garlic lured me to Hashem's Restaurant, open twenty-four hours and located in an alley, which had tables and plastic chairs spilling onto the sidewalk. My fumbling Arabic met with appreciation and smiles as men fried falafel and said "Ahlan!" (Welcome). Everyone in town knew the menu, which wasn't written anywhere and hadn't changed for years: falafel, *foul* (smashed fava beans), *hummus* (smashed garbanzo beans with tahini, lemon, and garlic), french fries, and sweet mint tea. Hashem's was so casual that no one used plates, napkins, or forks. It was all finger food, eaten wrapped in pieces of pita. The tables were rarely cleaned, and I ate off of pieces of paper. Dozens of sweetshops elaborately displayed stacks of baklava. Bakers constantly brought gigantic fresh pans of other sticky desserts out of the ovens.

Down the street, Rashid's Café is the popular place to watch traffic go by in the afternoons. When I walked up its dank and slippery staircase, I met a flourish of color. The interior, where groups of men sat playing cards and smoking *nargile* (a blend of tobacco and cured apple), was painted a gaudy, grass-colored green. The terrace, with its bright flags from around the world painted on the walls, could be seen for blocks–a splash of color in a sea of beige.

The Palace Hotel, where I called home, was a combination residential hotel for Middle Eastern businessmen and haven for backpackers. Men convened in the home-style living room on comfy armchairs and couches facing a television that reported news of war at all hours. Wars raged in two bordering countries, Iraq and Israel. Some of the men staying at the hotel were Iraqi. Most of the employees were Palestinian. Syria, just a short taxi ride away, was receiving streams of Lebanese refugees. What ground the region to a halt and had everyone horrified were the images coming out of Lebanon. Maimed children cried, their limbs missing, faces scarred, or bodies limp, as mothers screamed and sobbed. Of course, showing children might be seen as a deliberate tug on emotions. But from Iraq to Lebanon and among the Palestinians, it's common to have large families of eight to eleven kids. The ratio of children to adults is so high that when a street or apartment building is bombed, a disproportionate number of the casualties are children. Every day on the streets I saw mothers with their little ones in tow. Although some were light, others dark, some chubby, and others lean, those huge black Arabic eyes were a constant. They looked just like the eyes that haunted entire nations as little bodies were laid on stretchers.

In the hotel elevator, a man asked me, "Where are you from?" Abdullah was a balding middle-aged man dressed in a sports shirt, slacks, and loafers. He was from Aqaba (the Jordanian port where boats from Egypt dock) and said he wanted to sit down with a real American and hear my views about what was going on in the world.

Sitting on a couch, he told me: "My family is Bedouin and, although I am modern with a university degree, work as an engineer, and wear Western clothes, I seek to retain the best of my Bedouin heritage, the custom of hospitality to strangers. It doesn't matter how badly someone behaves, our greeting is still 'welcome,' and they are treated well. This attitude comes from the days when Bedouins traveled the deserts under the harshest circumstances. The only way to survive was to be given food and a place to stay by strangers, even if they were of an enemy tribe."

We talked about the absurdities of war, how pointless it was. The more I stayed in Jordan, a peaceful, secure oasis surrounded by countries that are troubled by strife, threats of war, and now steady streams of refugees, the more obvious the insanity was. Late King Hussein devoted his life to the peace process and was disappointed by events that undermined his efforts on both sides of the divide. People in Jordan loved him. His struggles yielded an example of people living in peace despite difficult circumstances.

Abdullah exclaimed, "Nobody wants war. It just destroys and disrupts the lives of families and innocent civilians who have nothing to do with the issues at hand, most of which are overshadowed by images of people getting killed over and over. Nothing changes, at least not for the better. It's all politics. People have nothing against one another. It would be crazy for anyone to blame the people of a country for the bad deeds of their government."

There was no shortage of exuberant men beckoning "Welcome," but I had yet to talk with a woman. I decided to head west and check out the fashions and hopefully meet some women at Mecca Mall, the largest in Amman. The entrance had a snack shop selling American-style candy by the kilo, muffins, cookies, and other junk food. Teenage employees sported the latest American-style hairstyles and jeans. This could have been anywhere in America, except for the tourists from Saudi Arabia; there were men in long white robes and checkered turbans and women in black *abayas* (loose overgarments that cover their clothes), headscarves, and face veils. Past the Starbucks and an internet café was a prayer area. People, mostly women, mingled easily. It didn't matter whether they were fully veiled, dressed modestly with a headscarf, or in modern-style jeans and sleeveless tops.

Most of the merchandise was from China, including the sparkly headscarves that lined the walls of the accessory shops. I paused to look at a makeup kiosk, when a woman attended me in Arabic. I responded, "Ana baki shuai Arabi" (I only speak a little Arabic). I was able to hobble along for a short time with the Arabic I knew, until she asked where I was from. I said, "Ana Amerki" (I'm American). She responded, but I didn't understand. Usually, people said things like "Welcome," or "We like American people but not your government." I responded generically, "Shukran" (Thank you).

She repeated in English, "I said America is killing Arabs." After tearfully telling me how she was separated from her family in Palestine, she invited me inside to try on makeup.

I met another woman, who was of the Christian minority. She had enjoyed a thriving career translating three languages, then met a Spaniard on the internet, quit her job and married him. Some of the men I had encountered told me that the only belly dancing in Jordan was in sleazy clubs. They emphasized by saying, "Belly dancing is not Jordanian. We do the *dabke*." (Dabke is a traditional folkdance popular in Jordan, Syria, Palestine, Lebanon, and Iraq.)

She disagreed, "Belly dancing is alive and well in Jordan, and families always ask their little girls to get up and dance," adding, "Our traditions are very important. There is little difference between the customs of Christians and Muslims. Our families cannot accept their daughters doing any type of dancing as a career, whether it's ballet or belly dancing. Jordanian women can study, work, and travel, but I agree that women shouldn't have complete freedom. If I had a daughter, she would be raised our way, with limits."

Caftan shops hired boys to stand outside and lure customers with promises of good prices or simply "take a look." Directly across the alley from my hotel balcony was a tiny shop packed to the gills with fancy caftans. The attractive owner, also named Abdullah, insisted that I drink Turkish coffee. He reprimanded me for eating at Hashem's and offered to show me what locals like. I thought for a moment, and then we were on our way to a towering Kentucky Fried Chicken. I told him that I don't like KFC, so he drove to Hardee's. I said, "I like Jordanian food." After passing Pizza Huts, Burger Kings, and the like, we wound up at a similarly shiny place that served exactly the same fare as Hashem's.

Abdullah pointed out a hotel that had been car bombed four months prior. Another hotel had been bombed during a wedding party. He said, "Everyone is appalled by these senseless actions." We stopped at the Crown Plaza and had mint lemonade in the café. On the way in we went through a metal detector. As a woman, I was led through an enclosed area and frisked by a female guard.

Politics came up and he bristled, "Don't get me started." Instead, he changed the subject to sex and settled on the topic of hymen reconstruction, an operation to make women "virgins" more than once, so they will bleed upon intercourse. On her wedding night, the bride's virginity must be proven, which is accomplished when she bleeds upon penetration. That blood must be shown to both the bride's and groom's families on a stained piece of cloth.

According to Abdullah "Most brides are virgins, but in case they're not, hymen reconstruction is big business. Without the blood, the least of her problems will be that the marriage is annulled, she is returned home, and her family is deeply shamed. At worst, her father or brothers will feel obligated to kill her to save the family's honor." These infamous "honor killings" have been outlawed by royal decree. Unfortunately, they still persist, as traditions run deep, and several people are arrested every year for killing their daughters.

Back at the hotel, I opened the *Jordan Times*, which ran an article about a woman who was axed to death by her mother and sister a day after having a baby out of wedlock. Then the two women walked to a nearby police station and confessed that they did it to save their honor. The paper said "This is the ninth honor killing reported in Jordan this year." I was surprised that women did the killing, not the father or brothers, but it really hit home how a woman's sexuality often doesn't belong to her.

Out of sympathy and mourning for the Lebanese war victims, nearly all cultural events were put on hold. I had been looking forward to the Jerash Festival, an annual week-long music and arts festival in a ruined Greco-Roman city outside of Amman, but it was cancelled.

I found myself in a city where literally nothing was going on. I was new and didn't know a lot of people. There were weddings and family celebrations, but I had no idea how to access them. I combed the *Jordan Times* in search of something to attend. Sometimes I felt like I was grasping at straws, but I occasionally found some bits of activity.

The Royal Film Commission listed an independent film screening on their patio. It was full, with both Jordanians and expats, to the point of standing room only. Due to a barrage of technical difficulties, the thirty-six-minute film started about the time it was supposed to be over. Meanwhile, we were entertained by a dozen repetitions of a short animated cartoon of belly dancers and nightclubs with drunks and mafia-like characters. "So that's what people here must think I do when I say I'm a belly dancer," I thought.

The much awaited film *Warning . . . Comment Ahead* was made by a young Jordanian woman. It was her way of speaking out about sexual harassment on the streets, primarily what she referred to as "catcalling." I thought it showed a sort of innocence. The catcalls were not nearly as harsh as what gets yelled out of cars by hormonal guys in New York or Miami. But the unsolicited comments definitely offended Arabic women's sensibilities. What kept coming up from the men interviewed in the film was: "Women want to be bothered, otherwise they wouldn't dress so cute," "They should cover more," and "Why are they wearing that dirt on their faces? Paint should be reserved for inside the home." The only two deterrents for sexual harassment with these guys were that it was un-Islamic and that it could happen to a woman in their family.

The filmmaker took one teenager to talk to the shaikh. "How would you feel if someone 'catcalled' your sisters and mothers?" she asked one man. Young Jordanian women, who had recently started wearing headscarves, said the scarves were no deterrent.

A lot of discussion took place afterward regarding the concept of women as property and how a woman who is not under the protection of a man is considered fair game. Men complained that they were deemed ineffectual if they didn't stand up and defend women they were with, even if they perceived that the offending man merely wanted to socialize. An American guy in the audience said that he was working with a group of Western women when someone approached one of them. His local boss reprimanded him for not doing anything about it.

A French woman named Angelique and I continued the conversation afterward. She was a blond-haired journalist and single mother to a six-month-old baby. Her wedding band did little to deflect the barrage of advances. I hadn't been catcalled, although I got a few marriage proposals from strangers. And there was the occasional married man who acted single and invited me for dinner, without his wife.

The mantra in Jordan is "eat." The night staff at The Palace would bring hummus and foul and insist that I partake. I had to cross the street when passing Mustafa's cookie store, otherwise calories would come back to haunt me. I loved a dish called *mensef*, made from dried yoghurt reconstituted while cooking lamb, and served over yellow rice. Even when I was stuffed, if someone was cooking mensef, I had to make room.

Thinking about the dangers encountered in this book project, I hoped to escape the Jordanian peril of going home looking like a bowl of hummus. With such thoughts swimming through my head, I made a beeline to Fitness One, the hip new gym near Mecca Mall everyone was talking about. Although many Jordanians don't speak English, the flyers and cards from this gym were all in English. That happens a lot with businesses in the West Side, as English-only advertising pre-targets a select clientele, not a cross-section of society. Many people spoke and socialized in English, and some offices even operated in English. On the East Side everything was written and spoken in Arabic first, though some signs were translated.

Nobody used street addresses. Instead, I would ask for the directions to where I was going. When taking a taxi to parts unknown, I usually handed the driver the address written on a business card. Since many cards were written in English, as was the case with Fitness One, I relied on my cell phone, putting the driver on with the receptionist.

We found the elusive gym on a wide and chaotic thoroughfare, behind a parking lot, in a small, nondescript strip mall. A nargile-smoking man pointed to the elevator. Women and men used separate floors. Female memberships included fitness classes, so I spoke to the manager, explaining, "I'm a belly-dance teacher and would like to teach class in exchange for gym membership."

When she asked "What is your usual fee in the U.S.?"

I responded truthfully "Belly dancers know me all over the world so I get $200 an hour plus airfare. But don't worry about that. I just want to work out."

She told me, "We need a substitute for an aerobics class on Monday," then gave me a membership card and said, "Come whenever you like and ask the receptionist for a session with a personal trainer."

How trusting she was. I, a complete stranger, walked in off the street with no proof that I knew how to dance, and she had no references or proof that anything I had just said was true.

All the women at Fitness One were covered, from the one behind the counter to the ladies stepping off the elevator. In the dressing room, layers peeled away; headscarves, long-sleeved blouses, and long skirts came off until everyone wore tight workout pants and shoulder-baring tops. While others worked out, some women took breaks to put on big white capes with matching head scarves and prayed at the edge of a row of machines.

My trainer proceeded to show me how to use the weight machines. I had been working out for five years but tried to listen patiently as she said, "Breathe, one, two, three . . . always remember to breathe." She then measured my body fat and, with a grave face, informed me that I was "obese." I thought, "Wow! Ten pounds ago I was considered a very fit dancer. Maybe obese has a different meaning in Arabic." I set to work as the *Pink Panther* theme played over and over on an amplified loop.

Serious attendants went from woman to woman as we used the machines, making sure we breathed and did the proper stretch before and after each exercise. These "stretch and breathe" police took their jobs quite seriously.

I took a belly-dance class, an aerobic version, to the latest modern Arabic pop songs. When it came time for the class I was teaching, which used classical sounding music from my Ikhwani Safaa CD and smooth movements, I thought they might think of me as a relic from a bygone age. Instead, the class was packed with all levels, from women who were stiff and seriously out of touch with feminine ways of moving, to those who, though they would never have performed in public, danced like professionals but did it for joy.

I felt I'd earned a treat and headed to an upscale West Side café called Blue Fig. Along the way, mansions were like square cubes: luxury surrounded by stark desolation, construction sites, and no vegetation.

Next to a two-story Starbucks with rows of luxury cars in the parking lot, was a defunct Planet Hollywood. On the other side, I went through a bag check and showed my ID, then was admitted into the Blue Fig. It was pretentious, with handsome waiters clad in black, sporting pseudosophisticated attitudes. Groups of young Jordanian women in hip-hugger jeans, tight tops, and streaked-blond hair sipped cappuccinos and sampled green tea cheesecake while hip young men in tight jeans sat nearby.

I descended to the basement to visit an English-language bookstore. The strapping young man at the counter said he hadn't seen a customer all day. He offered me coffee, then brought out a gold and white pot shaped exactly like the ones they serve coffee from on the streets of Zanzibar. The tiny ceramic cups were identical to those I drank from on the barazas of Stone Town. He told me, "This is Jordanian coffee."

"How odd," I said, as I sniffed the strong scent of cardamom, "it's just like the coffee in Zanzibar."

Coffee drinking spread during the time of the Ottoman Empire, after the Turks acquired a taste for the beverage in Yemen. I suspected the coffee we were drinking was similar to the original. In Turkey they add sugar and leave the grounds in the bottom of the cup. This coffee became popular throughout the empire, from Egypt to Greece, Lebanon and Bulgaria, and is widely available in Jordan. By way of the Turks, coffee made its way to Austria where the tradition of coffeehouses originated and spread to most European countries. Espresso took hold, the Europeans added milk, and the cappuccino was born. Fast-forward, following the coffee bean to Seattle for the birth of a new coffee-grinding empire (guess who), and back to Jordan, where you can sample the entire history of coffee in one parched city.

At the Palace, the door next to mine was wide open. Inside, a young man named Sam lay directly under an oscillating fan. As I passed by he moaned, "It's bloody hot in here."

I said, "It's cooler outside," and convinced him to take a walk to the Roman Amphitheater.

This was Sam's first time away from home and he hadn't gotten around town much. He didn't know about Hashem's or Rashid's Cafés. We climbed the stairs to Rashid's, and I offered to read the grounds in his Turkish coffee cup. I've always been intrigued by divination, and in 1987 a Romanian friend was eerily accurate when she read my cup. She told me I would go to Mexico to work and described exactly how it would be. When I got to Mexico City, I saw women reading "Café Turco" in dark little coffee shops and started to visit regularly to ask their secrets.

Sam warned me, "I'm an atheist and don't believe in anything that can't be explained scientifically." He was a disheveled intellectual, who wore baggy shorts and sandals with socks and walked with a slouch. He reminded me of a young absent-minded professor. With a master's degree but little worldly experience, Sam still possessed a great deal of naivety. My readings of the grounds in the bottom of his cup surprised him with an accurate assessment of his romantic situation back home. From then on, word spread at the Palace about his uncanny experience, and my reputation as a coffee cup reader began.

Waiting in line to tell the cashier what we had consumed, I looked up and saw muscles and a black T-shirt. My gaze continued to a scarred face with big round eyes. "Hi. I'm Mazen," a voice boomed. He insisted on paying our bill. Excited to meet an American, he exclaimed, "I'm moving to Brownsville, Texas next month." He gave me his number and an open invitation to take a spin around Amman in his Mercedes. Hmm. I pictured a luxurious tour in a top-of-the-line vehicle.

Back at the hotel I met Lisa, an American woman with a strong Tennessee accent, who had been traveling alone for several months. She'd been to Ethiopia, Yemen, and Dubai. Now she was mad! The window in her room wouldn't open. The fan didn't work. And it was so hot she ended up sleeping in the lobby. I said, "I have air conditioning." We became roommates. I told her about Mazen's invite and she wanted to meet him.

☾ ✩ ⁎ ✩ ⁎

Mazen drove up in a dilapidated 1969 Mercedes with lumpy white paint. It died, then started up after several tries. As we drove around,

Amman was ugly. To us, everything looked the same. Mazen's driving was jerky and erratic, unsettling our stomachs. The topography was based on eight traffic circles along a street called Zarana. Lisa asked, "Where's the fifth circle?"

Mazen said, "It became a tunnel." Other landmarks were an ancient Roman citadel overlooking the city and several five-star hotels. Police with fancy helmets periodically directed traffic. When the light was red, they signaled the cars to go. When it was green, we were ordered to halt. People drove fast, and lane markers were ignored with traffic merging randomly.

Heading out of town, we missed a turn-off and backed up a couple of blocks through oncoming traffic, down a hill, and around a couple of curves. Meanwhile, traffic continued forward, swerving good naturedly to make way for us.

Passing hills the same shade of stone as Amman, then a valley with olive, pomegranate, and fig trees, we reached a tiny village and the ruins of an old palace. The entrance was locked. Mazen didn't find it very interesting. "There are Roman ruins everywhere in Jordan. This is just a small one," he offered.

Mazen was a rough-skinned, tattooed kickboxing teacher. One of his forearms had acid burns that he had inflicted on himself when he broke up with a woman whose name was tattooed on his arm. He worked in Iraq as a kickboxing instructor and gym trainer at a U.S. army base. Through the help of those army contacts, he planned to move to Texas. I didn't understand how he got his visa, since the U.S. has an abundance of kickboxing instructors already. Certainly, being Arabic didn't open the doors any easier. I asked how he came to work with the U.S. military and he explained, "One night, I was terribly drunk and signed an agreement, then woke up and said 'What have I done?'"

Mazen had been married twice. The first was arranged by his family when he was nineteen. His parents took him to her house for tea, and they met for five minutes. She was shy, but he said, "Ok." He told us, "On our wedding night, she cried and said, 'I'm not a virgin.' Normally, the man returns the girl to her family, but I didn't send her back immediately because there was no telling what her father would do. She was afraid of getting killed." He continued, "A few years ago, men only got six months in jail for honor killings. Now, they're sentenced to life in prison." He didn't want to be her husband, so they came up with a plan. "After ten days, she went home to her parents, crying that I was a terrible guy and she couldn't live with me." Next he married his cousin, but that ended in divorce too. He explained, "She was too religious and no fun."

I was still sleeping when Lisa came in with the grounds of her Turkish coffee stuck to the bottom of her cup from breakfast. Through a sleepy haze, I read the meaning as best I could.

Soon after, one of the room cleaners knocked on my door with his cup in hand. Hamed, a slight Palestinian man from Jericho, looked North African and smiled a lot with a sweetness that made me like him immediately. I couldn't explain the details of the reading with my sketchy Arabic, so Lisa took notes for him to translate later. He took out his camera phone and showed us photos of his children, then invited us to meet them.

Hamid led us through a complex series of bus rides, until we ended up in a distant and dreary suburb full of terminally unfinished buildings. In many poor countries, the houses are always under construction because people build as they can afford it, take breaks to save money, and continue building at a later date.

His extended family lived in several apartments stacked upon one another. With many curious children in tow, we traipsed up a rough cement staircase. The interior looked like a palace, with ornate furniture, plastic flowers, lots of knick knacks, and stuffed animals. Luma, his wife, served glasses of Fanta followed by Turkish coffee. Hamed asked me to read Luma's cup. Lisa wrote the reading on a piece of paper in English for future translation. On the rooftop, blessed by a cool breeze, we sat with several women. My Arabic was improving. When necessity knocked, long-forgotten Arabic words surfaced. We ate watermelon, managed to converse, took photos, and thrilled the kids by showing them their photos on the camera screen.

We were severely entertainment deprived so when I heard about a pro-Hezbollah demonstration outside King Hussein Mosque, Lisa and I figured, why not check it out? No one else seemed very interested. A guy at the hotel said, "It is over." Two police officers who were setting up a road block said, "It should be in an hour or two." We didn't venture far and heard nothing; it passed with little fanfare and we missed it.

This was on Friday, the Islamic holy day. Most of the shops were closed, and the streets of downtown were as quiet as a Sunday in small town USA. Lisa and I were enveloped in a fascinating conversation while walking a deserted sidewalk, when a man heaved huge amounts of spittle at us. I jumped out of the way in the nick of time, but Lisa, who got the brunt of it, thought it was a leaking air conditioner. I joked, "He's probably a pro-Hezbollah demonstrator, and this may be an act of retaliation," then pointed out, "That's the guy!" He was spitting at someone else down the street, so we knew it was nothing personal and was not because we were foreign. He was merely a crazy, random spitter.

Mazen had an unlikely buddy named Samir, who was a balding government official. Together, they became the unofficial welcoming committee for our ever-expanding circle of traveler friends. Sam's older sister Tabatha came from England, and Mazen took several of our backpacking neighbors under his wing. The crowd could be joined predictably at one of three locations: Rashid's Café, Hashem's Restaurant, or roaming the streets of Shemayzani, the cruising area of Amman where neon fast food signs screamed for attention just as loud as the booming tape decks in passing cars. The streets were packed with families and men but never groups of unaccompanied women.

Every day Mazen repeated his offer to take us cross-country to the Nabataean ruins of Petra in his sputtering car. He said, "Then, we'll go camping in Wadi Rum, a famous desert." I wanted to see both places but didn't trust Mazen's car or his driving. Sam and Tabatha were going. Samir said he would take the bus and meet them in Wadi Rum. Lisa stayed behind, attempting to get a visa to Iran and I opted to take the bus with Samir, then continue to Petra alone.

The bus to Wadi Rum took five hours to reach a lonely stretch of road. Samir's serious air vanished shortly after he took off his suit and tie. Throughout the bus ride, he bent my ear with stories of crazy bar-room brawls he and Mazen had gotten into and details of his hot internet affair with an American woman via webcam. I worried about what kind of company I was going to be in the desert with and called Mazen, asking to speak with Sam and Tabatha. When we arrived, Tabatha came in the car with Mazen to pick us up.

A multicolored glow illuminated the big rock formation behind our camp. Each crevice was lit with a different color. I expected the same isolated natural beauty as the Egyptian deserts, but this camp was set up for city folks. It had electricity and all the amenities: several tents, tables, a dance floor, bathrooms, and showers.

Camp employees cooked chicken under the sand, and Samir put on quite a show dancing for us. It was sort of a belly dance, with understated hip movements and the arms held high in the air. Mazen, Tabatha, and Sam drank vodka mixed with Fanta, and we all smoked nargile. I soon realized that instead of savoring nature, this camping trip was a rather listless party.

The electricity went out at midnight, and all was pitch black except for the twinkling stars in the sky. Mazen cranked up the stereo in his car to provide earsplitting musical ambience.

Khaled, the cook, was drunk and bumbling something to me in a mixture of Arabic and unintelligible French that turned out to be a come-on. Samir had a talk with him and said he would sleep near me as protection. Just what I needed! Now Tabatha and Mazen were behind a big rock, and Sam had drunk himself under a table. I was on my own to contend with either Khaled or Samir. I felt like I'd stepped into some sort of adolescent spring break with no way out. I laid a mattress in the middle of the dance floor under the stars, so there would be absolutely no privacy. Khaled brought me blankets, and I fell into an uneasy sleep. Soon, Samir was next to me, complaining of the cold and wanting to share blankets. I was cold too, but was not willing to share. Married with kids, he started up again about his webcam affair, her husband, and their ridiculous shenanigans. Sometimes the worst of America is what gets out. This was like the Jerry Springer Show exported overseas then regurgitated to me in the middle of the desert. Yuk! I asked about his wife and whether she minded the fact that he was always out with Mazen or his going camping without her. He said, "She likes to be the keeper of religion at home, doesn't want to come out, and is very pious." Mazen piped up from somewhere, "The cousin I married was that way too. That's why I divorced her."

By morning, I was anxious to go. The scenery was beautiful like the American Southwest, with red sand and towering rock formations, but not as awe inspiring. The best sights were probably farther into the desert. Our group wasn't capable of appreciating them anyway.

Mazen's car was a disaster. Samir pushed it to get started because it was almost out of gas, and Samir reminded Mazen that his oil was completely dry. When we stopped at a gas station, he forgot to buy oil. Later, the police pulled us over because his brake lights were out.

I asked to be let off at the nearest bus stop and felt relieved to be out of their clutches. An old man led me to a bus headed to Petra, gave me tea, and my day improved dramatically.

☾☆ . ☆ . ☆ .

I took a starlit evening walk with a group of people I'd met at Petra's visitor's center. The entrance to the ruins was a narrow canyon lined by candles casting a pretty glow from the inside of paper bags. We reached the Treasury, an imposing structure carved out of stone by the Nabataeans hundreds of years before Christ. Candlelight from hundreds of bag lamps and Bedouin flute music emanated from inside the ruin. Then an old man sang and played a one-stringed instrument called *rabab* as we drank glasses of sweet tea.

By day, Petra was magical from the first step. Bedouins had lived amid the ruins in caves until the mid-1980s when the government built a new town for them and made them move out for the sake of tourism and archeological preservation. It must have been amazing to meet them in the old days.

Entering Petra, I walked on the same path as the previous night, but it was a completely different experience. The crunching sound of my footsteps echoed along the trail, which was so peaceful until the small canyon opened up to the Treasury. I looked up at the well-preserved structure with columns and cupolas that had been cut from the cliff. This stone was pink, whereas other areas were golden, and some of the tombs inside were cut from stone with multicolored swirling stripes. An onslaught of camel drivers and kids with donkeys appeared. For awhile I wanted exercise and chose to walk but later decided to support the local economy by taking a camel ride followed by a donkey ride. Bedouins from the new village were allowed to work in the ruins, taking people on camel, donkey, horse, and carriage rides. Little girls sold pieces of rock, and there were small shops and women with stands selling jewelry. Some older people sat with fires, making tea. I was beckoned to sit and drink tea eleven times throughout the day. My favorite kind was "Bedouin tea," a smoky concoction of sage mixed with black tea and lots of sugar, cooked over an open fire.

On parts of the trail, huge paving stones leading to the tombs are still in good shape. Petra was built across a vast area when the Nabataean people were pagans. They had devised a way to control the floodwaters, creating an artificial oasis. The ruins were only partially excavated, but there was a lot to see: tombs, a treasury, a monastery, sacrificial alters, and early Christian churches. Only one of these churches could be visited, because they had to have a special roof to protect their precious mosaics from the elements.

I walked, climbed, and rode camels and donkeys for ten hours, not feeling the fatigue or realizing that I hadn't eaten since breakfast. Most of the self-styled guides told me they had been overseas or had a relative who had married a Western woman who had taken him to her country or fallen in love with Petra and stayed. With the onslaught of tourists, the odds were good that a local guy could form a beneficial relationship. Being a woman alone, I was constantly pestered by guys hoping to hit the jackpot.

I was invited for yet another cup of tea, in the shop of a man whose name I couldn't pronounce. Translated into English it was "Help." He seemed classier and not as sticky as the three guys who sat outside waiting to walk behind me. I asked "Help" to take me to a wedding. He gave me some tea with eight herbs that was supposed to "do wonders for the digestion," and said he would find out if any weddings were going on that night.

In town, I spotted a little restaurant. The women's area was dark with a ratty carpet and I was the only person inside. They didn't want me sitting outside, because of concerns about people bothering me, but I insisted. David, an Australian traveler, was eating alone, so I asked to sit with him. The restaurant staff looked stunned (women don't sit with strange men) but took it in stride. He turned out to be a fascinating and well-traveled man who could talk about history, current affairs, and had learned to speak Japanese.

We were deep in conversation when "Help" came over and drank tea with us. He had hired a driver and rented a pickup truck to take me wedding crashing. David opted to stay behind, so "Help," his driver and I plied the backstreets of the government-built Bedouin village, asking around for weddings. We finally stopped in front of a plain cement house. Some men sat in a yard, smoking and talking. I was led down an alley to the side of a house where the women's party was in full swing.

Women and children sat around on mats in a cement floored room. Several teenage girls, mostly in modern clothes (jeans, long denim skirts, dresses over bellbottom pants, and very few head coverings), danced dabke, which is a line dance that has simple steps unless you are the one in the lead. The leader usually improvises fancy stomping footwork, and the others follow.

Wedding festivities can last as long as a week. This party was a celebration held by the groom's family. I couldn't figure out which of the groom's father's two wives was the groom's mother, but both women seemed in charge. The Egyptian wife was enormous, with a strong character to match. She wielded a stick, which she alternately used to dance with and to control teenagers. The local Bedouin mom was just as big, and the two wives seemed to get along well. At one point, there was a break in the recorded music and the two moms sat with some teenagers singing songs of praise for the bride. Afterward, headscarves went around the hips and below the buttocks. It was time for belly dancing. Many of the younger women worked in Petra selling jewelry and spoke quite a bit of English. I was urged to dance, though I doubt they expected me to know how.

When dancing in social situations, I take on a different style from when I do a show. Home style belly dancing involves little in the way of arm, head, or upper-body movement. Although the music at this party was strong, from southern Egypt, most people didn't move fast and furiously as is expected in the West. It was earthy and sensual. The women danced well and were surprised when they saw my dancing. Some girls bumped my hips hard with theirs, but the stick-wielding lady kept them at bay. She wanted me to dance for her. Some of the ladies videotaped with their camera phones. One girl asked for my video camera and proceeded to film me dancing. I got close enough to an amazing old Bedouin woman in a traditionally embroidered caftan and a scarf that was tied around her head like a bandana, that she was caught on camera too. She placed four tea glasses over her fingers and clacked them together like cymbals to accompany her dancing. Luckily, there was enough of her in the video that I could edit myself out and give a rare glimpse of this woman's dance.

Eventually, "Help" wanted to leave. The women's party was in full swing, but he was bored on the men's side and wanted to go. The stick lady refused to let me out, holding the stick to bar my way. I didn't want to leave anyway, so she was a good excuse. Another man came, and I played dumb. They said, "You can spend the night if you like, but your ride wants to leave now." I should have spent the night but thought about my promise to meet David in the morning. Sometimes it's a toss-up between being considerate and not letting opportunities for special experiences slip away.

The following day, David and I decided to take the bus back to Amman together. While looking out the window at flat expanses of desert, I warned that he might get bored and informed him of the necessary stomping places—Rashid's café and Palestine Juice. Soon after arrival I showed him Hashem's Restaurant, where we ran into Mazen, Samir, Tabatha and Sam.

Tabatha told me that Mazen's car had a lot of problems on the way back, not the least of which was that a wheel popped off making them skid a long way down the road. Luckily, no one was hurt.

☾ ☆ ⋆ ⋆ ⋆ ⋆

David and I looked at books sold on the sidewalk, recognizing the faces on the covers as Hitler, Che Guevara, and other revolutionary or infamous world figures. A man approached, introduced himself as Abbas and invited us to try *kenafi*, a local Palestinian dessert. He led us to an alley where I had seen people lining up. Now I knew why. We were treated to a sticky and delicious mélange of crispy wheat, white cheese, and sweet syrup served on paper plates that sagged under the weight of so many calories.

Abbas claimed to be a retired police chief, and told us how "King

Abdullah appears on the street, sometimes dressed like a Bedouin or driving a cab." King Abdullah, a large British-looking man, would surely be recognized behind the wheel of a taxi. Abbas gushed, "I love the king so much that if he asked me to kill my own child, I would." He added, "When King Hussein died, I cried for five days . . . King Hussein would go to people's homes and ask to come in for tea." I don't know how he expected us to believe these stories, since King Hussein's bodyguards were a constant presence, having averted numerous attempts on his life. David tried hard to get rid of Abbas, but he stuck to us like glue for the rest of the evening, telling more fish stories.

We had to get up early the next morning and catch a bus to the Dead Sea. "Are you going swimming or fishing?" a man asked as David and I boarded the bus. After an hour we were dropped off at a stand that sold candy and drinks. The vendor pointed us down a path to a dismal construction site with remnants of shelters. We mutually determined "This place is so ugly it can't be one of Jordan's top tourist destinations."

The same vendor offered to take us, for a hefty fee, to a more appealing area in his van. We passed several luxurious resorts but settled on the public beach, which looked like a fancy Californian rest stop. After we stepped over sharp stones and burning sand to enter the water, the stones got even sharper. It was a struggle to get in and out, but it was so much fun once we started to float. The water was 30 percent salt and bright blue, and it had calm waves. Dry brown mountains in Israel were visible a few kilometers across the water. Given enough time and fewer security obstacles, we could have floated across the border. There was no need to swim, as one could not possibly drown.

The eclectic array of bathers included Western women in bikinis, modern Jordanians in long shorts and tops, and women completely covered in black robes and headscarves. One woman had her face and hands covered in mud, then everything else covered in black cloth. People of all nationalities reveled in the saltwater, slathering masques from the natural grey mud they picked up from under their feet. A guy floated by, face caked in mud, talking on his cell phone.

I'd never paid attention to the perfume stall on the corner of the alley leading into the Palace Hotel, but David was headed to Israel the next day and wanted to buy some gifts, so he commissioned some "designer perfumes." The wall had bottles of oils that smelled like all the famous fragrances. A young merchant mixed aromatic oils, alcohol, and I-don't-know-what-else using a syringe. He added something to make it bubble up, then shook it up and put on a cap. Voila! Chanel No. 5 for the equivalent of three dollars.

With David gone to Israel and Lisa off to Iran, I thought about how budget travel is a strange phenomenon. Perfect strangers can spend days stuck together like I did with Lisa or David, sharing many details of their lives, problems back home, and hopes and dreams. Then, when it comes time to leave, we rarely stay in contact. If one meets a local or a settled expat while traveling, the probability of maintaining the relationship is much higher.

As a dancer, I often find that the best way to meet people and get connected is through the arts. As I stepped off the tourist trail and started digging deeper into life in Amman, three people were instrumental: Dr. Mohammed Rawani, professor of music, and author; Angelique, the French reporter who shared many an exploration with me; and Luna.

Angelique invited me to her house to eat lunch and to meet a French belly dancer named Luna, who had studied with top teachers in France and Egypt. We talked about the local attitudes toward our profession, and Luna said, "Since my French Moroccan husband has a responsible and important job, a lot of people are shocked that he allows me to be a dancer." In Jordan there are strong taboos against being a professional belly dancer or even just being a female performer. Even so, upscale weddings often have a belly dancer, which is considered prestigious as long as she is a foreigner.

Russian women have a dubious reputation throughout the Middle East, as many have found prosperity plying the world's oldest trade. Russia also exports multitudes of belly dancers. I'd heard about Russian "belly dancers," with little training, working at cheap bars. But according to Luna, the best belly dancer in Jordan was a Russian woman named Tatiana who performed at the Marriot by the Dead Sea. I had to see her dance.

Angelique and Luna picked me up, then we met Tatiana, a plain young woman in overalls and a backless shirt. She didn't conjure up images of glamour.

We descended past steep hills into a deep valley. As the sky darkened, the harsh dryness softened, and the drive became beautiful. At 418 meters below sea level, the Dead Sea is the lowest place on earth. Amman is about 1000 meters higher.

The Marriot was a luxurious treat. Tatiana, who taught herself to belly dance, had been there for several years. With a strong background in ballet and Russian folkdance, minimal makeup, and an elegantly simple costume, she was a stunning performer. She and Luna talked about how agents go to Russia to hire dancers: "Many are go-go girls, not belly dancers, but most places don't care how good they are as long as they dance for cheap."

Luna had a show at the Turkish Bath House, as part of a wedding celebration. Her style was authentic Egyptian, with just the right blend of subtlety and spice. She entered dressed in a caftan, playing finger cymbals and balancing a lit candelabra on her head. Later, she emerged in a beautifully beaded evening gown. Finally, she changed to a folkloric dress and did a traditional, earthy Egyptian cane dance, inviting well-heeled women in designer caftans to join. Too "classy" to actually dance well, or to admit it even if they could, they danced stiffly, looking like Westerners who'd never had a belly-dance class.

Afterward, we went out "clubbing," an activity that was highly unusual for women. We were both aware that nightclubs in Jordan aren't known for being wholesome, but wanted to see what went on so we could understand why our profession raised eyebrows in polite circles. Luna spotted a poster of a dancer on the door, and we heard music wafting up a staircase. We braced ourselves for an adventure and descended. The club was full of hookers, had a lone organ player, and lacked both customers and pizzazz. The mafioso-looking manager begged us not to leave. It looked like his bodyguards were going to block the door, but we got out first.

Nearby, we found a cheap club with fluorescent green light emanating from the basement. A huge mural of belly dancers graced the entrance. They assured us that the belly dancer would be coming soon. One wall was stenciled with "Merry Christmas 2000." Tinsel hung from the ceiling. The music was earsplitting, with a singer and a man on a synthesizer. At least a dozen chubby women in short shorts and high platform boots milled about. They were curious about us and came to our table. Most were Moroccan, which is common. Morocco is famous for exporting prostitutes to other parts of the Middle East. One with short blond hair and a big belly spoke fluent French and serenaded us with a popular Algerian song. Her voice was as good as that of a professional singer. Each table had several women hovering around. Their outfits epitomized kitsch: from shoes to tight shorts and ruffled minidresses. One girl who came to our table to shake hands looked about fifteen.

Suddenly, a crowd of women rushed to the door. A man entered who must have been a good client because every working girl surrounded his table. We sat, eating peanuts and fruit from the plate set before us, watching the scene unfold.

After about an hour, Ameera, a curvaceous young dancer, appeared. Her costume was nice, although most of the skirt was missing. She had black briefs and a transparent black skirt over the top, but the skirt didn't cover the front. With harshly damaged dyed-black hair (most of it glued in), her eyebrows painted in artificially high arches, and face plastered with white makeup and lots of eyeliner, she looked ghoulish. I couldn't tell whether under the makeup she would have been pretty or not.

Ameera danced fairly well, going from table to table, collecting tips, and doing provocative things like very deep backbends into men's laps, in-the-face shoulder shimmies, and big hip circles, often pushing her butt toward the customers. Her dance was definitely about titillating and collecting money. She was not a prostitute, but she helped liven up the men so they would hire girls. Everyone had a purpose in this hidden nocturnal society. The announcer went from table to table, calling customers from the audience by name, adding on the title of "shaikh." I had seen this kind of place in the Tunisian film *Satin Rouge*. It's a lifestyle in which people seem almost like part of one another's surrogate families.

Angelique and I visited the exquisite home of a Palestinian woman who had a museum-like collection of dresses from each region of her country. Most were valuable antiques. Her home contained an impressive array of handmade furniture inlaid with mother of pearl, rugs, and the like. Antique photos gracing the walls looked like they were from vintage *National Geographics*. Studying a rug that was a map of pre-1948 Palestine, Angelique told me how the Israelis razed villages they took over, destroying homes and ways of life that had been passed down through the generations.

"People now feel such attachment to their villages, even if they no longer exist. They may live in Jordan now but hope to return to their village one day, even if they've never been there and only heard about it from grandparents."

She told a story of one man who went back in search of his home. It was gone, and all that was left was the lemon tree. He took three lemons, dried them, and kept them to remember his home. His sons still hope to go back to that place.

Two waves of Palestinians came to Jordan, one in 1948, and one after the 1967 Arab-Israeli War. Amman is approximately 65 percent Palestinian. They range from wealthy merchants to members of a poor underclass, who live from menial labor.

I didn't want to leave Jordan without setting foot in a Palestinian refugee camp. Near the beginning of my stay, I had met a pharmacist who worked for the UN in one of the camps. Suleman had grown up in such a camp and received a scholarship for his studies. He said I wouldn't be able to go in unauthorized. My main reason for getting together with him was to find out about going to a camp. His motive was to explore the possibilities of coming to America, so our friendship fizzled from the start.

Later, Angelique told me about a famous fortune-teller who read coffee cups and lived in al-Baqa'a, the oldest refugee camp in Jordan. She contacted Abdusalam, who spoke French, Arabic, and English, to accompany us. Angelique didn't have the woman's address and the phone number she had no longer worked. It was a blind search, which began with a visit to Ali, a Palestinian who had been adopted by a German family. Angelique spoke German with him as we ate fruit in his home.

Ali was a portly man who returned to the Middle East after twenty-eight years in Germany. He said, "Europe never felt like home. I was out of place." He is now a guide and lives with his wife and kids in this camp. Inside, their home was a nice middle-class apartment. His wife, a teacher in the local school, dressed in conservative beige and brown pants, jacket, and headscarf. The couple said they didn't approve of fortune-tellers and Abdusalam didn't believe in them either, but one of their daughters had some leads on finding the coffee cup reader.

We followed the girl to a store that sold junk food to crowds of kids outside the school. The owners, a warm and engaging older couple who looked African but were Palestinian, sent a little boy to ride with us to the woman's house.

The child asked around the neighborhood, and then turned to us saying, "Sometimes they do magic and spells, and take away curses. She got in trouble with the police and is not supposed to do readings anymore." We knocked on her door and were told that she had gone to visit her brother for two months. No wonder her phone was cut off. A little girl told us about someone else, and another boy climbed aboard to show us the way.

A corpulent woman, swathed in white scarves and dress, beckoned us into her simple cement-floored house. In a dark and windowless room with mattresses on the floor, a patient lay flat, jars and candles on her stomach. The lady in white removed them and placed them on her lower back. The patient already had five daughters, hence this procedure to help her be able to bear a son.

For the reading, no coffee cups were needed. We were merely asked our first names and the names of our mothers. The fortune-teller then prayed, sometimes jerking her arms. Suddenly, she started speaking. There was some accuracy, but she understood little about our world, which made it hard to know what to do with the information she received. All was good though: happiness, plenty of money, successful projects, and a nice, tall, skinny, dark man for me.

About 100,000 people live in Baqa'a, which was built in 1950. Despite the UN vans, it looked like a vibrant, though humble, neighborhood. I sneakily filmed from inside the car window as we drove toward the exit. Angelique said, "Keep your camera down. The police don't let anyone film in the camps without a special permit."

☾✩ ⁎ ⸰ ✩ ⸰ ⸰

Luna and I watched Al Jeel Jadid, a dance company representing the Circassian minority, during rehearsal. Circassians were dispersed throughout the Ottoman Empire when a war with Russia (1722-1865) forced them to escape. The agreement was that Russians took the land and Ottomans took the people, converted them to Islam and resettled them in various countries of the empire. Today, there are Circassian communities in Turkey, Lebanon, Israel, and the United States. They first came to Jordan around 1875, and Amman became a Circassian settlement. Jordan's Circassian population originally numbered 4000 and has increased to 120,000. They strive to maintain purity because they hope to return to their homeland one day.

Yinal, director of the Al-Jeel Jadid, was a tall, swarthy Eastern European looking guy, with a warm and intelligent way about him. Cigarette in hand, a booming voice, and shaved head, he kept his group of sixty-eight dancers, ages sixteen to twenty-two, disciplined with a clap of his hands. Women floated gracefully with elegant arm movements and, sometimes, fancy footwork. One dance included women dancing with daggers. "Usually, that's the domain of men, but the Circassian women were also warriors." Yinal told me, and then added, "There's a theory that the fabled Amazon women were actually Circassian." Men did dances landing on their knees, and both sexes turned very fast and landed on the front of their feet, with the toes curled under. All of this was done with no ballet training and on a hard stone floor. Ouch! A few girls wore white headscarves. It looked amazing when they spun fast across the floor. I loved the *kachak*, a wooden instrument held in each hand consisting of six thin pieces of wood tied together and shaken.

Yinal told me that he'd been back to the Circassian homeland in Russia ten times. "We don't call ourselves Circassians. Our homeland is known to us as the Adyghe Republic." He explained, "Circassian women have more freedom than their Jordanian counterparts. They have strong positions in society." The first president of the Circassian Club, which is the social hall where his group practices, was a woman. The first woman in Jordanian parliament was Circassian. Circassians have three seats in the parliament and many are guards for the royal family. Before Jordan became a country in 1921, the only language spoken in Amman was Circassian. I attended several rehearsals of Al Jeel

Jadid, each lasting six hours. I wished I could have seen a performance, but all performances were cancelled because of the war in Lebanon.

Luna said she had seen tribes of Gypsies living on the edge of town and wanted to meet them. My friend Ahmad, an intellectual tour guide who had guided me to Starbucks a couple of times, knew about many things. Using the term "Gypsy" is quite sensitive. In most European countries, "Gypsy" is a misnomer and can be considered derogatory. The preferred term is *Rom*. The Arabic word in this region is *Dhom*, although I later met Dhom who called themselves Gypsies when speaking English.

Ahmad said, "They live in small groups in tents and move around. Though they have been here for hundreds of years, they aren't even considered Jordanian, and are the bottom rung of our society. You can recognize the Dhom by the way they dress." He agreed to take Luna and me to try and meet them, with no guarantee of success. Soon after, we climbed aboard Ahmad's SUV and scoured the industrial areas outside of town.

Most people I'd spoken to about Jordan's ethnic groups talked about Bedouins, Palestinians, Circassians, recently arrived Iraqis, and even Chechens. There was little mention of Dhom and none of Turkmen.

We found groups of extremely poor nomads living in a no-man's industrial wasteland, introducing themselves as "Turkmen." They said, "We're not Gypsies." In a rundown industrial area, we came upon colorful tents made from patches of bright fabrics that livened up the dismal scene of a cement factory, wind-blown garbage, piles of rocks, and a used-car lot full of dust covered vehicles.

Everyone was friendly. Children ran to us with excited squeals. Kids were dirty with matted hair. Young men dressed modernly, with jeans and T-shirts or tank tops. Women wore tunics reaching just below the knees over pants with ruffles on the bottom. The fabrics and colors were vibrant, trimmed with braid or metallic cords. Women and little girls wore long thick braids and heavy makeup. Some girls and babies had red spots on the center of their foreheads, like the Indian "third eyes." Many kids crowded around, pointing to our cameras and motioning "picture." When we tried to click, they jostled to stick their faces in the camera. If I raised the camera, they jumped up and down, waving their hands in the viewfinder. We showed them their photos on the screens.

One of the young men explained that their language is "ancient Turkish, an old dialect no longer spoken in Turkey."

Later in the day, we returned and sat with one of the families. We saw a tent being made, a child washing clothes, and a woman washing dishes. There was neither a source of water nor electricity. Tents were loosely constructed with two sides and a rug on the ground, though it didn't cover the whole floor. Each family lived in one tent. Ahmad translated in Arabic to some men, but the women rarely learned Arabic. A man explained, "The longest we stay in one place is six months. Sometimes, when we set up camp on private property, they ask us to leave soon after." In the summer they live in tents, but in the winter their homes are constructed of corrugated metal.

They claimed their heritage as being Turkish, "We had to leave during one of the wars, went to Palestine, then came to Jordan in 1948. Now we have Jordanian passports and ID cards." Their main source of income is selling inexpensive items from China, such as sunglasses, on the street.

Ahmad showed distain for the Turkmen and said, "Their information is most likely wrong, and they are just trying to tell us what we want to hear." We were told that their chief was staying in Abu Alenda. Luna and I wanted to seek him out. According to the people we spoke to, there were about 15,000 Turkmen in the Amman area. One man said, "We have an emperor in Turkey. Luna looks like the queen."

A few days later we convinced Ahmad to take us to Abu Alenda in search of the Turkmen chief. We found his house, which was on a construction site, partially built of cement blocks and roofed over by Mickey Mouse fabric. Two children brought me inside, where several hammocks hung from nails. The floors were bare cement and colorful comforters with gold-colored designs were folded and piled against the wall. Judging from the unfinished mansion next to this structure, they were most likely squatting in what would be a garage, guest house, or storage area. The chief was out of town, so we played with his kids. They were fascinated by my earrings made from Tanzanian bottle caps. I showed head slides and hand circles to the little girls. One of them did even better hand circles than I did. I thought, "There must be some good dancing going on in this culture, if only we could see it."

Several days had passed when we returned once again in search of the Turkmen chief. Ahmad was tired of taking us, but Angelique's friend Abdusalam was happy to oblige. Once again, the chief's wife said he would be back the day after next. A man followed us and had me targeted, insisting that he must "cure" all of my "bad luck." He handed me a string and said, "Tie three knots." The only way to stop the pestering was for me to tie the knots. He motioned for me to tighten my fist around the knotted string, made some incantations, and motioned for me to open my hand. The knots were gone. He said that my problems were resolved and I owed him fifteen dollars. He then said, "It's fine for you to be in our camp, but we aren't interested in helping with your book."

The chief's wife added, "We won't be able to read it anyway, so why should we care?"

The magic man insisted I put my hand in a bowl of water to "Take off the dirt of your tomb that is inside of you."

I insisted on asking questions like why they had a big satellite dish and how they got electricity to watch TV (sometimes from a car battery, other times generators, or if they are close to town, they get it from the wires); how far they traveled when migrating (they stayed around Amman); how they worshiped God (some went to mosques and others to churches); what about weddings (they sign papers to make it legal, then they make a big party and everyone dances); and if the kids went to school (no).

Finally I put my hand in the water. He placed a towel over the bowl, removed it and the water was clear. He motioned for me to put my hand in the water again, and the water turned to mud. "That mud came from inside of you!" he exclaimed.

☪ ☆ ＊ . ＊ °

On the way back to town, I decided to ask Abdusalam about djinns. He said, "They are definitely real. Some believe in God and are Christian or Muslim, just like people, but others are evil and believe in nothing, or in Satan." He told how they enter during sex and that married couples are supposed to say a prayer before sex.

We stopped at the Cave of the Seven Sleepers. There were some unkempt Nabataean tombs by the side of the road that were full of garbage and graffiti. Nearby were more, better cared for, ruins that had a new mosque behind. Abdusalam noted, "People come from all over the Muslim world to see this, though it is not in most guide books. During Roman times, seven people escaped into this cave and fell asleep for two or three hundred years. When they awoke, the area had become Christian, so they were no longer afraid. One man went into town to buy food, but people couldn't understand why he had such old coins. It was then that he realized that they had been sleeping all that time."

I met a music professor named Dr. Mohammed Rawani through Lubna, who worked with the Jerash Music Festival, which is normally held every year amid ancient Roman ruins. This year, it was cancelled because of the war. She said the professor would be a good contact. As we sat in his elegant apartment with lavish gold draperies and ornate furniture with two of his sons, Mohammed told me who was who in the Jordanian music world (it was extremely small), and detailed some of his projects. The banquet table in his dining room was covered with manuscripts of a thousand-page book of songs and Jordanian musical history that he was writing. He'd won awards for a book about the life and work of the late Abdu Musa, Jordan's most famous Dhom singer.

One of the singer's grandsons, now a student of Dr. Rawani, was working on a PhD. When I expressed interest in learning more about Abdu Musa, Dr. Rawani arranged for Luna and me to meet the Musa family. We picked up Abdu Musa's eldest son, Sobhe, and Sobhe's son, the handsome and well-mannered eleven-year-old Moayed, who was carrying a violin case. We then went to the home of another of Abdu Musa's sons, Mohammed.

The sitting room was absolutely beautiful, with rich brocade couches, fringed cushions, and crystal chandeliers. Mohammed served Arabic coffee, orange drink, tea, and Turkish coffee. The water and Arabic coffee were taken communally: three cups for seven people to drink coffee and one glass for all to share the water. This wasn't from a lack of cups or glasses, rather it was a custom of sharing. Luna and I were instructed to sit in the center of the room as guests. Only the men were with us. The women sat in another room.

Sobhe had a huge dark mark on his forehead which was from touching his head to the ground in prayer five times a day. All of Abdu Musa's sons were impeccably groomed. Moayed already knew how to act with adults and was refined and well mannered.

Mohammed's wife, Diba, came to sit with us. A high school English teacher with a college degree and articulate English, she looked very religious wearing a brown coat, white headscarf and no makeup.

Diba shared her family's history with us, "After his father died, Abdu Musa was raised by my father, who was his older brother. Mohammed and I are cousins." Marriage between cousins, when the man's and woman's fathers are brothers is acceptable and sought after in many parts of the Arab world.

Abdu Musa's seven sons were respected because their father was Shaikh of the Dhom in Jordan. Even the Turkmen called him Shaikh. Abdu Musa's son Fathe, a former singer, assumed this role and tried to help people who came to him with legal problems and paperwork. He was currently running for parliament and wanted the Dhom to be represented in the government.

Diba's father had had five wives, but not all at once. Divorced several times, he had twenty children. Diba told the story, "When my father was on his death bed, he asked Abdu Musa to sing his favorite songs, which was so hard for him. How could he sing while the man who had been like a father to him lay dying? He did so out of love and respect."

Abdu Musa sang and played the rabab, a one stringed instrument. Diba exclaimed, "He was the pioneer and there has never been anyone better than him! Nobody in his family was a musician, but he was found to have exceptional singing talent and became famous. When he worked on the radio, one of the government ministers hired a tutor for him because he couldn't read or write. All of his sons became educated; daughters studied until they got married."

Diba talked a lot about being Dhom and how, in Jordan, people discriminate against them and make it difficult for her kids to admit their heritage in school. Diba and her family rarely said the term "Dhom," using "Gypsy" instead. She spoke little of the language and her kids spoke none at all. She had no traditional Dhom clothes and preferred to dress Islamic, keeping her head covered even in front of her husband's brothers but removing her scarf when among her immediate family. She said, "I got married in a white Western-style dress but became more religious later. Hopefully, my husband and I will go to Mecca next year."

We were treated to an impressive violin concert by Abdu Musa's grandson, Moayed. His fingers were calloused with peeling skin because during school vacations he practiced ten hours a day. With a repertoire ranging from Classical to Arabic folk, and music from Egypt's "golden age," this extremely talented boy played songs from Egypt's great singers and composers—Om Khalsoum, Farid El Atrache, and Lebanese diva Fairuz—plus an Eastern European Rom medley.

Diba, Luna, and I talked about Dhom in Jordan. Diba said, "Nobody helps them. The government has no money." I pointed out that there are many programs for poor people, such as the Beni Hameda weaving project that employs Bedouin women and other cooperative projects, but she said, "The Gypsies have been neglected." I opined that they needed leadership to make a plan and ask for help. She was surprised when I told her about Rom congresses, conventions, and governing bodies in other parts of the world, where people gather from Europe, India, and the Americas. Jordan seemed to be out of the loop. Luna told us about a Palestinian Dhom woman who has done a lot for the people there and promised to bring information from her organization's website.

Luna, Diba, and I decided to meet again and brainstorm about what could be done to help the Dhom. This time, Diba was uncovered and so were her daughters. Diba said, "My father was designated a Pasha by the government. He helped the Turkmen get Jordanian passports. Turkmen aren't related to us, but we help them just the same."

We talked about "kidnapping" marriages among the Dhom. "When a girl wants to marry a man of another tribe against her parents' wishes, they call it *khatifa*. Fathe is the person the family goes to for help with this problem."

When asked about dance, Diba said, "Gypsies in tents do special dances and play the rabab. Women sit in one area and men in another, but they see one another. Dances are difficult, with shoulder moves and *zagat* (finger cymbals)." We were invited into the living room to watch the video of Diba and Mohammed's wedding in 1980, which had not been watched in years. A seventy-year-old woman in a long dress did earthy belly dancing with strong shimmies and flamenco-like barrel turns. This was the first time I'd seen the use of finger cymbals in Jordan.

A recurring theme kept coming up: "People say we are better than the Jordanians, but there is still a stigma attached to being Gypsy." The house was beautiful and spotlessly clean. Her kids had perfect manners and excellent social skills as well as good grades. They dressed Jordanian and were ideal examples of good Muslims. The daughter was attending college, with plans to be a doctor. She had excellent grades and conduct, but complained, "I can't tell my friends I'm a Gypsy." Abdu Musa's musical talents gave his family the opportunity to become educated and move up to middle class, but they were still trying to prove their worth and to show that Dhom could make it in the world. Trying so hard to assimilate, they were losing some of their own culture.

Diba said, "The Gypsies and Turkmen need schools and doctors, but they don't have money to pay. Education can solve so many problems."

Changing the subject, Diba brought out a black head scarf and wrapped it on my head. Mohammed used eye liner to paint my face with designs that local Dhom women of their mother's generation had tattooed onto their chins and foreheads. He fetched a camera and asked me to pose for photographs.

I'd heard about a Bedouin custom called *tahia*, in which the men chant in low voices, reaching a crescendo as a woman dances, her face covered, wearing a black robe and wielding a sword to defend herself against the men's advances. According to Lubna, the woman at the Jerash Festival office, "Tahia is done at weddings, but originated when the warring tribes invaded one another trying to take the money, land, food, and women of another tribe. If a woman was beautiful, they tried to touch her. If she was able to defend herself and ward off men, she was a fine woman and could be taken as a wife by a high ranking man. If one of the men was able to catch her, he could keep her. Now, the dance is done as entertainment at weddings, and the woman is never caught."

Lubna referred me to Mr. Sanawi, head of the Ministry of Culture. He told me about a Bedouin poetry festival in the town of al-Kalbiya that would have a performance of tahia. I called Angelique, she came to pick me up, and we were soon headed out of Amman. Suddenly, in the middle of nowhere, there was a traffic jam. A man waved lighted batons to get the cars to stop. A bus and small truck almost ran him over as they barreled past at least a dozen tanks on flat bed trucks speeding toward the Syrian border. When we arrived at the little town of al-Kalbiya, a young man noticed that we were lost and got in the car to direct us to the festival. Men in crisp white robes and red checkered turbans took turns orating. Cardamom coffee, tea, and water flowed as we sat through hours of poetry echoing out of a loud set of speakers. It was animated and dramatic, and the audience responded with loud "aahh's," and other expressions of enthusiasm. We didn't understand a word.

Eventually, the tahia group came onstage. The music consisted of men's hand-claps and vocals—no instruments. Some songs had chanted words, while others consisted entirely of synchronized guttural grunts. One man had a sword and another held a cane. A little girl danced, waving her hands with skipping steps. Unfortunately, we didn't see the real dance because grown women only dance if every man in the audience is a relative. Traditionally, a woman would dance with a sword, but this show was adapted for public display.

It was time to renew my Jordanian visa, and I had a choice between hours of bureaucracy or a visit to Syria, just a short drive away. A ceasefire with Lebanon had taken effect a few days earlier and warnings of the war spreading to Syria had subsided weeks earlier. I already had a Syrian visa in my passport, so the choice was clear. This would be my first journey into the "Axis of Evil." I wondered how I would be received.

Up the hill from my hotel were several storefront agencies selling passage to Syria in old American made cars. I climbed into a bright yellow one and waited for it to fill up with passengers.

The road into Damascus was lined with unpainted cement brick buildings, becoming increasingly modern as blocks of black and white buildings took their place.

I stayed on a cute little street, not far from the historic area, that was lined with vines and old guesthouses. A beautiful citadel was closed to tourists and, unfortunately, the moat running alongside it was dry and full of garbage. Once inside the old area, tiny streets steeped in history were paradise for the few tourists who ventured to Syria. Absent were the hearty welcomes and easy conversations with strangers. I found people reserved but not unfriendly.

I was followed several times. One guy showed me an ID written in Arabic with his photo, which he unfolded. It was in tatters, and he said, "I am from the police and must accompany you." It was surely a scam, so I got rid of him. Others were hangers-on, and one of them left when I gave him a mean stare. I saw very few uncovered women and was glad to be wearing an oversized skirt and top.

I started out telling people I was Colombian, until Fadi, the owner of a carpet store, commented, "Many Americans say they are from elsewhere, but you should just say you're American because Syrians have nothing against you." I was busted and embarrassed, but said, "I used to live in Colombia." He showed me beautiful textiles from Uzbekistan, including colorful Atlas silks. Syria was the end of the ancient Silk Road from China, and Atlas silk has been sought after ever since those trading days.

He invited me for tea. When I needed to use a bathroom, he opened a double glass door and ushered me past his private collection. A maze of room after impressive room displayed carpets, lamps, and wall hangings. Fadi spoke little English, but I understood his gist, "War is about money and only between the leaders, not reflective on the people as individuals."

The next day, I walked around the old section of Damascus, exploring covered souks, exquisite fabric stores, spice and herb sellers, varieties of olive-oil soaps, and lots of sweets made from apricots and pistachios.

Most important of the numerous historical churches and mosques was the Umayyed Mosque, a huge marble complex containing ancient gold mosaics that were crafted in a Byzantine style by imported workers. To one side was the tomb of Saladin, lit by green fluorescent bulbs. Properly known as Salah-al-Din, this 12th-century Muslim political leader, who was Kurdish-Iraqi, founded the Ayyubid Dynasty and ruled Egypt, Syria, Iraq, Yemen and parts of Arabia. Best known for recapturing Palestine from the Crusaders, he is widely admired in the Arabic culture to this day.

I passed two *hammams* (Turkish bathhouses) in the old section. One had a sign outside saying "This Hammam is 800 years old." I thought how, by comparison, the U.S. is only 230 years old!

The doorway to the bathhouse I visited was covered by a rug. Inside, they had a steam room and stone fountains from which to pour water on oneself from metal bowls. People lie on the floor, and a woman scrubs layers of dead skin away with a rough mitt, followed by another who gives a brief massage with oil. Women outside were eating lunch and invited me to join them.

After midnight, on my way back to the hotel, I was uncomfortable because I felt someone following me. When I got to the street of the hotel, my suspicions were confirmed. He ran away when I turned and started following him. A man came out of my hotel and saw me safely inside. When I explained what had happened, he said, "I sensed something was wrong and went outside to check." Hossam was an engineer from Iraq, living in Cairo. For awhile the front desk clerk translated, but once he walked away, we kept talking for almost two hours. My Arabic was terrible, and his English worse, but somehow we could communicate. I found that this happened more and more in my travels, and later puzzled, "How did we talk about so much without a language in common?" Then again, children barely old enough to talk understand each other when adults have no idea what they're saying. So language must be only one of many ways to communicate.

Mohammed, the music professor, had arranged for me to attend a wedding in the small Jordanian town of Ar Ramtha, near the Syrian border. I went to a parking lot full of service taxis headed out of Damascus and waited for one to fill. On the way to Ar Ramtha, the car stopped at a butcher by the side of the road. We stayed half an hour while all the men from the car smoked, socialized, and bought meat.

They stopped again to buy cigarettes and food, then hid everything under the seats. Inspectors were paid off as we went through several border checks. Getting out of Syria was a long and tedious process, with several police and security checks, as well as auto inspections and opening of bags. I was concerned because Mohammed's friend Bilal was supposed to take me to the wedding and would be waiting across the border, and, to top it off, my phone battery was dead. We arrived an hour late and, luckily, Bilal was still waiting by the border.

Bilal was an entertainment agent whose own folkloric troupe worked all over Jordan. Mohammed called after Bilal had left me with his wife Samia and two children. "Samia would like you to stay overnight with them," he said. Samia asked me to dance for her, and then she danced for me. She was as good as any professional.

Samia was dripping with gold jewelry: three hoops in each ear, at least a dozen bangles, and chains of gold around her neck. Her teeth were adorned by precious stones stuck on by a dentist: two diamonds and one sapphire. Without my glasses, I thought she had braces.

She stood on the balcony, chain smoking, and said enthusiastically, "I love my neighborhood. It's quiet and there isn't much traffic." Her house, across the street from the local graveyard, was pleasingly eccentric with a homemade fountain and funky decorations made of rocks. To my outsider's eyes, this house was the only distinguishing landmark in a nondescript, dry and dusty neighborhood lacking in personality. Like many graveyards in Islamic countries, this one contained plain slabs of stone, some standing straight and others fallen sideways. There was no vegetation, just bare dusty earth. A van passed with the back door open. Four guys sat with sad expressions, flanking a blanket wrapped body. Samia explained, "Here, we don't use coffins, and the body isn't dressed. It's merely wrapped in white cloth, so you leave the world the same way as you came."

Bilal and Samia's cute eight-year-old daughter, Nihad, became my constant companion. We walked to a neighborhood wedding that was just beginning. It was on an intersection that had lights and a miniature imitation Eiffel Tower in the middle. Loud music could be heard for blocks, but it was early and there were only a handful of people. Women, mostly in elaborate cross-stitched caftans and headpieces with coins and tassels, sat on one side of the street, while men sat on the other. We stayed a bit and later had coffee with the next door neighbors. Bilal came to drive us to a second wedding, which his group was playing at.

In a dusty open lot, dozens of women in caftans and headpieces danced a simple *dabke,* a traditional folk dance, holding hands in a line that circled half the field, and stepping a one-sided series of steps. Each area has its own style of dabke, and I was told that you can tell what village a person is from by how they dance A keyboard played loud music, and there were heavy drums and a singer. They got me into the line immediately, and we all synchronized around the vast expanse of open dirt. Soon, all the women sat and the men danced. Women can only dance among men they're related to. Since most of the town was invited to this wedding, they interspersed men dressed as women into the line. These men wore the same caftans and coined headpieces as women but covered their faces with the red-and-white checkered turbans. A drummer twirled on one leg, dancing, and beating his big drum with sticks. A big man in white robe and checkered turban animated the party, dancing among all the guests. Men in vests, hired as part of the entertainment, served bitter cardamom coffee.

Events in Jordan always included pouring tiny amounts of bitter coffee. If one drinks it all, the hosts must keep pouring more. The only way to stop getting served is to return your cup with a few drops of coffee in the bottom. Others, with tall flower laden pitchers attached to their waists, poured *tamer* (a date drink that tastes like cough medicine). They started dancing and twirling, then someone carried a big picture of King Abdullah and danced with it overhead. I'd been to weddings around the world, but none as festive as this. The lot was decorated with Jordanian flags and pictures of King Abdullah and had strings of bare lightbulbs draped overhead. Women sat in one area, and men in another.

A group of men carried a table laden with a pan of flowers and candles, signaling that it was time to put henna on one of the groom's hands. Suddenly, plastic snow poured down, strings of canned plastic goop spurted from all sides, and candy was thrown for kids to scramble and pick up. Men danced with others sitting on their shoulders, and some did so with big drums.

Samia told me, "Tomorrow, the marriage will be consummated and the bloody cloth shown to both families. If the bride doesn't bleed…" (she motioned her neck getting slit), "she dies," she added with a non-chalant giggle.

I asked, "How do you feel about that?" and she gave me a puzzled look. After a few moments, she replied, "I never thought about it."

We discussed the concept of honor killings, then she concurred, "Maybe it's not such a good idea." I mentioned that it's illegal, but she pooh-poohed, "Everyone in this town belongs to two families. We protect each other."

Bilal took me to Amman, where his group was performing at another wedding. The men were in one banquet room and the women in another. His group, consisting mostly of teenage boys, filed off a bus and met us in the fashionable hotel's lobby. He abruptly motioned me to go into the women's party.

For a long time I sat, completely ignored. Conservative women wore headscarves. Some had nice clothes, while others were serious, severe, and nun-like. Younger women wore modern clothes: jean skirts or evening dresses, with no head scarves. One belly danced beautifully from table to table in a flowing silk dress she later told me was a Fouad Sarkis (Lebanon's top designer) evening gown.

The band was all male, as were the waiters. It was clearly a women's party, and they were comfortable completely ignoring the men who served them. Older women did a Bedouin dance, holding scarves in front with both hands, rocking back and forth. A line of women did the dabke, in a slightly different version from Ar Ramtha. It took awhile for people to warm up to me, but later I met several women, including Nadia and Majda, who were friendly, and I even received invitations to visit one of the local villages.

I thought Bilal's dabke group would dance for men, but there was no music in the men's party. The women's party was far more animated. I sat and waited for about three hours. Finally, the dabke group entered in matching green and black satin outfits. A flourish of drumbeats and a screeching synthesizer accompanied as they held hands in a line, stomping and shimmying their shoulders. The show was nice, but the previous day they had been in their element, doing something similar, but infinitely more interesting because it was part of their culture and real lives. Now, they were on display as a show for the city folk.

I accepted a ride out of Amman with Nadia's family. Upon entering her home, Nadia blurted, "I hate men! I don't sleep with my husband and I never let him kiss me." At the age of fourteen, she was married off to a wealthy man in his 50s with whom her father was doing a business deal. Although they stayed married for many years, she never met his first wife. He gave Nadia everything money could buy, but eventually she left him for another man and consequently gave up her children. In cases of divorce, most Muslim countries award the children to their father, and the mother returns to her family's home. It is assumed that the father can offer greater financial stability and that he will have a mother and sisters who can take over caring for the children.

The next morning, Nadia brought me to visit Sara, a pretty and statuesque woman with streaked-blond hair. She answered her door wearing a slip that showed lots of cleavage and then changed into a long skirt. She soon went to her room and came out in a ruffled micromini dress. Someone brought out a tape deck, and Nadia and I danced. Sara reemerged in an evening outfit of black bellbottoms and a top with rhinestone accents. Her husband came home from work, changed into a cotton robe, and plopped down on the couch. Nadia said, "Sara hates her husband too. She loves another man but can't leave or she will lose her kids."

Upstairs, lunch was served on a big platter on the floor: chicken and rice, salads, and yoghurt. Two brothers sat with us, one with his wife (who is his cousin) and their baby. The younger brother teased, "My wife is better looking," and both brought out photo albums of their weddings, asking me, "Which bride is prettier?"

When they discussed why I wasn't married, one brother piped up, "It's harder for English (he called everyone foreign 'English'), because they expect to stay married for life, and the men don't sleep with other women."

On our way out, we found Sara in yet another outfit. I commented that she changed clothes a lot. She said, "I always do this," and covered herself with a beautifully embroidered caftan and headscarf, and we went into town.

Majda picked me up with her young daughter in tow, and we wound up at a cell phone store, where a corpulent woman swathed in black ushered us next door inside an apartment. Majda said, "I want you to tell me who is better, him or my husband." There was a bearded man seated on cushions who wanted her to leave her husband and become his third wife. She explained, "He is supposedly religious, but he beats his wives, and loves the second one more than the first." I remembered my conversations with Mr. Bambang in Indonesia, as well as further readings that said if a man has more than one wife, he must treat them all equally, which is difficult to do, so it is preferable to only marry one. I refused her requests to dance for him and she kept asking, "Which one should I choose?" The first wife served coffee. The second had gone out. We sat on low cushions in the sitting room with the wife and her daughters. One was eighteen years old and about to marry for love. Everyone was friendly, but the scene felt surreal. Majda kept hounding me, wanting to know my opinion of this guy.

Later, Majda wanted me to meet her group of friends, who were all gathered in her kitchen, chopping and cooking. I didn't get a chance to put my bag upstairs before she insisted I dance for her friends. They all started belly dancing: one while washing dishes, another as she cut the cucumbers. I helped by cutting potatoes and drying dishes. It was a communal effort, which I thought was for a special occasion. It was only lunch for us. The three women were sisters, each on her second marriage.

One of the sisters was a beautiful, fashionably dressed forty-year-old, wearing full makeup and a creatively wrapped sequined headscarf. At one point, she was praying in the bedroom while everyone else dressed and put on makeup. She had married at fifteen, had her son at sixteen, and then couldn't have more children. Her husband wanted more, so he took a second wife, and she asked for a divorce. She'd been remarried for two years, but again her husband wanted kids and took a second wife. This time, she stayed and decided to go to college. Having just graduated as a teacher and about to try teaching school, she said, "My first day is tomorrow. If it's ok I'll continue, but it is more important for me to be beautiful and keep the house and my clothes looking perfect, so my husband doesn't leave me for his other wife. If teaching makes me frazzled, I'll quit."

Another sister was only thirty. She said, "I love American actors! Mmm . . . Tom Cruise and Leonardo Di Caprio," then teasingly said, "I want an American husband." She was on her second marriage and complained that, "My husband says he wants to hire a cheap prostitute, have sex with her and call me on his cell phone while in the act so I can listen to them," then went on, "I started studying English, but he made me stop. I have no choice but to put up with him, or I'll lose my children."

The third sister sat quietly, dressed plainly in a neutral-colored headscarf and oversized blouse, breast-feeding her baby.

Although Majda was fairly well off, the gas stove was barely functional, and she spent a lot of time underneath trying to light the oven with a burning napkin. Finally, a man with a new gas canister came in, and they hooked it up. It looked so dangerous; he almost forgot to turn off the lit burner before connecting the gas hose.

I tried to help set up a sitting room for lunch. One of the women gave me a giant roll of plastic wrap and motioned me to do something with it. I was confused until she came over, moved the coffee table out of the way, and unrolled some plastic, stabbing at it with a knife until it ripped. Then she motioned for me to open it. This roll was wider than we would use to cover leftovers in the refrigerator and was specially made to cover the floor, so we could sit and eat on it. We set out the chicken, salad, and kebab, and some spoons and plates. All the children sat and ate with us.

In Jordan, women's lives revolve around rites of passage, primarily weddings and associated social events. People seem to constantly be getting married, and marriages are for the whole community to celebrate. Majda invited me to a henna party.

"Hurry and get ready," one of the women said breathlessly. A frantic dash upstairs ensued. We had an hour before leaving, but the sisters liked to primp and try on different clothes. They put on massive amounts of makeup. After I applied what I considered heavy evening makeup Majda asked, "Is that all the makeup you're going to wear? Don't you want to put more?" Even the little girls wore eye shadow, lipstick and liner. One of the sister's eight-year-old daughters wore a sleeveless top, miniskirt, and full makeup. Majda was still in house clothes but donned so much gold that it looked like she was getting married. She said, "I bought this all today," then put on a tight red spandex jumpsuit. A black abaya on top gave her a properly cloaked appearance for arriving at a party.

The celebration was in a tent. Several corpulent and serious-looking women sat in a row, dressed in traditional caftans and wearing flowered scarves on their heads. The bride-to-be was the eighteen-year-old daughter of the man with two wives who wanted to marry Majda. She wore a giant satin dress with a hoop and sat with henna on her hands atop a throne decorated with hearts.

Both of the father's wives were hosting the party. The second wife was very personable, wearing an all black abaya and a headscarf adorned with tiny red roses. She led a dabke and made sure everyone was comfortable.

Teenagers started appearing, first in tight jeans and tops, then some in spandex dresses and miniskirts. They danced up a storm, put their black abayas back on, and left. The third and most conservative sister commented, "That was embarrassing. People only used to dress like that at home. Now, they watch Lebanese and Egyptian videos and imitate them."

Luna, Diba, and I had a meeting to discuss ideas about what could be done for the Dhom. Diba said that the Jordanian Dhom make special knives and sew their own clothing. I told her about a project in an area called Beni Hameda where Bedouin women were organized into cooperatives to hone their age-old skills as rug makers and their wares were sold around the globe. Before I left Jordan, I promised to research the Beni Hamida weaving project and find out how it helped empower so many women, improving the economic situation of an entire region. It hadn't occurred to me that I had no idea where it was or how to get there.

Several days earlier, I'd been impressed by the friendliness, intelligence, and fluent English of a cab driver named Firoz, even though his best English came out when he spurted, "I look at your president and I see the devil!" He had given me his card, and I hired him to drive me for the day.

Taxis in Amman ranged from beautiful, new, and spacious to that belonging to Firoz. His shabby little car bumped and rattled all the way through Madaba, a historical town famous for mosaics. As Firoz chain-smoked, his taxi huffed and puffed past dry terraced hills and winding dirt roads. We wound through a dusty village to Beni Hamida. The building stood out as the only modern structure in this area of earth-colored mountains. Its classy, though traditional, showroom had been donated by a Canadian group. Halime was the woman in charge. Dressed in black with a headscarf, she spoke limited English. Firoz was very helpful, translating and coming up with questions of his own.

Halime explained, "The Beni Hamida project was established in 1985, and it has changed the fourteen villages in our area. Previously, few women finished high school, and mixing with men was restricted. Minds were closed but they have opened due to meeting new people from Amman and the outside. Now, local women have become nurses, government employees, police, and civil servants. Since the project began, it has changed life both economically and socially. There is more money, as well as more motivation. Thinking has changed. Now, young women are more determined to continue their education."

She continued, "Rug weaving was a tradition. Only old women did it, but once the project began young women learned to weave too. They work at home on everything except dyeing the yarn, because that requires special machines. This project was designed to help women economically while they stay home with their families. In the beginning, many women weren't allowed to leave home and go to work. Besides their earnings, people became more open. Without this project," Halime said, "I would not be sitting with you."

She added, "When people from the U.S. visit our project, I get a different idea about them than what's in the news about bombs and helping Israel." She met foreigners and gained firsthand experience. She said, "We are not terrorists or violent people. We're more peaceful than people would believe. The prophet said 'Don't cut a tree or kill animals needlessly. Don't destroy wells or set grain on fire.'" (She was referring to the rules of war outlined in the Qur' an.)

Traditionally, when a woman married, she was given a rug to bring as furniture. This was woven by women of her mother's family. The groom gave her gold snake bracelets and a necklace of coins.

243

The women in this region had no measurement scale for yarn or rugs, such as feet or meters. Rather, things were measured by the rounds of each woman's head.

Halime said, "In the beginning, the locals were afraid and thought people were coming to exploit them. Most women were against the project, but a few gave it a try. When they were successful the others changed their opinions and wanted to take part too.

"The organizers started by having a general meeting for all the women of the area. They said, 'You are good weavers and we will pay you and help improve your life.' They gave natural wool for them to clean. The foundation brought tools and separated the jobs: cleaning wool, dying, and weaving. The hardest and most skillful work is dying the wool."

How do the men feel about all these changes? She said, "They liked it because there was more money coming in. Now, men work in the army, government, farms, health care, schools, and government. There are fewer farmers now due to little rain and no water for irrigation. We had sheep and goats, but many animals died in the drought because there wasn't enough food for them. The government started nature preserves, which reduced the farmland too."

We stayed more than two hours, and Halime told me, "We want to attract the type of tourism in this area where people stay with families and learn about traditional Bedouin life." She added, "This area is quiet and good for tourists who want to experience nature and history. We want visitors who want to live with us: milk cows, go to weddings, or do home stays." I wished I'd met her thirty-eight days ago. I'd been trying so hard to get into local life and would have loved to do a home stay with a Bedouin family. Unfortunately, my forty days were almost over.

It was time for her to go home, but Halime accompanied us to a vantage point overlooking the Dead Sea. She showed Firoz some medicinal plants, which he picked to ward off the evil eye and to lower his mother's high blood pressure. In the distance were the remains of a palace where John the Baptist was imprisoned and legends say that Salome danced.

A sign at the beginning of the trail read "Memorial of the Prophet Yahya (John the Baptist)." We followed a path up the hill, alongside an old wall, and past caves that looked like they'd been inhabited centu-

ᅟ

ries ago. Though now dry, deserted, and nurturing only scrubby plants, the scenery was stunning. Terraces wound up and down the majestic mountainous terrain. Some might be geological, but vast amounts of terracing looked man-made, like ancient farms. The castle appeared to have slight attempts at restoration, though with little authenticity. Some stumps from ancient pillars still remained, but the towering pillars were obviously modern reconstructions.

The dungeon where John the Baptist was imprisoned looked like one in an old silent film version of *Salome*. There was a flat area where Salome may have danced, although her name is not mentioned in the bible. Maybe someone created the movie set based on this ruin. In any case, the open area was a perfect place to dance, and Firoz videotaped me doing so on that same spot. Mysteriously, the tape got irretrievably tangled up in the camera and could not be seen.

The palace looked no larger than an upscale house in Abdoun, but, compared to the lifestyles of the day, it must have been opulent. Firoz, who was never without a cigarette in his mouth, was exhausted by the climb but fascinated at the same time. He'd never heard about this place or read the stories about John the Baptist or Salome.

On the way back, far from Beni Hamida's cluster of villages, were many shepherds and Bedouin tents. Firoz asked if I wanted to stop and visit a family.

We approached a black and beige tent located in a dry field of dirt. Whereas the Turkmen lived in colorful camps where everyone shared one big open space, each Bedouin family lived a distance from the others. Poverty was comparable between the groups.

At this dwelling, a woman named Fatme and her three young sons greeted us. Her husband was off tending sheep.

She told us about their lives: "We live outside of Madaba in the summer and travel to the Jordan Valley in winter. My husband, three kids, and I live in this tent during the summer. In the winter, the tents have plastic covering to protect us from the rain and mud. My sons, three, five and six years old, don't go to school because we would have to stop traveling, and my husband wouldn't be able to work."

She continued, "Our livelihood is a herd of thirty sheep. In the winter, we sell milk. If we need money, we sell a sheep. I travel with my husband's family. His parent's tent is on the other side of the road. Our day starts at 6 or 7 AM, when we drink tea with milk. At 11 AM, I cook on an open fire. The family eats meat once a week, and chicken once a week as well. For a big feast, like a wedding or other celebration, we kill a sheep and make mensef."

I asked about the television and she explained, "We watch TV using a car battery for power and use kerosene lamps for light. We look healthy and like everything is fine, but it's not true. Life is difficult. Of course, I would love to be settled in a house." When the time comes to move, her husband rents a big truck that takes the family, their sheep, and all their belongings to the next grazing place.

Neither Fatme nor her husband had been to school, though she said, "He knows some reading and writing." She was twenty-three at their wedding; she went to a salon to fix her hair and wore a white gown. The ceremony was in tents. She said, "We've been married for seven years. He is two years older than me and I love him. I'm happy with my husband and my marriage."

After a delicious dinner in a Lebanese restaurant in Madaba, I read Firoz's cup. He told me "My life is over and now I just exist." He seemed to have given up on life and had been nervously chain-smoking all day. I asked if he wanted to talk about it, and he asked if I was willing to listen for a long time.

Firoz said "I lived in the U.S. for ten years, during which time I was caught and convicted of transporting cigarettes across state lines from Virginia to New York. I spent three months in prison, and was on probation for a while. I hadn't violated probation at all, but felt something bad was going to happen. The federal government took me in 2003 and I was held in a windowless six-by-nine-foot cell for one week. By the second week, I was stripped naked and had to sit in forty-two-degree cold with no furniture. Then they gave me two options: deportation, or await my hearing which might take a year." He chose deportation and returned to Jordan, miserable and unable to adjust.

My Jordanian experience ended without fanfare, with a tea party at Luna's spacious house in the suburbs with Angelique and several

French and Jordanian women who Luna had wanted to introduce me and my project to. I told them how Jordan seemed like a series of cultural experiences tied together by the fact that everyone was on an island of tranquility in the desert. Not only had the Nabataeans, Greeks, and Romans made their marks, but so many people had escaped the perils of life in Russia several generations ago, or lost their homeland when Israel became a state at the Palestinians' expense, or, in the case of Iraqis, simply wanted to get out of the line of fire. Life in Jordan was a case study in Bedouin hospitality and magnanimity, where everyone was welcome, and everyone I met echoed that sentiment with a "Welcome." The surface was dull, or overrun by foreign corporate influences who had been welcomed along with everyone else. But a few scratches beneath revealed a fascinating multicultural blend as well as a balancing act.

Getting from Jordan to my last destination, China's westernmost province of Xinjiang, was no easy feat. First, I had to get a Chinese visa and supply a letter from the U.S. embassy stating who I was and why I wanted to go to China.

The level of security at the American Embassy was astounding. Traffic couldn't come near the building, as there were cement barriers and an extra lane separating the building from traffic. There were three checkpoints. I had to turn off my cell phone and they took it and my two cameras away at the front. My handbag was searched, and then I went through the x-ray and was frisked by a guard with a metal detector.

I was given a number, #80, and passed a security guard who directed me to American Citizen Services. The room was packed like a can of sardines and they were only on number six. I asked the woman behind a thick layer of glass about the letter the Chinese Embassy had requested of me in order to issue a visa. She handed me a piece of Xeroxed letterhead that barely had ink and said, "Write it yourself and the consul will sign it for $30." I handed the paper beneath a slot with wind blowing it back—in case a person's documents contain poisonous powder, it will come back in their face. The employees spoke through the bulletproof glass on phones while wearing headsets. There was almost no personal contact or way to get information or ask a question.

I asked several travel agents to book my ticket and got responses ranging from "No. We don't sell tickets there." to "Where? . . . never heard of it."

Ahmad-the-guide's uncle had a travel agency and he booked me a ticket from Amman to Abu Dhabi, then to Islamabad, Pakistan. He said, "I reserved your ticket to Kashgar (in the Xinjiang Autonomous Region of China), but it's cheaper if you buy it in Islamabad."

Abu Dhabi is in the United Arab Emirates, not far from Dubai. I only scheduled a two night layover, but it was packed with appointments to see very special people. I wrote to Sabriye, the belly dancer who let me stay in her hotel room in Cairo. Now she was working in Abu Dhabi! I had been writing to my pen pal, Ravi, for thirty-two years. Originally from Sri Lanka, he had been living in Saudi Arabia for eleven years. Saudi Arabia borders the Emirates. His entire family of four took the bus to Dubai and we met, at long last! I also learned that Ali Abdella Buaisha, the composer of "Afkari" (the song played by Ikhwani Safaa that inspired me to visit Zanzibar), lives in Dubai. I called and he invited me to visit his home.

On the way to Abu Dhabi, the airline lost one of my suitcases and, for security reasons, refused to keep it at the airport if it showed up. Luckily, it was located. I pretended not to get the message, so they had to keep it.

The Emirates is oil rich, hypermodern, luxurious, and full of shopping malls. In Dubai, they even have one with an indoor ski slope. Sabriye drove me an hour from Abu Dhabi to Dubai. The city is planned and built on a square grid, except for a posh waterfront strip that contains the world's most expensive hotel, shaped like a giant sailboat.

Ali Abdella Buaisha's twenty-three-year-old daughter Zahra picked me up in a fancy SUV. Covered with a black abaya and headscarf, she said, "I'm comfortable with a few limitations and I don't mind. Sure, I have to be home early and cannot do everything my brother does, but it is more important to me that I can work and go to school." Ali Abdella Buaisha was about eighty-one or eighty-two years old. Wearing a white turban with black cords around it and white robe, he looked like the Arabs from the Gulf.

We sat on ornate couches in his sitting room as he told me how he left Zanzibar and came to Dubai: "Soon after the revolution, one of the soldiers forewarned me that I was on the list to be hung. He urged me to flee. Many people died in wooden boats trying to get to Arabia from Zanzibar, as boat captains would be forced to take as many as fifty people on a small boat. Many of these sank, but I was lucky to be taken on a ship. The king of Dubai refurbished an entire neighborhood and gave free homes to Zanzibaris who fled for their lives."

"Last year, I went to Zanzibar as the guest of honor for Ikhwani Safaa's hundredth-anniversary celebration. My father, who died when I was two, was one of the club's founders."

After all my visits were over, I went back to the Abu Dhabi airport. I identified my bag, sent it through to Pakistan, and checked in. The ticket agent said, "Where is your Pakistani visa?"

I said, "I will only be transiting."

"Then you must have your ticket to China," he responded.

I was caught in a tangle because his boss confirmed that I could only be considered "in transit" if I had a ticket onward already purchased. The Chinese airline only sells tickets where they fly from, so I needed to wait and buy it in Pakistan.

A crowd of airline employees was forming, all interjecting their own reasons why I would have to give up my flight. "You cannot board," a menacing man said. Later, I was taken to a special office to buy an extremely overpriced ticket for the short jaunt from Islamabad to Kashgar.

I got to Islamabad and had a few hours to kill. I was told "We do not allow people to wait inside the airport," and shuffled out the door. It was funny and ironic that I was locked out of the airport without having been issued a visa or having my passport stamped. Fortunately, taxis were abundant so I hailed one to take me sightseeing in Islamabad. There wasn't a lot to see because this was a new city that was built specifically as a capital, but the elaborately painted open-sided trucks that passed, full of men in billowing white pants and knee-length shirts, were interesting and the taxi driver took me home to pass the time drinking tea with his father. They made me promise, "Next time, you write a book about Pakistan, Okay?"

THE
XINJIANG
AUTONOMOUS REGION OF CHINA

"Pursue knowledge from birth to death, even to faraway lands such as China."

—Prophet Mohammed PBUH

A conveyor belt in the tiny Kashgar International Airport of China's Xinjiang Autonomous Region sputtered under the weight of Pakistani rugs and other cargo on their way into China. I had checked two suitcases in Abu Dhabi, but only one arrived. After the last giant bundle was tossed off the belt and onto the floor, I realized my other bag was lost somewhere over the Silk Road, between Islamabad and Kashgar. When I asked to fill out a report, the manager glared and spat, "Not our problem. Go back to Pakistan and look for your own bag." I stubbornly refused to leave without some paperwork. He crumpled my claim slip and tossed it on the floor. Standing alone amid piles of unclaimed merchandise, I couldn't protest. I simply had to swallow my anger.

That was my introduction to the Chinese occupying force: a force that won't let go of its largest province, even though most people in Xinjiang aren't ethnically Chinese and they never wanted to be part of China.

How did I find out about this sparsely populated outpost? One day while visiting Hong Kong, a huge photo of dancers in sequined silks and bejeweled hats beckoned me to try a new restaurant called "Silk

Road." Fascinated by the dancers they had brought from Xinjiang, I heard about a dancer, teacher, and former movie star named Pasha. Soon, she and I began to exchange lessons. On a brief tour of China, I had an opportunity to visit and meet Pasha's family in Xinjiang. From that moment I wanted to share this beautiful land with readers who were, maybe, like I'd been, unaware of its existence.

Xinjiang is Mandarin for "new frontier." This area has long been inhabited by a diverse mixture of Muslim peoples, the majority being Uyghurs, who speak a language similar to Turkish. Until 1949, less than five percent of the area's population was Han Chinese, but since the Communist revolution, many demobilized soldiers have been sent in as settlers. Han Chinese now comprise about 40 percent of the population. These immigrants dominate industry and administer some of China's worst prisons. Now, they have spawned a new generation of people who are resented by the local population. It's a virtual apartheid, in which Han Chinese and Uyghurs live in completely separate areas, and rarely work together or shop or dine at the same places.

In the airport, I was waiting for Melissa. I'd met her on the internet. A belly dancer from New York, she spoke Chinese and offered to travel with me for part of the forty days to help translate.

Having forgotten to discuss the difference between "Beijing" time and "Xinjiang" or "Uyghur" time, I wondered if she would be there to meet me. This always has to be specified, because Beijing time is two hours ahead of local time; all of China is officially one time zone, but many locals don't adhere to that. Everything official, such as government offices and banks, operate on Beijing time. Socially, people refer to Xinjiang time. It's easy to misunderstand and wind up missing one another. I scanned the airport for a young Chinese woman with New York–style and a bit of belly-dance flair. Suddenly, a tall foreigner in a headscarf hovered overhead. "Tamalyn?"

Melissa is Polish and Lithuanian. She learned Chinese in college, spending part of her studies in China. Her translation skills were needed immediately. "I'm going to find that nasty baggage manager. Can you talk to him?"

The cantankerous man led their discussion in circles. She became more exasperated than I had. "I've hit the 'Great Wall'! That's what makes people crazy in China. You'll understand soon enough."

I had to approach this section of the book delicately, because if I went to officials and said, "I'd like to film and write about the lives of Islamic people in China," they would have shown me a very controlled version of reality, if I were allowed to do the project at all.

Instead, I had to do some hit-and-miss touring around, hoping to find legitimate excuses to peek into people's lives. People practiced not saying anything critical or self-incriminating, and I wanted to be sure not to get them in trouble if they said things they shouldn't.

A lot of hotels are "Chinese only." Melissa heard about a place that was good and cheap, but they turned us away because we were foreigners.

We crossed the street to the Seman Hotel, formerly referred to as the "Russian Embassy." British and Russians used to play spy games in this remote corner of the world. In the late 1800s, the Russian and British empires expanded, coming close to each other in central Asia. There were personal rivalries for information, influence, and Silk Road antiquities. Consulates became listening posts, remaining in use until 1949, when the People's Republic of China was founded. Now, a foreigner visiting Kashgar can choose between staying in the former British consulate and the former Russian consulate.

Uyghur taste is elaborate in every way. Women wear long sequined dresses by day. Colorful, filmy, and sparkly headscarves are more of a fashion statement than a pious religious adherence. The lobby of the Seman was resplendent with carved wood, and floral and paisley marble designs. A relief mural of dancers and musicians decorated the wall behind the front desk. Nearly every inch of the walls and furniture in the budget area was frilly and ornate. One would expect people to be milling about in tuxedos, but most of the clientele were mountain climbers or adventurers who came overland from Pakistan or Tibet. Even more over-the-top was the deluxe section. That was frequented by tour groups from China's large and prosperous cities: Beijing, Shanghai, and the like. Five internet cafés, which doubled as trekking tour agencies, were scattered throughout the hotel premises.

Melissa soon fell in love with "John's Information Café," located just past a carved grape trellis, near a parking lot lined with giant gleaming tour busses. Foreigners congregated there to discuss the best way to bike across Tibet, cross the border into Kyrgyzstan, or find convenient bus routes to Inner Mongolia. By the time Westerners get to Kashgar, they've been almost everywhere else in the world.

The name *Kashgar* conjures up a special mystique, even for the most seasoned travelers. Two years earlier, I'd made a brief visit to Kashgar and been disappointed. Most of the old traditional mud architecture had been torn down. The town was one big dusty construction site with open sewers. Most of the traditional homes that remained standing were in a historic area that tourists had to pay a fee to enter. Square modern buildings built of the typical Chinese bathroom-tile-looking material were springing up like mushrooms on wide new boulevards throughout the city.

This time, the old plaza and its surroundings were reconstructed in theme-park style, like a fantasy version of *1001 Nights*. It was apparent that Uyghurs had become a tourist attraction. Western visitors tried to find real Uyghur life beneath controlled tourist markets, restaurants, costumed camels, and decorated sheep posing for tour busses. Large groups of domestic tourists wore matching hats and were led by flag-waving guides.

Amid the feeding frenzy of clicking cameras, local life continued. Someone had set up a stereo playing Uyghur music. At least thirty men and boys gracefully stepped and twirled, honing their traditional dance skills. Uyghurs are famous throughout China for their joyful music and dance.

We wandered onto a street too narrow for tour busses. "Peddlers Street" was where metal smiths, melon vendors, and instrument makers plied their trades, much as their forefathers had. It was alive with music as instrument makers tested out strings, and metal smiths tapped and clanked while making tools, heating metal to bright red, cutting, cooling, and then reheating. A sewing-machine shop displayed rows and rows of new treadle machines. We dipped beneath a row of *dutars* (one of many varieties of long-necked relatives of the lute) and watched a young man concentrate on the finishing touches of a *rawab* (a stringed instrument with a snakeskin cover). Lining the wall was the dried skin of a giant snake at least twenty feet long. A man started to play virtuoso rhythms on a *dap* (a frame drum made of snakeskin lined with rings to make a jingling noise).

Forging ahead, we found a park with a giant lighted Ferris wheel, a neon fountain, a man-made river, and fake fireworks made from tiny lights. A group of boys, thrilled to get a rise out of two foreigners, tried to unleash a scorpion from a jar onto our laps. We screamed and ran, then walked on and found a back way to the old area of tiny streets, bypassing a ticket booth set up by the government. It was pitch black and we could barely see two steps ahead of us.

On wide boulevards, towering modern buildings with neon signs written in Chinese characters lit the sky. Uyghurs write in Arabic script. We saw many small signs and announcements in Uyghur, but the biggest, loudest, and most overwhelming signs were all in Chinese.

We looked up at a giant statue of Mao hovering overhead. Melissa said, "'People's Park.' Every town has one."

Two yellow arches framed a neon sign in English: "Best Food Burger."

I was torn between lamenting the Chinese big-money glitzy façade and enjoying the visual feast. On one hand, all the lights and glam were modern-day extensions of the looming Mao statue, telling the Uyghurs "we're in charge" with one big stomp. On the other hand, it was Uyghurs who were milling about the parks; they weren't rejecting this extension of China's megalomania, they were just resigned.

We had arrived on time for the famous Sunday market. This is where farmers, driving everything from horse and buggies to electric cars, sell produce and trade goods ranging from tires to metal boxes, clothes, and animals. Unless they plan to scale a mountain, most foreign travelers arrive in Kashgar, hit the Sunday market, and head out the next day. It looked like Melissa and I might stay awhile, awaiting my big suitcase making its way over the Khunjerab Pass.

First thing in the morning, I made a beeline to the hotel lobby, hoping to track down my lost bag. After several attempts, using a little red pay phone, I managed to get a call through to Abu Dhabi. Luckily, the person who answered was Yajie, a Chinese woman I'd had brief contact with. She said, "I'm the only person who would believe that the Kashgar Airport doesn't have a computer and that they refuse to make a report. I understand because I'm Chinese." She assured, "It's not in Abu Dhabi, so it must be in Islamabad." She told me to send a fax and promised to talk to her boss, adding, "Then all we have to worry about is getting it to China. There's only one flight a week to Kashgar, and it rarely has space in the luggage compartment." Despite the odds, I remained confident that gravity would not have permitted my suitcase to fall off the planet. It contained costumes for a theatre show I would be producing in Miami and all the paperwork for over $20,000 in grants that I had to administer.

Although the trekking agencies advertised all sorts of travel services as well as long distance calls, I had yet to meet anyone working in one who had been on an airplane. One employee sensed my frustration. After I told him my lost bag story, he carefully explained the process, "When you arrive at the airport, there is a moving belt. That's where you should look for your baggage." He was earnestly trying to help, but I was torn between laughter and anger.

A young woman sat, eyeing me intently. I was so perturbed by my suitcase situation that I paid her no mind. On my way out of the lobby, she walked behind me and I heard a quiet voice say, "Can I come with you?" Wearing a homemade A-line dress with cap sleeves and a high neck, she was obviously local. The design looked like something out of the early 1960s. The fabric was traditional Atlas silk weaving, which incorporates multicolored stripes into uneven patterns. She had light brown hair and light eyes, but there was still an Asian look to her appearance. The girl, Aynur, spoke in soft, gentle tones so measured that I often had to wait for her to speak or respond.

"I'm going to the livestock market. You must have been there a million times."

"Can I go?" she asked again.

Melissa breezed across the lobby in a flowing skirt with a sparkly Uyghur scarf on her head. "I see you've already started shopping," I said.

"Belly dancers and glitter . . . that's a dangerous combination!" She laughed while tightening the knot under her hair.

I added, "We're going to the livestock market."

She grinned. "Cool!"

We hailed a cab and sped down a smooth highway. Two years prior,

I couldn't spend much time at the livestock market because I had felt sorry for the animals. This time, I was fascinated by the humans. It was interesting to see farmers in all sorts of traditional hats: square ones covered with embroidery, tall caps lined with sheepskin, and felt hats like American gangsters wore in the 1930s.

There were rows of fat furry butts. They belonged to a special breed of sheep, sought after for their globs of pure fat. Once their wool was trimmed away, the sheep looked scrawny. Little tufts of fur and a flourish of fluorescent pink paint were added to their hip bones for decoration.

Donkeys kicked up dust. Vociferously protesting cows were led onto pickup trucks with ropes around their necks. It was noisy and smelly, and our lungs were lined with dust. Aynur looked with curiosity at me, then Melissa. There was no shortage of foreigners with telephoto lenses clicking away; ranchers went about their business as usual, used to the fact that they might appear in magazines or coffee-table books in some far-removed European country.

Aynur was a student of hospitality and tourist services. She asked, "Is this what foreigners are looking for?"

Melissa replied, "People want to experience real Uyghur life."

A man was cutting slices from huge *hami* melons (which seem somewhere between a cantaloupe and honey dew). Another man stretched and tossed moistened flour, shaping it into a big circular rope that was soon to become traditional *lagman* noodles.

Kashgar has definitely been discovered, and its exotic allure brings such crowds that the mystique is becoming mainstream.

The Sunday market, Bazaar Yildiz, is an attempt to co-opt what the Uyghurs, Kyrgiz, and Tajiks have come together to partake of for centuries: trading, bartering, and eating melons. What used to be an empty lot is now enclosed in a square cement structure. Neat stalls sell traditional Atlas silks, instruments, hats, and a wide array of household goods, each in its own designated row.

The multiethnic Turkic–Central Asian multitudes didn't bother with this new building, preferring the chaos that ensued outside. Dust-covered streets and a few remaining vacant lots were alive with barter. Piles of produce lay on tarps, cartloads of merchandise ambled by, and people slept amid the melons they were selling. The surrounding streets were packed with people, donkey carts, and horse and buggies. Villagers climbed aboard motor-tricycle driven platforms to ride out of town.

We climbed onto a flat-bed donkey cart. There was nothing to hold on to but each other. The driver, whose donkey was handsomely adorned with bells, flowers, and metallic cords, raced by making his donkey outrun other carts as we struggled not to fall off. Aynur perched on the edge, looking puzzled again. Her eyes darted from Melissa to me.

She said, in a serious tone, "I don't do this."

After the wild ride, Aynur asked, "Do you like *samsas*?" She sat us on a bench. A man was chopping lamb meat and piling it on a wooden tray. He grabbed white globs from a mound of sheep fat, which was as large as the pile of meat, and stuffed both ingredients into small crusts. Aynur said, "Sheep fat is good for health." Melissa and I looked at each other and gulped. The fatty little meat pies were cooked on an open fire.

Aynur then marched us to another set of wooden benches. The main attraction was an outdoor television that dozens of people sat glued to. A woman shaved ice with a small rake-like instrument; put the ice in a bowl; and added a couple of ladles of yoghurt, some sugar syrup, and a bit of water. She tossed the liquid high into the air to mix it, and voila! A refreshingly sweet and sheepy-tasting drink called *duq*.

Later, I went to find a restroom at the market. All the glitz in China can't mask the smell of a bad bathroom. I put some rose oil on my fingers as I held them to my nose. The small, unventilated room was curtained from public view. Three women at a time pooped simultaneously into the same sewer, and then they primped in a cloudy mirror, ignoring the stench.

I started every day trying to scale the "Great Wall" in an ineffectual search for my suitcase. Sometimes I wondered if it actually *had* fallen off the planet and floated away to another galaxy. I searched by phone, internet, and fax. In one internet café, computers seemed to have molasses inside. The seemingly never-ending wild-goose chase led nowhere.

I met a Pakistani gem dealer from Hunza. I figured, the more people I spilled the story to, the more likely someone would eventually find a solution. He told me: "Most people's bags don't come with them. They arrive a week or two later. Traders pay at the airport in Islamabad to have their packages go first. If there is room left, they will load passenger's luggage." I thought how cinematic meeting a jewel trader from Hunza sounded. But he was just a nice, normal man sitting at a slow computer in a booming metropolis along the ancient silk road. I realized I'd reached the point where exotic illusions had melted away.

The weekly flight from Islamabad was scheduled to arrive, so I asked Melissa to come to the airport and wield influence over the mean employees. There was no bag, but at least I learned a new expression. Our young taxi driver wound in and out of traffic, enjoying moments of rowdy irreverence. When passing the airport's gate guard, he hurled an insult by calling him a "turtle egg." I thought how much more creative and articulate his road rage was compared to English words that are usually limited to four letters.

Sitting in one of the internet cafés after being told to send yet another fax to Abu Dhabi, I wished someone would come along so I could let off steam and yell "turtle egg!"

Suddenly, a devastatingly handsome man with coal-black hair sensed my discomfort. He was Pakistani and transported motorcycle accessories between Pakistan and China—probably one of the turtle eggs who'd paid to get his merchandise on my flight, thus causing my luggage to fall off the planet. He took me to a public phone and made about thirty calls to contacts in airports, airlines, and even air-traffic control. He got the same runaround; nothing was accomplished. Then he took me out for a Pakistani lunch.

When he asked about my work, I told him I teach dance, organize shows, and am writing a book. I reached the moment that enthuses most people: talking about how the Islamic world is misunderstood in the U.S. and most of our information is oversimplified, and how I want to share the voices of Islamic people with American readers. He interjected, "Have you met Michael Jackson? He's the greatest dancer in the world!" Luckily, I had, so he was duly impressed.

A sign in the Seman hotel lobby read "Traditional Dance Performance Nightly." One night, we attempted to go but were told it didn't exist. We heard drums and a horn and went running toward the sound. The dance group did one song for a busload of Japanese senior citizens. We followed the performers down several passageways and asked one of the women for a dance lesson.

They led us to a hidden theater where we agreed to trade belly-dance moves for Uyghur steps. A woman, who had red hair with long braids woven in, showed us a few simple-looking moves, which proved difficult when I later practiced in our cramped bathroom, dancing into hanging towels and the shower head.

That evening, a "bowl dance" was about to begin. Each woman's hair was styled in at least five plaits, braided to reach below midthigh. Traditionally, Uyghur dancers weave their grandmothers' hair, shed during brushing, in with their own to add length. Each dancer walked in quick, tiny steps with a plate in each hand and a stack of six breakable bowls balanced on her head. They removed them one by one while dancing, and then— surprise!—water was poured out of the last bowl.

Aynur suggested we go to a restaurant.

"We've been going to restaurants every day," I countered; then changed the subject to the delicious *polo* we'd eaten every day for the last three days. Polo is the Uyghur rendition of pilaf, *pulao* in India, *pilau* in Zanzibar, or *paella* in Spanish. Our favorite place cooked the rice with chunks of lamb, pumpkin, dried apricots, and plenty of sheep fat, and served it with yoghurt and a shredded salad. This dish is claimed to have just the right combination of "heating" and "cooling" foods needed to make the body function properly. I still didn't understand the need for dripping sheep fat, but it tasted surprisingly good.

Aynur said, "Let's go dancing." Our ears perked. We hailed a taxi, which swerved onto the sidewalk to fetch us. She told the driver to "take us to a restaurant."

Brass-lined staircases led to an elegant hall that had a marble floor and flashing neon lit arches. It wasn't packed, but there were a few big tables, including a boy's birthday party with a lot of little kids running around.

A lone keyboard player played for an array of Uyghur singers doing local cover tunes. Dancing ranged from traditional Uyghur, with people dancing their own improvisations focused on the elegant hand and arm movements, to couple's slow dancing done mostly by people of the same sex. Kids jumped and rolled on the floor among them. The most popular style was waltzing to Uyghur songs. One song had a Russian beat, and people kicked and jumped. Whenever the blinding disco lights began, along came an ultramodern beat. Disco dancing was done with finger snaps and arms held high.

On one of our futile attempts to track down my suitcase at the airport, I met a man named Anwar, and he gave me his card. "I am a government official, in charge of tourism. I'll have no problem pulling the necessary strings to bring your suitcase home." I thought, "How lucky to meet a Uyghur who works in the government."

This seemingly important man invited us to a party at a restaurant, with a promise to show us Uyghur culture in action. He met Melissa, Aynur, and me outside and escorted us up an elegant staircase to a circumcision party. In Turkic cultures, circumcision is cause for celebration, and the boys are old enough to enjoy their party.

Everyone at the party ignored us, and it was apparent that Anwar didn't know anyone. Most big restaurants have a banquet hall as well as several private rooms. The hostess led us down a hallway flanked by private rooms. Behind a closed door were four middle-aged men sitting around a coffee table laden with several dishes. They sat quietly dazed. It was obvious that they had been drinking a lot. We were introduced to each by job title he held and government office he was in charge of. What an incredibly boring bunch of bureaucrats! They thought we would be impressed. When asked where the women were, Anwar replied, "The dancers will be coming later."

Aynur said, "I won't be seen here!" We orchestrated a speedy but graceful exit without having to run down the maze of hallways or open random doors until we found our way out.

Melissa had a cold. We told her "keep coughing" to make her illness seem dramatic. Anwar and buddies were too caught up with their own self images, thinking they had snared two foreigners and a college student, to notice that Melissa was hacking to a point where normal people would have called a medic. We feigned panic, exclaiming, "We must take her back to the hotel and straight to bed!" Anwar hailed a taxi and paid to get us back to the hotel. A short distance down the street, Melissa took a deep breath, laughed loudly, and said in perfect Chinese, "Take us to the disco instead."

Aynur directed the driver to a disco. It had one shift in the afternoon, from 3 to 7 PM, and another in the evening, from 7 to 11 PM. At a table, we were given wholesome snacks: dried fruit, almonds, and a bag of microwave popcorn. The concept of going out dancing is different for the Uyghurs than for Westerners. It meant just that—dancing—not drinking or finding a mate. You buy a ticket that's valid for one shift, dance the night away, and leave with the people you came with. A singer belted varied songs, from waltzes to Uyghur traditional, as people danced, circulating around the floor in unison. The décor had detailed columns and low lighting. By any country's standards, this was a nice club. We smiled at our escape.

One day, while walking along a large boulevard in Kashgar, I passed a large white building whose sign, in three different scripts, said Uyghur Traditional Medicine Hospital. "What's that?" I wondered. I have always been fascinated with alternative forms of medicine and have read about Ayurvedic medicine from India and benefited from Chinese medicine, but I didn't know that Uyghurs had their own traditional healing practices.

I told Melissa about the hospital, and we each decided to seek help for our minor infirmities: Melissa's cold and my water retention. A puzzled nurse ushered us into a room and gave us numbers. It appeared that this might not be a place to seek traditional medicine, rather a regular hospital where traditional people go. The doctor was Chinese, not Uyghur, and two people walked around with casts on their arms. We tried to ask if the place provided traditional or modern medicine, and the only answer we could get was "Take a number and wait your turn." We asked the same question of a receptionist; she replied, "Take a number."

We enlisted Aynur's help and she got us into a doctor's office. His cell phone kept ringing, interrupting our questions, so we were sent up several cement staircases to the top-floor administrative office of a Dr. Anwar. (Anwar is a common name, and we had already put our boring-government-official experience behind us.) We sat in dark polished wooden chairs beneath organizational charts painted on the wall as Dr. Anwar patiently introduced his ancient profession.

"Uyghur medicine has a long history, about 2700 years, and is related to the ancient Greek medical system. First, we take your pulse, which can be fast or slow and have different qualities. There are four characters of people, which follow the four elements that are present in everything on earth. These are: water, fire, air, and wood. There may be some similarities with Chinese or Indian medicine, and often a doctor will decide if you should be treated by Uyghur, Chinese or Western medicine. This hospital is integrated, with all three."

He continued, "There are a couple of ways to learn Uyghur medicine. The Urumqi Medical University has added Uyghur traditional medicine as a specialty. In Hoten, it is a four-year program specializing in Uyghur medicine." That was where Dr. Anwar had studied. Hoten is a small city on the edge of the Taklamakan Desert known as the home of Uyghur Traditional Medicine. He added, "Another way is that people learn from their elders with information passed down through generations."

Melissa and I wanted checkups. He said, "Come tomorrow without eating breakfast."

When we arrived the next day, Anwar was in a meeting, so we waited in the hallway until he came out. He took us to a doctor who checked Melissa's pulse. She was given several prescriptions for herbs to improve her digestion and change her sleep pattern. Balancing the humors in her body would rectify her sinus cold.

He checked my pulse and said, "Everything's fine." He asked, "Do you live alone?" and guessed correctly that I am single, mentioning, "That can aggravate an imbalance." Two tonics were prescribed for general health, strength, and digestion.

We asked about the four elements (a.k.a. humors) that need to be in balance, and the status of ours. There are four combinations: dry and hot (fire), dry and cold (wood), damp and hot (air), and damp and cold (water). I had too much cold, while Melissa had too much heat and dampness. We were both told not to drink anything cold. He told me I needed to eat more fats, especially sheep fat and lots of meat, to heat my system and balance the cold. Melissa needed to add milk and honey to her diet.

Anwar accompanied us from window to window as we paid in one place, dropped off our prescriptions in another, and picked them up at another. Melissa ended up with a big bag, while I had just two things. One bottle contained tiny round herbal pellets with instructions to take five in the morning and five at night; the other contained "honey plaster," which is an herbal paste in a sweet base, to be taken by the spoonful.

I read up on herbal medical practices and learned that ancient Greek medicine, which was created around 430 BC, is philosophically virtually the same as Uyghur medicine. The idea of different humors is also used in Chinese, Indian, and even one form of Vietnamese traditional medicine. The prescription of sheep fat to heat the body is used in Chinese medicine as well. Indirectly through their conquests, Arabs got their medicine from the Greeks. Xinjiang was mentioned as one of the places involved in this information exchange. I wondered if this ancient medicine survives in perhaps its purest form in Xinjiang.

In the plaza surrounding Id Kah Mosque, Mohammed, a traditional Uyghur doctor, was crouched on the sidewalk mixing up a fragrant herbal remedy by combining plants with a giant bag of sugar and putting it through a press. Out came a dark green paste that the practitioner said was for heart patients. He had many herbs, as well as jars of Nescafe, in his shop. I asked what instant coffee cured. He answered quite seriously "It is to make money."

Mohammed's shop was a popular place, so we waited our turn, looking at teas and discussing the names of herbs and plants. Finally, he sat and patiently answered my list of questions.

He told me "I studied in Hoten for four years with Abdumejit, a famous doctor," then wrote down the doctor's telephone number for me. He said "I prefer to learn from firsthand practice rather than books," then urged me to visit Hoten and meet his teacher.

Mohammed's explanation of the history of local medicine was that it originated with the Uyghurs and is similar to ancient Arabic medicine. There was mutual exchange of information between many cultures after that, which accounts for the similarities between the various medicinal traditions.

"People respect Uyghur medicine now more than before because it works better than Chinese or Western medicine. A respected political leader once had vitiligo, where the skin loses pigmentation in patches, and was cured by Uyghur medicine. Since then people see it in a positive light. Uyghur medicine was more respected before the Cultural Revolution, then the government said it was archaic. We never stopped practicing, and now it's gaining popularity again."

I asked why he used sugar with the herbal mixture. He said, "Sugar is good for you. When mixed with some herbs, it can increase their effectiveness."

When taking my pulse, he used four fingers because each finger feels something different. He couldn't shake my hand socially because he was devoutly religious, but pulse reading was acceptable because he was a doctor. Two years ago, I'd been taken to visit an old Sufi, who checked my pulse through a plastic bag over my wrist.

"The four elements of fire, water, air, and wood should be equal and in balance. They affect each other." Mohammed seemed to be using more intuition than anything as he looked at both hands and decided which to check. He told me, "Your type is cold and damp. Combined, we call it 'water.' Eat meat, fat, honey, and walnuts, but stay away from milk and yoghurt." I asked about the snakes, lizards, frogs, and seahorses, which were dried and in jars. Aynur translated that they were for strengthening the body. Pointing to a big jar of pearls, Mohammed said, "You heat them over the fire, grind, and mix with egg white to apply to the skin."

One thing I wanted to understand better was which foods heat the body and which cool it down. He gave me some examples, which relate to temperament rather than temperature: some foods that are cooling are chilies, most Chinese teas, fruits, vegetables, milk, and yoghurt; some foods that are heating are meat, fat, polo, kebab, soup, samsa, nan bread, honey, sugar, nuts, coffee, and black pepper.

☾ ☆ ⁎ ⋅ ⁎ ⋅ ⁎ ⋅

Reality sunk in and I became resigned to the fact that I might never see my suitcase again. Melissa and I decided to explore other parts of Xinjiang, starting with Urumqi, the province's largest city and where my friend Pasha's family lived. It had an airport in case my bag was located.

I looked around and reminisced a bit about Kashgar while waiting for a set of bus tickets at the internet café–travel agency combo where I'd made many a phone call, always having to explain where Abu Dhabi was.

I looked out the door, wondering why the sidewalks were so wide that cars often parked or even drove on them. Then I did some people watching. A lot of Uyghurs have light honey-colored or even blue eyes. Eyebrows that grow straight across the forehead in one line are a sign of beauty, but few women have them naturally, so some people pencil them in over the bridge of the nose. Some women were swathed in thick headscarves, covering their necks and, at times, even their faces. It's typical of Kashgar for women to place a brown square of thickly knit fabric over their heads, covering the entire face, eyes and all. It's often worn with a long brown coat. More often, women have adopted a more liberal version of the Islamic dress code, keeping their arms covered with sleeves, which can be transparent. Headscarves are often transparent, showing hair both in front and back. Sometimes women wear ankle-length nylons with knee-length dresses. Many young women are good Muslims but don't follow the dress code at all. Aynur was an example. Although she would be considered demure by U.S. standards, her arms were uncovered and she didn't wear a headscarf. This didn't lessen her resolve to follow her spiritual practice.

I did a last minute e-mail check while we waited. Surprise! Yajie, the woman I'd first called in Abu Dhabi, had located my suitcase in Pakistan and was having it shipped to Kashgar on the next flight! I sent an e-mail begging her to have them forward it to Urumqi instead.

The double-decker sleeper bus to Urumqi was full of bunk beds, crisp white sheets, and chrome railings, and had televisions on both levels. I commented, "It looks like a hospital on wheels."

Such sterility was only inside the bus. Laying down for over a day was tiring, like being in a sick bed. I was relieved when we stopped for breakfast at a dusty truck stop. It was full of melon vendors hanging sheep carcasses, for chopping later, and people dicing vegetables for a spicy stew that was served with dumplings, in a synthesis of Chinese and Uyghur roadside cuisine. Upon reentering the bus, all passengers had to remove their shoes and put them in plastic bags.

Going to the bathroom was an adventure. In the wee hours of the morning, my stomach was in pain. I had to go—desperately. At last, outside of a small town, the driver stopped and made a motion. I could see no visible sign of a bathroom. Another lady walked me to the edge of a mud hut, where a low metal fence surrounded some dirt that had a small indentation full of all sorts of defecation. She did her business, in plain view.

There were all manner of pits throughout the day: deep ones that didn't smell too bad and the non-pit toilet au natural. I thought I was being smart wearing slip on shoes for the bus ride, even though they had a high platform. Little did I know that I would have to hike through broken stones, dodging poops of all sizes and wads of toilet paper decorating the scrubby desert brush like white flowers. Men headed one direction and women another. The places were all in view of passing traffic, but people were used to not looking.

We passed an area of wind farms, hundreds of huge modern windmills harnessing energy. After twelve hours of so many people sleeping, snacking, and removing their shoes repeatedly, the bus stank. For the most part, the scenery was dusty and drab, stark and grey.

☾ ☆ ⁎ ⁎ ☆ ⁎ ⁎

After twenty-six hours in horizontal mode, we arrived in Urumqi, a metropolis that's claim to fame is being "the world's farthest city from any major body of water." A big, modern, predominately ethnically Chinese metropolis, Urumqi is also one of the only places in Xinjiang where you see all thirteen of the province's nationalities in one place. These groups include the Tajiks; Turkic speaking Muslim groups including the Uyghurs, Kazakhs (some are still nomadic horsemen), Kyrgizs, and Uzbeks; and the Muslim, Mandarin-speaking Hui.

One section of Urumqi is still Uyghur. A walk of a few blocks showed an amazing contrast. Whereas urbane Chinese women dressed in tank tops and any length skirts, once we entered the Uyghur area, appearances changed completely. Uyghurs were always more conservative than their Chinese sisters. Men wore traditional square hats. Women could be seen in headscarves, along with high rhinestone-studded platform shoes. The Chinese area had upscale boutiques; Uyghurs shopped at street stalls and winding bazaars.

Once again, Uyghurs were treated as a tourist attraction for busloads of well-heeled Chinese tourists from more populated eastern cities. They descended on the International Bazaar, perhaps better described as "Uyghurland," en masse. The new fantasy reconstruction was built in the style of Aladdin, complete with minarets and domes. Tourist shops lined the open area. An obese camel, dressed in Atlas silk and roses, posed as tourists climbed aboard it for a fee.

Near a Kentucky Fried Chicken and an underground Carrefour megastore, we waited in line for yummy traditional Uyghur nan bread. This was the best I'd ever had, although it was also adapted for the Chinese taste and came with a special gift box. The tour groups were formidable, jostling in front of one another in line, grabbing the bread before I could, and shoving bills over my head. Abdusalam, one of the bread makers, told us that he worked twelve hour days, making between 2000 and 2500 pieces per day. Behind a glass window with a sanitation department certificate on it, another guy formed the dough and then handed it to Abdusalam. Abdusalam patted it some more, dipped it in a mixture of milk and sesame seeds, then placed the dough on a round stone with a cloth cover, which was used to plop it against the salt-covered wall of a deep coal-heated oven. Using a metal stick, he removed each one, brushed it with melted butter, and then returned it to the oven.

Each time a piece came out, a clamor ensued. I usually lost. The woman by me had taken five, so when the next came out, Abdusalam placed it slightly out of her reach. I was armed with a plastic bag that he tossed the bread into before she could reach across. I handed the attendant the equivalent of twenty-five cents and walked away munching. Melissa said, "You have to show some muscle in China, especially when dealing with tourists."

Across the street, visible from the tourist market but seemingly miles away, there were many beggars: old women, limbless men sitting with their stumps exposed, and quadriplegic people laying on wooden carts unable to move. I became angry, wondering what happened to the premise of helping the poor in a country that still claims to be communist. A child, about twelve years old, was wrapped in hospital bandages with scarred and diseased skin exposed. He or she was unrecognizable, lying on a wooden wagon with a box for people to put money in. The sidewalk was packed with people pushing carts of merchandise and rushing to get places; this very ill child had been laid out helplessly, in the middle of it all, by someone who would be collecting the money at the end of the day.

It was getting dark and we looked up at the sky. A death-defying tightrope performance was taking place three stories overhead between two buildings. Below, groups of Chinese tourists ate a sumptuous banquet. The only safety net provided for the tightrope walkers was made from the many bowls of noodles on three hundred people's plates.

A man and woman dressed in folkloric Uyghur clothing walked the rope, holding a long stick for balance, executing feats of increasing difficulty. First, it was walking forward, then back. Then they did acrobatic splits and headstands and pretended to fall, landing with the rope between their legs. Finally, the woman sat in a chair, posing in difficult contortions, and the man rode the rope on a unicycle and then executed a dance, jumping around on the rope.

We were straining to watch and film while trying to survive the perils of big-city life in Urumqi: dodging tour busses driving on the sidewalk, and avoiding getting stepped on by a fat camel that worked the crowd with its bored-looking driver in tow.

September 11, 2006, marked the first anniversary of my *40 Days & 1001 Nights* project. It was a very good day. Melissa brought some delicious nan bread from Abdusalam. We each ate a spoonful of rose jelly from Mohammed, the traditional medicine doctor in Kashgar. Purported to be healthy, it tasted delicious on fresh nan.

"Nothing is easy in China" was our new mantra. I couldn't make heads or tails out of buying a new SIMM card for my phone, and we couldn't call outside the hotel from our rooms. Melissa was experiencing a bout of homesickness for her husband, so we took to the streets in search of a landline. In the street market, there were lots of kiosks and tables that had little red telephones. It took several tries to get a call through. When we hung up, a bell rang to indicate how long we'd spoken.

Great news! My bag had arrived! The ride from downtown Urumqi to the airport took forty minutes, through neighborhoods of high-rises and industrial sprawl.

At the airport, a guard told me to show him my ticket so he could let me in. I had the boarding pass from Islamabad to Kashgar, but that wasn't enough; I needed an actual ticket. I had the receipt for the trip from Abu Dhabi to Islamabad. It was shaped like a ticket, and since he didn't read English, it worked. I saw my familiar bulging tan duffle bag in the distance. The sixteen-day suitcase saga had reached a happy ending. Yay!

My friend Pasha is known as one of the most beautiful women in China. Her family, whom I had met two years before, invited Melissa and me for lunch. Just in time to celebrate! We climbed an ornate golden stairway curving to the top floor of this restaurant that was the pinnacle of Uyghur elegance. Chandeliers, rich brocade and fringe curtains with crystal-gauze linings filled our eyes. Even the wicker chairs were unique and full of detail.

This was an experience in Uyghur restaurant etiquette. Even in fancy places, you pay when the order is taken. The waitress put down a brass teapot and Pasha's sister, Kamelia, a construction company director in a tailored business suit, set about taking care of the table's needs. She poured a bit of tea to clean each cup and then tossed the liquid into a plastic container shaped like a miniature waste basket. She then filled our cups with the fragrant golden colored brew and cleaned each saucer thoroughly with a napkin. It is customary in Xinjiang for the host or head person at each table to clean dishes and utensils before eating. I wondered if this custom came from the old days in the desert when everything was covered with a layer of dust.

Whenever our tea ran low, Kamelia poured more for everyone. As each of the many dishes arrived, she took a pair of chopsticks and served a few bites in each saucer. People don't pass food or utensils. It isn't seen as rude to reach or lean across the table. Even at this most fancy of places, the waitress piled a bunch of tissues and pairs of disposable wooden chopsticks at the end of the table for Kamelia to distribute.

Dishes of food were brought at random, starting with big skewers of lamb kebab, deliciously spiced with red pepper and coriander. Each kebab contained three chunks of lamb and two chunks of pure fat. The proper way to eat them is to either bite the meat directly off the skewer or to slip it off with chopsticks, which is more difficult. Water was not served, but tea pots were constantly refilled. Sweet and salty dishes were served intermittently. I thought, "In the U.S. we have sweets *after* a meal, and in Indonesia, they commonly eat sweets before." In Xinjiang, dessert was eaten *during* the meal, which made sense because some dishes were very spicy. The sweets cooled the palate, so we could taste our tea again. We had some spicy noodles and green vegetables, then crepes filled with walnuts and sugar, followed by eggplant and a meat dish, then sweetened cakes of corn and peas, and lastly, mutton-filled ravioli-like dumplings in broth. It seemed like the dishes would never stop coming. Leftover food is rarely thrown away; it's poured into clear plastic bags to be taken home.

Kamelia took us to a vast hall of costume makers on an upper floor of the fabric bazaar. They took measurements and sewed on location, using foot-pedal machines. Walls lined with dozens of small stalls offered all varieties of folk and belly-dance costumes. Each cost $50 to have handmade to one's size and specification. The cost would've been at least $700 for the same thing in the U.S. We each ordered four costumes and dance shoes with gold floral designs sewn on the toes.

Pasha's niece Sameera said, "This is the big city. We even have low-fat samsas. There is a restaurant which replaces the fat with chunks of onion."

Down an alley in a room with simple tables and the dirtiest floor I'd ever seen, they served us tea. Sameera rinsed the cups, as her aunt had done the day before, dumping the tea into a plastic garbage pail, then pouring more for us to drink.

After several days in Urumqi, we decided to move on to Turpan. In Urumqi, the hotels had been square and drab with equally dour staff. Two and a half hours to the east, in Turpan, we were escorted down a street with grape trellises overhead to a hotel that had something for everyone: cheap dorms, midpriced rooms, and luxury for those who could afford it. It was gorgeous, with ornate carved architecture and grapevines all around. As we wound through an expansive complex of pastel-colored domes and pillars, we heard music from a folkloric dance performance and hurried to see the show.

Rows of young women created formations, floating then spinning with utmost precision. After a series of regional folkdances (including some acrobatic men's dances and a reenactment of romance amid the grapes) a flute player played a song with strange and amazing effects, simulating conversations between different species of birds. Sometimes he played so fast that I wondered how he breathed. The percussionist went a mile a minute on his dap, which is held in one hand and drummed delicately with the fingers of both hands. It requires great strength to handle. A *qalun*, like the ganun played by Ikhwani Safaa for my CD in Zanzibar, was played with hammers. In Zanzibar, they plucked the strings with metal finger pieces.

When an audience participation part came, the entire cast encouraged Japanese, Chinese, and Austrian tourists to join a circle and do a chicken dance. A dancer deliberately dropped her rose, choosing a man from the audience to kneel down and pick it up with his mouth. Finally, there was normal Uyghur music and dance. The lead dancer was shocked that I knew some moves and told everyone else. After picture time, they surrounded Melissa and me, asking questions and giving us their phone numbers. The troupe wanted us to demonstrate our dancing but there was no music. We danced silently—me doing Arabic-style belly dance, and Melissa doing Turkish.

Soon, the dap player, a rounded middle-aged man, executed some agile hip circles, picked up a *dumbek* (Middle Eastern drum), and played Arabic rhythms at hyperspeed. In Uyghur music, playing really fast is a well-honed skill. In Arabic music, taking time to savor the feeling is essential. It was hard for me to turn up the speed, but we must have done something right. The entire group adopted us immediately, and we were whisked away in a minivan to eat dinner with them.

Outdoor night markets are the best way to sample local foods anywhere in Asia. At a most attractive, brightly lit outdoor night market, we ate delicious food at long tables. One dish after another was laid on the table and then washed down with tea. The adorable dancers were between seventeen and nineteen years old, tiny, delicate, and bubbling over with enthusiasm. Two of them were daughters of the flutist. Their mother sold tickets at the door. They explained their daily routine: rehearsal for three hours in the morning, home to rest and eat lunch, back at 2 PM to do their makeup and get ready for the evening show. It never varied. This was what they did, seven days a week.

The next morning, our first dance lesson was held under one of many grape trellises. The two lead dancers taught us beautiful and difficult combinations. Gulipari, who had just graduated from performing arts school, demonstrated a series of backbends where she literally folded herself in half again and again. Anipa, at 37 years old was the senior dancer of the group. Wearing a skirt just above her knees and high heeled shoes, she led us across the cement dance floor combining elaborate arm patterns with steps and turns.

We had liked our time in Kashgar and Urumqi, but Turpan had something special. It seemed to rotate on a different axis. Drivers were courteous. Ethnic groups got along. People were gentle and the place was peaceful. Even the dancing was more refined. We had to rethink our statement "Nothing's easy in China." Life was starting to flow.

Turpan is full of "grape streets." Our hotel was along one and the trellises overhead had bunches of grapes hanging from them. It was illegal to pick the grapes because they were needed for shelter and decoration. Turpan is unbearably hot in the summer, so grapevines provide much-needed shade.

Melissa found another John's Information Café, right across the grape trellis from our hotel, We recognized an interesting group of Austrians from the previous night's chicken dance and drank milk tea with them. Yakub, the leader of this small personalized tour, had been part of the Haight-Ashbury scene in the 1960s. Now, he is married and has six children and a grandchild. For the past twenty-five years, he has lived in an area of India near Tibet and has a specialized following of adventurous souls who patronize his tour business. In my journeys through the Islamic world, the subculture of world travelers who aren't afraid to forge their own paths has been a compelling part of the journey. So many people find freedom to live unconventional lives on their own terms, seeing beyond the fear factor.

He leads his groups to exotic out-of-the-way places such as Yemen and Tibet. When we met them, the group consisted of three white-haired adventurers who started in Islamabad, went through Hunza, and traveled overland to Kashgar. One couple had camel-caravanned across the Sahara in Niger and the single grandmother had recently traveled the backroads of Sumatra. Yakub invited us to join them on a jaunt around town in a horse carriage.

We heard bells and the clattering of hooves on the slippery cobble-stone street. A heavyset man in a Uyghur hat arrived driving an ornately carpeted flat-bed cart. His bell-laden horse skidded to a stop in front of John's Café. We rode out of town, past mud houses and multi-colored, ornately tiled mosques. Even the mud and dust looked clean. People were friendly and waved as we passed.

Suddenly, the cart stopped. We got off and entered a private home made of mud. Thousands of bunches of grapes hung from ceiling to floor to dry. This was part of the raisin-making process.

Two healthy-looking white goats lay eyeing us as the family went about their business, kindly letting us snoop and ogle. It seemed strange to enter someone's house like this, but they seemed to like our enthusiasm. Yakub knew the residents of several homes and often brought tours inside.

The baffled driver had no idea why Yakub was leading him onto out-of-the-way dirt roads. He tried to take us along the paved roads to tourist sites, but Yakub had other ideas. When he pointed down a dirt road, the driver protested, "It's too dusty for you."

We chimed in, "We don't mind."

Yakub didn't speak Chinese or Uyghur, but he had no problem communicating with the locals. Soon we were in another home, which had a colorfully decorated bed on wheels and a teddy bear at the entrance. Melissa pointed out a bicycle next to a giant mound of coal and said, "That's a scene you'll find everywhere in China." (Coal is still a main source of heat and cooking fuel throughout China.) There were even more grapes hanging from the ceiling. The mother started to make tea, but a neighbor came and invited us over to see her baby.

The three-month-old baby named Arafat lay in a traditional Uyghur cradle made of carved wood. His pants were open to reveal a wooden cap on his penis, attached to a tube that drained into a container hidden beneath his cradle. To keep him from pulling it off, his arms were strapped down. He was rendered completely immobile by two wide embroidered straps. This may sound cruel, but it's a tradition. And although it seems like it could stunt development, Uyghurs grow up moving beautifully. Arafat was alert and happy; he didn't cry at all. His eyes twinkled when one of the Austrians sang a lullaby in German and when I practiced Uyghur dancing for him.

For miles around, every house had limitless hanging grapes. There were grape fields as far as the eye could see. The horse cart took us on more dirt roads, past fields of grapes and a graveyard where the tombstones were made of mud bricks piled in triangular formations. Islamic graveyards are often simple and natural: just bare earth and plain stones, no flowers or fancy carvings.

Back in Turpan, we all shared a bottle of white wine made in Loulan, a town where ancient six-foot-tall Xinjiang mummies were found. It is now home to the famous Lop Nor nuclear testing site. The wine tasted good, but I hoped it wasn't radioactive. We said our goodbyes as the Austrians caught a bus to Dunhuang, the next province over, to see ancient Buddhist caves.

By the time we returned to the hotel, it was show time again. We intended to go to the show every night. After it was over, Gulipari, the lead dancer, invited us to go out with her group. The flute player motioned us to his van, but Gulipari refused to go. We never knew why. The group took us to a fancy outdoor restaurant with dancing. It was like the places in Kashgar that had a keyboard player and several singers.

Everyone sat around the table, and loads of food rotated on the lazy Susan. Some dishes were good and others odd, like sheep innards and thousand-year-old black, pungent eggs. It was the nineteenth birthday of one of the male dancers. Some of his friends came, and most of our group left suddenly, without taking us. We were puzzled.

Anipa, the dance mistress, sat with us and really wanted Melissa and me to belly dance. I happened to have a CD, so we danced to one of my songs from Zanzibar. Everyone went crazy. The dance floor filled up, and people's dancing was so polished that I suspected this restaurant was a hangout for professional performers. Men danced passionately with proud and elegant posture. They also danced in couples, sometimes men and women together, other times in pairs of men or pairs of women, doing waltzes and couple dances. Wild Spanish bubblegum (teenage pop) music played, and the dance floor turned into a frenzied free for all.

The next day, Anipa invited us to her home for lunch. Weathered beds with no mattresses were set up all over the courtyard of her modern-block complex. We learned that in more traditional homes people sleep on the roof in the summer, move to the yard in September, and then inside for the winter. This custom carried over into modern city life. When the beds were not being used for sleeping, small piles of peppers were laid on them to dry.

We climbed six flights of stairs to Anipa's apartment, which she shared with another friend. There was no clutter, which was true of every Uyghur home we visited. I thought about how this reflects people's lives. For example, Anipa was thirty-seven and danced for a living. That's what she'd done all her life. She wasn't running around multitasking, with her energy dispersed in all directions like we are in the U.S.

In her apartment, she set up a traditional Uyghur welcoming table that was low and surrounded by cushions and set with fancy dishes of nan bread, cookies, sweets, dried fruit, and candies. We watched VCDs (inexpensive DVDs which cost about $2 in China) of Uyghur dancers, ate polo, and got sleepy.

Melissa woke me up on time for the hotel's dance performance. So far, we hadn't missed a show and joked "We'll soon know it by heart." We were completely baffled when the drummer's wife, who took care of the front door, wouldn't let us in and rudely closed the curtain to block our view. Melissa and I had always been willing to pay, but the woman had repeatedly refused to accept money. We didn't know what was going on. This sudden and unexplained switch from adoption to rejection was a mystery which hurt and disappointed us.

Anyway, we left and ran into the horse and buggy driver from a few days before. He offered to take us to "the best place in town." Crossing Turpan in his cart, he dropped us off at the outdoor restaurant where we had partied with the nineteen-year-olds. A woman in a sparkly dress named Jamila kept asking me to dance. She took photos and invited us to have a traditional Uyghur meal in her home the following day.

Jamila lived several blocks away in a five-floor walk-up apartment house. Constructed bathroom-tile-style on the outside, it was fancy inside. It was in keeping with Uyghur detail-oriented style and their love of elegance. The apartment had absolutely no clutter. Most rooms were unfurnished, making them spacious and comfortable. The only real furniture was a dining room table and chairs. All the other rooms had thick wall-to-wall oriental carpets on the floors and some of the walls. Ornate chandeliers lit the rooms. Every inch of the remaining walls and ceilings were papered with floral-patterned metallic wallpaper. Doors had carved details as did the moldings and the archways between rooms.

There were no beds. In Xinjiang it is common to sleep on mats, which are tucked away in a little alcove by day. Three suitcases stacked in a corner held some belongings. Jamila had a large television, on which we watched what looked almost like a Chinese version of *American Idol*. A guy who sang songs by Queen in Chinese with a troupe of male backup dancers in zebra-print suits won.

We sat down at the table, which held nan, dried fruits, and sweets. Jamila's gentle, accommodating husband did the cooking and served noodles, pies with Chinese cabbage inside, and assorted skewers. Later he made a delicious noodle and lamb soup.

Jamila invited us to a circumcision party held by one of her friends. She was late and we weren't comfortable going in alone. Across the street was a *department store*. It had several floors of stalls selling sneakers, electronics, and clothing. It looked similar to American department stores, except that each department had a different owner and many departments sold the same items. We returned to the banquet hall and saw the recently circumcised boy running around chasing his friends. He was seven years old, the age of circumcision in Xinjiang. They say it's easier for an older boy to take care of it and not get an infection. His mother and sisters greeted guests in what looked like bride's and bridesmaid's dresses and updos, like helmets, sprayed with glitter hairspray. Jamila led us to one of many tables with a lazy Susan and laden with the requisite sweets, nan, fruit, nuts, and rose tea. Children twirled and played on the dance floor.

Lights dimmed and a show of Xinjiang-style dancers began. They changed costumes and did a Bollywood number, then a belly-dance piece with candles in each hand, to one of the songs I had performed to on the *Bellydance Superstars* DVD. Bootleg versions of this DVD are sold all over China, and some of the women were thrilled when Melissa told them that it was me that they'd been watching in their living rooms.

The hostess asked me to dance. Jamila explained, "If they like the way a person dances, she gets a scarf," adding that if I danced well, it would give the hostess good "face," a Chinese concept that is a little hard to understand.

Since Uyghurs use mostly upper body movements when they dance and Arabic-style belly dancing is more earthy and sensual, I requested a Uyghur pop song by a girl band, then focused on my hands, arms, and quick spins. I was awarded a big piece of Atlas silk, so they must have liked my dancing.

The mother and her sisters motioned for Melissa and me to join the family lineup. The boy, who was dressed in a safari suit, had stripes of glittery paint in his hair. Poised and self-assured, he took the microphone and gave a speech. Translated, it went something like "Thank you mother and father for taking care of me. When I am older, I will send you to Mecca."

Melissa, Jamila, and I were all given scarves. Many men asked us to dance with them, but Jamila stopped Melissa at one point and showed her how to put her hand on her chest, bow her head, and gracefully decline. She explained that "it is improper for a woman to dance with the same man three times, unless she is his wife."

☾ ☆ ⁎ ⁎ ⁎ ⁎

Toyuq is known locally as an important Islamic pilgrimage site, and some Uyghurs say that going to Toyuq seven times is as good as taking the pilgrimage to Mecca. Jamila said, "It is best to do both at least once in your life." When we tried to arrange a car to Toyuq, she insisted on taking us instead. "To visit the holy pilgrimage site of Toyuq, you must go the hard way and not let anyone take you."

At the gate to her apartment complex she said, "My husband left for Urumqi today. He will study there for one year but has to leave once a month to come home and visit." She had often mused about how wonderful he was and that she had a lot of freedom. Now, she added, "My friends envy me, but I'm not satisfied. So I have other men." One always assumes things get lost in translation, so when she said her boyfriend was driving, we hoped this was a misinterpretation. It wasn't. He picked us up in a company car. He wasn't friendly. He just drove and didn't pay us much mind. Nor did he show any interest in the holy site; he sat outside in the car.

On the way, we were stopped by the police for illegally changing lanes. That was absurd considering that the other cars and busses scooted about randomly, making four lanes out of two. The officer took away his driver's license and gave him a fine. We thought we would have had to turn back, but instead, he took the back roads.

Built of mud bricks in a pretty valley, Toyuq looked like a medieval town. There were several onion-domed tombs along the uphill path, ancient Buddhist caves in the surrounding hills, and a turquoise-colored mosque in the village.

Before entering, we were given plastic vessels of water and sent to the side of a mud building to wash amid a pile of animal poop and parts of a dead chicken. Jamila instructed, "First our hands, then our private parts." Luckily, we wore long skirts because we had to do this outside. We then washed our hands again, feet, face, and mouth. Jamila washed fervently. Some older ladies nearby washed just as thoroughly. Melissa and I commented as we squatted, "It's not common to find someone who is willing to share this kind of travel experience."

We wound our way up a trail to the symbolic tomb of the first "Uyghur who became Muslim." Then we entered a small tomb, a Mosque-looking place that had verses from the Qur'an painted on the walls.

Multicolored rugs decorated the floor. A pile of bills indicated that donations were accepted. Jamila had disappeared, but we spotted her dainty gold sandals beneath a narrow stone stairway. Three old men invited us to sit, and one started to chant.

After some time Jamila emerged, backing out of a small cave-like opening and down the stairs. Her eyes were swollen from crying. A man struck her lightly all over her body with a padded, fabric-covered stick.

Melissa and I were motioned to go up the stairs past a gate and crawl through a tunnel to an inner sanctum. The tiny room was packed with people seated with their hands facing up. One man prayed out loud and everyone cried. Once finished, we were told to back away and down the steps. We waited in line for the man to flog us, which was said to be "good for health." A listless chicken lay outside the door. Money had been placed on the dirt floor of a side room where plastic water bottles containing small amounts of liquid had been left as offerings. Up the hill was a big mound of cloths tied together. Jamila said, "If you want to bring someone you love closer, write their name on a scarf and tie it there."

On our way out, one of the old men took a big knife to the chicken's neck and extracted blood as a remedy for a young woman. Jamila said, "She had too many fears, so they put some of the blood on her forehead for protection." I wondered whether the chicken died and the people ate the meat, or if they kept it alive and extracted blood until it was too weak to handle more slicing.

Visiting Toyuq was an intense experience! I was surprised that they were open enough to allow us foreign, non-Muslims to take part. As Melissa put it, "We were there but didn't know exactly what we were seeing. It was like looking through a dark mirror."

I described our experiences to Bambang, the Islamic lecturer in Indonesia, and he wrote: "What you saw was not Islamic. I think the rituals were some sort of local custom, interwoven with Islamic teachings. Blood is considered dirty and impure in Islam. The names written on cloth are not found in Islamic teachings either, although it is okay as long as that thing is not worshipped. Alterations and modifications of true Islam are common, considering that Islam was spread from Mecca to faraway lands through people with different customs.

It would be strange if in every corner of the world Islam had a single precise form."

We decided to spend a day on the tourist trail and caught a cab to Jiao-he, a ruined Buddhist city. It was beautiful, with mud-brick walls still standing, deep wells, and a complex of Buddhist temples. The setting, a plain overlooking poplar-lined valleys and grape drying houses, was picturesque. There were signs on the most important buildings written in English, Uyghur, and Chinese, explaining about the region's Buddhist past.

Our next stop was the Emin Minaret. The adjacent mosque was wood inside. Surrounded by grape fields, the huge minaret with fancy mud-brick work was overly restored to the point that it looked brand new. It was full of tourists. The most interesting were a group of Korean monks in face masks and grey robes over baggy pants.

Grape Valley was next on the agenda. Entering this huge tourist complex that catered to package tours, we were sold a book of five tickets, each to a different "scenic spot." We spent the rest of the afternoon rubbing elbows with busloads of Chinese tourists. (It was kitschy and fun.)

Down a poplar-lined street, we passed what had once been rural villages. These villages had found themselves within the boundaries of the ticketed-tourist area. At the gate, our driver was instructed to stop only at the five ticketed destinations, not between. The first consisted of pretty trails full of grape trellises and a sea of camera-toting Chinese tourists. One grape alley was for fruit tasting, while others were lined with souvenir and scarf sellers. I suppose Westerners had stumbled in before, because many vendors tried to use English to entice us. They beckoned, "Just looking," thinking it was a greeting.

There were dozens of varieties of raisins for sale. Some had names that translated into "scent of a man," "scent of a woman," "raisin king," and "mare's nipples." There were tiny ones made from champagne grapes, and long golden brown ones. We bought a bag of delicious rose-scented red raisins.

The third stop was a museum dedicated to composer Wang Luobin, a singer and songwriter whose series of Chinese-language *Silk Road Love Songs* was popular throughout China.

Fourth was Afanti Village. Afanti was a hero of humorous Xinjiang folktales whose popularity has spread to the rest of China and parts of the Middle East. At the village, a guy dressed like Afanti posed, and a poor restless donkey with fake flowers on its head was tied to a tree. The park was pretty. Some little boys picked flowers and gave them to us.

Another ticket admitted us to more grape trails, leading to the "World's Largest Nan Bread," which was actually made of cement. "The World's Largest Nan Oven," was about two stories high. Our driver said, "For large tour groups, they use it to roast a whole herd of cows." Melissa giggled, "Pose by the nan." Then she pointed out a sign that said "Best photo spot" in three languages, and sent me there for more shots.

On our way back to town, we visited a house that served as a restaurant, where the waitresses also danced. The affable owner showed us his grape fields. He said that they allow tourists to come and pick, but at the moment, the fields were picked over. He sat us at a low table and served melon slices, watermelon, and plates of grapes. Pasha had told me that when she was growing up in the 1970s people were starving and begging for leftovers. But everywhere we went in Xinjiang, tables were laden with more food than could possibly be eaten. It seemed to be a Uyghur custom.

A tour bus full of Taiwanese tourists filed in, and the owner sold them kilos and boxes of many varieties of raisins. He told us, "We do this about six times a day."

☪ ✩ ✩ ✩

On our last night in Turpan, all the dancers from the hotel's show descended on us. They took pictures, hugged us, and were sad that we were leaving. Obviously, they liked us, but we were still mystified by our banishment from the show.

We tried going to the show again. This time, after Melissa finagled a bit, we were admitted to the front row. The lady taking tickets said, "It's not my fault. The director didn't want you here." We never found out why. Anyway, we watched the show and danced, then said our goodbyes to the dancers.

Back in Urumqi, we stayed in a conveniently located, though charm-less, high-rise business hotel. Kamelia had arranged a discount for us. Every night the phone would ring. Inevitably, a woman at the other end asked, "Massage?" We usually hung up without saying a word, but one time I said, "No." She asked, "Sex?" Melissa and I laughed our heads off, but then I thought more seriously about the social im-plications. All over China, it's so common for prostitutes to call hotel rooms all night that men often unplug the phones. Making cold calls to strangers shows a lot of financial desperation. Then again, someone must say "yes." "What does that say about the clients?" I wondered, "Are they so lonely that they don't care about seeing who they are go-ing to sleep with?"

Kamelia took us to a place specializing in Atlas silks. Xinjiang is famous for this style of fabric, which is woven with a technique called *ikat*. The word is from Indonesia and means "to tie." It uses a process similar to tie-dye before the threads are woven into a pattern. This process is used in Indonesia, parts of India, Japan, Latin America and along the Silk Road. In Xinjiang, the fabric was sold in long narrow pieces of six meters by about twenty inches. She explained, "They come from Ho-ten, and that is the width of the looms."

Hoten is in southern Xinjiang and so is Kashgar. Hoten is also home base for Uyghur traditional medicine and has an extensive Sunday market that doesn't attract tourists. I thought of my next destination and all signs pointed me toward the long bus ride back to the south.

China was different from the other places I'd visited for this book in that I felt totally without communication. In other countries, either I knew enough Arabic to keep a basic conversation going for a few minutes, or more people spoke English. It was helpful to have Melissa translate. She also had insights on Chinese culture because she had lived in China.

The time for Melissa to leave was approaching. I wondered how things would change once I was reduced to sign language. Hopefully, some of the Uyghur words had stuck. In Hoten, they would speak Uy-ghur. After Hoten, I planned to go to Tashkurgan, a Tajik area where their language is related to Persian, a totally different linguistic family. My language comprehension skills seemed to be deteriorating. It seemed like once I learned a bit of a local language, it was already time to leave and tune my ears to a different set of sounds.

Kamelia, Melissa, and I spent our last night together at the Grand Bazaar Restaurant. It had the most famous dance spectacle in Xinjiang. Everything was huge. Huge is synonymous with China. The sparsely populated, expansive province of Xinjiang was overwhelmed by towering buildings and masses of visitors. This restaurant, holding over three hundred people, was packed nightly. Elaborate stage backdrops ranged from mountains to grapes, changing throughout the show. Dozens of dancers descended from high, carved, spiral staircases in elaborately embroidered costumes of sequins and silk. This was a lavish production of Vegas proportions, although it was folk-based and the women were comparatively covered. A belly dancer used my *Superstars* song again; she danced with a live snake wrapped around her. I really liked the Tajik opening, with performers in red and black Islamic dress, and the men's hat-shaking dance, where they wore big fuzzy hats and shook their heads in unison.

Throughout *40 Days & 1001 Nights*, I'd arrived in each country alone and had to find my way. Traveling with another person had added a new dynamic. It took away the solitary struggle of having to process my experiences alone, often feeling isolated and like a fish out of water. Verbal translation meant I didn't have to rely on body language, but instead had an instant source of communication. Body language is such a raw form of communication that when you get your point across, it's honest. It's difficult for either party to lie, and you don't have the luxury of "she said . . ." whether it's true or not. Actions become the means of communication.

Traveling with a companion gave me a chance to compare notes. Together, we had two heads to figure out how to get where we were going. A woman alone often elicits either a desire to help or at least curiosity, but sometimes people didn't approach us as easily, assuming that we didn't need help.

I was curious how the dynamics would change on this trip as Melissa headed to the airport and I caught a cab to the bus station—the *wrong* bus station, I later learned. A woman in official uniform escorted me across two parking lots to a bus. I bought my ticket from her and got on. It was a sleeper bus with brightly colored mattresses on the beds. The music was good and played loud like a disco. Boom! Soon after we hit the highway, we had an accident. As one lane closed and our bus was moving over, a big truck zoomed by and broke the big side mirror. The drivers had a big argument, blocking both lanes of traffic until workers moved the flag-laden rope to let the other cars around. The two men stopped arguing and became friendly while waiting for the police.

After we got moving again, the bus picked up more people at another terminal, and the driver's assistant motioned for me to move to another bed farther back. I thought that was silly, then noticed that the sheets on that bed were stained as if someone had had their period or some other accident on it. A lot of the beds had dirty sheets. I didn't want to move but finally conceded and walked almost all the way back until I found some clean sheets.

One woman motioned for me not to go back there. I realized why. Xinjiang had some permeating smells, and the concentration increased the deeper one went into an airtight bus. The smell of sheep fat, drying grapes, and musty socks became overwhelming. After some deliberation, I spotted a top bunk farther forward and grabbed it. I noticed that men were in back and women in front. There was a lot of yelling as the assistant kept rearranging people and telling them to change bunks. Some men were up front and he wanted them in back, but a lady had to move back too. Passengers weren't cooperating and the assistant was frustrated, shouting orders that went unheeded.

By dawn, I began to wonder if I was on the right bus. The road to Hoten was supposed to pass dramatic dunes of the Taklamakan Desert. I saw only flat nothingness. Twenty-five hours went by before we arrived in a town. I asked the driver, "Hoten?" He motioned something which I interpreted as "stay on the bus." Other people I asked pointed another direction but motioned for me to stay on.

The last stop wasn't Hoten. As I took my bag, one of the drivers said, "No Hoten." He made a sleeping motion with both hands under the cheek. I understood that as "spend the night here and take another bus tomorrow." I stayed cool and collected as a wave of raw determination came over me. Having come so far to see the Sunday market the next morning, I wasn't going to miss it. Remaining steadfast, I made sure they understood my dilemma. A crowd of curious onlookers gathered. If I'd lost my cool, I would have lost my crowd and gotten no cooperation. My ticket was written in Uyghur and Chinese scripts, so I couldn't read it. It must have said "Hoten" because the concerned driver rushed me to what looked like a metal school bus. He paid my fare and the fares of three other people from our bus, then gave me some money back. I sat near a guy who I could communicate a little with, though he didn't know any more English than the six words I knew of Uyghur.

The bus dropped us in a town and he said, "Kargilik." He motioned that I would have to spend the night. I don't speak many languages, and those that I do are only useful in Latin America, but at least I'm stubborn. I repeated "taxi" and "Hoten" like a broken record and slowly shook my head every time the word "hotel" was uttered. I knew that by local standards a taxi would be exorbitantly expensive, but at this point I didn't care. I wanted to get to the Sunday market! The guy I had been sitting with took me to a lot where taxis congregated and negotiated a price. It was only a couple of dollars more than the money that had been refunded to me, so I said, "Rakmat" (thank you), and sat in the front seat.

Three guys got in the back, and we drove past farmers on carts, foot, and three-wheeled motorized tricycles that were loaded with produce. Absent were the tour buses, bathroom tiles, and big buildings. Driving down a road with poplar trees making shadows in the waning sunlight is a typical scene from Uyghur music videos. I felt like I'd stepped into one of those scenes. Poplar trunks glowed, and the trees were so dense and tall that they leaned toward us. It was like a tunnel.

We drove for hours in what became pitch blackness. Trucks came head on with their bright lights glaring. Donkey carts, bearing lopsided piles of goods, had no illumination. I hoped that, with so many blindingly bright lights, we wouldn't plow into a cart or an unlit bicyclist. We passed one poor horse pulling two carts extremely overloaded with giant bags.

I thought the farmers must have been headed to the famous Sunday market and assumed that we were near Hoten. Not so. We drove for hours! At one point, without even a star to light the sky, the taxi came to a dead stop. The men opened their doors. I looked around, realizing what a vulnerable position I'd gotten myself into. Gone were the carts, trucks, or any sign of human life. I opened my door too, but the driver uttered something and motioned for me not to get out. I sat, as if on needles, wondering what they were up to, as everyone disappeared into the darkness. They returned in much better spirits, and I realized that it was a potty break, for men only. At midnight Beijing time, I wound up in the parking lot of a hospital where a local cab awaited.

I said "Hotel," and he asked "Hoten?" I certainly hoped we were in Hoten, or at least that he was going to take me to Hoten. Within minutes, he pulled up at the Hoten Hotel, a big shiny place that looked like a budget buster but was cheap and comfortable!

It was the night before the beginning of Ramadhan, and I had only eaten a few crackers all day. I was happy to be in a nice, comfortable room in yet another frilly Uyghur-style hotel full of marble and carvings. During Ramadhan, I was always more thirsty than hungry, but if I didn't find something to eat, it would mean two days without food. I motioned with my fingers to my mouth, making a chewing motion and ended up at a Chinese-looking "People's Park" lined with red lanterns. Strings of bright lights and a few tables indicated the presence of a night market. A gang of street kids was tormenting a mentally ill homeless man. This was the first time during my stay in Xinjiang that I'd seen a mentally ill person wandering alone or pint-sized street gangs.

During Ramadhan, the first couple days of going without food or water from sunup to sundown are the hardest. One must keep busy so as not to think about the hunger or thirst. I was relieved by the distraction of the Sunday market. People were much quieter about Ramadhan in Xinjiang than they'd been in Indonesia. I started to wonder if I'd gotten my days mixed up as I watched some kids eating. No adults ate. Kebab grills had no fires, so I surmised that it was, indeed, the fasting month.

While in Indonesia for Ramadhan the previous year, I had seen advertisements for fast-breaking foods long before the fasting started. The idea was "You should break the fast with something sweet." In

Mohammed's time, that was dates. Now, sometimes people eat Oreos. Conversely, Uyghurs usually break their fast with nan and water.

The call to prayer was ever present in Indonesia, but in Xinjiang, it was noticeably absent. Indonesian mosques broadcast long lectures over loudspeakers in the wee morning hours. Everyone knew when fasting started and ended via wailing sirens, chants, or public announcements. In Xinjiang, I had to find out for myself when to start and stop eating, which wasn't easy without the aid of language.

The Sunday market was a feast for my video camera! I couldn't stop filming. Every time I put the camera away, I had to take it out again. There were absolutely no tourists, so the camera was a fascination for many. I inevitably drew a crowd of old and young, many from the countryside who were fascinated with watching themselves in the viewfinder.

The whole town was a market; each area specialized in selling something different. One street was full of birds, chickens, and a few cats and dogs. I was surprised to see that people had dogs as pets, since they are considered dirty in Islam, thus not allowed in the home or given much affection. Eating dogs is taboo in Islam, so they were definitely not sold as food. I heard that some people in Xinjiang kept them in courtyards but not indoors. I saw dogs playing with children and being run on leashes, like pets anywhere in the world.

Markets enveloped street after street. One large area was overrun by jade sellers. They sold rocks, from pieces that were tiny to up to a foot in diameter, of Hoten's famous white jade as well as green and black. Stones were laid out on tables, on the ground, and in wagons or sold from trunks of cars. Young kids roamed about, holding little pieces in their hands offering them to passersby near a dry riverbed where people searched for jade on a daily basis.

Rug sellers opened large red, pink, and purple pile rugs in a building that looked like a smaller version of Kashgar's Bazaar Yildiz. Rows of women sold Atlas silk. I struggled to restrain myself, as I planned to buy plenty when I visited a famous silk factory outside of town.

Men carved trunks then embedded them with gold sequins. There were metal smiths who beat tin into large cans, boxes, and pans. Topplingly full carts of lettuce ambled past, and one backstreet had a proliferation of onions. I'd never seen so many in my life! Drivers climbed over the onions and stepped on them as they tumbled on the ground.

A gas station for motorbikes consisted of two large metal drums full of gasoline. When someone drove up, a young woman in a sequined dress would scoop the gas into a smaller pail and funnel it into the vehicle's gas tank.

I hailed a cab and motioned "spinning silk," then "weaving on a loom." The driver sped out of town, stirring up dust on the unpaved roads to Jiya. Making Atlas silk is the mainstay for most families in this mud-brick village. A typical piece is spun of many colors. Each six-meter-long piece is woven on a narrow loom measuring about twenty inches across, so that is the width of the fabric. Spanning 2000 years of history, this style of multicolored silk can be found from China to Syria and everywhere along the ancient Silk Road.

Jiya's Silk Factory had been a failing state-owned Atlas silk mill. Tureaili Haji, a local villager, saved it from bankruptcy, converting it into an attraction for the few tourists who make it all the way out to Hoten. At the factory, people can see the silk being loomed by hand and dyed with all-natural dyes. When I arrived, three women were working outside, soaking silk worm cocoons in water, unwinding fine filaments, and spinning the filaments into thread.

A handful of men and women wove silk fabric on rustic wooden looms that were pedaled by foot. Threads were put in place with a small wooden pick. This natural silk was completely different from what I'd seen in markets all over Xinjiang. Most of what I'd seen and bought as silk was actually synthetic, and the colors were different because of the chemical dyes that were used. This was my first time seeing the real thing.

Wondering about all the other silk makers of the village, I asked the driver (via gestures) to take me to see private homes with silk looms. He asked several locals who pointed to different houses. One was locked up. Another had some silk thread, dyed and just laying in a pile. Still another family was making synthetic pieces with a machine. They invited me to come in and watch.

On our way back to Hoten, a thought occurred to me, "Did Hoten have a livestock market like the fascinating photo-op in Kashgar?" If so, it certainly wouldn't have foreigners with zoom lenses capturing the "real experience" like they were in Kashgar. I looked at the driver and said, "Moo." He smiled and mooed back. Determination took over once again, and I "mooed," "baahed," and "hee-hawed" until he snapped his fingers like "I get it!" turned the car sharply and went in another direction.

We made it to the livestock market just before it began clearing out. Men were piling sheep, several deep, in trucks, donkey carts, horse carts, and anything with wheels. The sheep protested as they were tossed onto piles, like the onions I'd seen earlier in the day. I felt bad for the sheep but thought of how people deal with terrible things too, risking their lives hanging off of packed buses and squishing into hot subway cars unable to move from under the arms of smelly passengers. An outdoor butcher was hanging a butchered fat-rump sheep on a metal hook. I filmed as he cut off the butt and hung it from a separate hook. The body was lean, but the rump was pure fat.

At the People's Park I passed a ride that had kiddie cars and played electronic Christmas carols. These songs are pretty common in Xinjiang, where "Jingle Bells" and "Santa Claus is Coming to Town" attract toddlers to merry-go-rounds and coin-operated rocking horses. In a Muslim area of a communist country, the songs completely lose their meaning.

I sat at a table and ordered two small kebabs, some melon, and a duck egg. The duck egg was cooked in the shell over an open fire. It was much bigger than a chicken egg and had a delicious smoky flavor. After I ate my kebab, I left the chunk of fat. A well-dressed woman approached, holding a plastic bag, and pointed to my skewer. I motioned that I was done, and she took the chunk of fat, put it in a plastic bag, and then went to another table to comb for more scraps. Soon a man approached doing the same. These people looked so clean and decent that one would never imagine that they were actually starving.

Mohammed, the herbalist I'd interviewed in Kashgar, had recommended that I visit his teacher, Abdumejit, in Hoten. I couldn't communicate with anyone, so Mohammed had made arrangements (via long distance) for a translator from a small language school that had recently opened in Hoten.

Abdurahman, the translator, showed up at my hotel with a man who turned out to be his boss. I was surprised when this slight young man spoke the best English I'd heard so far in China. In fact, he was one of the few people in Hoten who spoke any English at all. He even knew idioms like "It's raining like cats and dogs" (it rarely rains in Hoten) and "That's the way the ball bounces" and used them often.

Abdumejit's office was humbler that I had expected. I imagined him to be an old man in a big center, but he was about thirty and looked a lot like Mohammed. His office was one of many similar herb shops in the Chong Kur Bazaar, a sprawling complex of fabric sellers, dirt streets, and herbal-medicine stores. Medicine shops lined his street. Rustic wooden folding tables contained metal boxes filled with varieties of herbs. Inside, the walls were lined, floor to ceiling, with old-fashioned yellow cabinets full of small drawers; it looked like a pharmacy from America's old west.

Hoten was on the edge of the Taklamakan desert so everything in the town was covered with dust. The herbs on Herb Street of the Chong Kur Bazaar were no exception. People seemed used to breathing and ingesting dust.

A young man came into the shop holding a large lizard on a leash, hoping to sell it. Abdumejit's shop contained a few dried animal species, but not as many as the doctors in Kashgar had. He weighed the reptile, inspected its body, and rejected it. As people came and went, he consulted a thick "book of knowledge." Its cover was cut from a cardboard box. He explained, "For over two thousand years people have tried herbs to find out what worked and passed their experiences on to the generation after generation. This experience accumulated and became the body of knowledge it is today."

He continued, "The Qur'an says that Allah sent the knowledge of medicine through a man named Hekim Lokman. He was the founder of the medical profession and had a deep understanding of herbs and drugs. In 1100 AD, doctors of Uyghur medicine wrote *The Book of Medical Knowledge*. To this day, doctors continue to document their own experiences and the book is always growing as doctors pass their experiences to one another."

He explained, "There are two roles in Uyghur Traditional medicine: that of the therapist and of the healer. Therapists learn to recognize the herbs and their role, and how long the raw materials last.

"Healers learn four ways to diagnose: one, questioning the patient on how he feels; two, smell, from their mouth, ears, urine, etc; three, pulse, there are several places on the body, but 90 percent of information is gathered through the wrist; four, observation of eyelashes, fingernails, body shape, and skin color."

I asked if they use intuition, and he said, "No. We depend on experience and concrete information."

Abdumejit was generous with his information and offered to take me to meet his teacher who ran a clinic for Uyghur traditional medicine.

We sped on motorbikes. The staff, wearing white coats, gathered in the reception area to see me. I was quite the novelty. His teacher, the director, took my pulse, checked my eyeballs, made me stick out my tongue, and asked if I had a pain in my back. He pointed to the spot where I have had a mild pain for ten years. He motioned "camera," and had staff members take pictures of him taking my pulse as I posed with my arm out. Nearly out of the pills and plaster I had been given in Kashgar, he wrote down several items on a pharmaceutical pad instructing me to take a series of sweet, spicy pills and instant herbal teas that dissolved in water. I started a new regimen, which seemed to be an intestinal cleanse since it gave me diarrhea. Fasting, not drinking water, and diarrhea wasn't a good combination, so I cut out one of the medicines and felt fine. It did help me lose a few pounds though.

Abdumejit invited me to his home for dinner to break the Ramadhan fast, spend the night with his family, and eat breakfast with them in the morning. Of course, I didn't want to miss that!

We returned to his office where he piled bags of herbs on top of each other and brought in the boxes. Up and down the street you could hear the folding of wooden tables and the metal-and-earth sound of herb cans being dragged inside. He shut a wobbly metal accordion-style gate and locked it with a padlock. We dumped a big metal bowl of grapes into two large plastic bags. I rode sidesaddle down an outlying country road on the back of his motorbike with a lap full of grapes. Passing a clinic, he pointed to it and said something I couldn't understand.

We stepped around a big delivery truck and a huge pile of corn husks to enter his parent's yard. The outdoor table was laden with melon, noodle soup, and dark yellow corn on the cob. Abdumejit's son, Elias, was an adorable twenty-month-old with a wide face, shaved head, and split pants. Throughout China, most children don't use diapers. They simply have their pants split exposing their bottoms and genitals. It gives them the freedom to pee and poop by squatting in gardens or over the edge of sidewalks into gutters. Elias was the center of attention. Everyone doted on him with kisses and hugs.

We sat on a raised platform with fabrics laid out and brocade mats on top. Very little liquid was consumed, though an occasional bowl of hot water was served upon request.

Mohammed motioned for me to follow him. I thought we were going into the house, but we walked down the street with his wife, the baby, and a young woman, reaching the clinic he'd pointed to earlier. That was their home. The central area had an open-air latticework ceiling with several sleeping platforms and a few rooms. Homes would never be built like this if there was much chance of rain.

They brought me into a room, which hadn't been inhabited in a long time, and wiped a thick layer of dust from the glass coffee table and the rug-covered chairs. I was motioned to climb onto a hard sleeping platform covered with bright green felt. A teenage girl entered, holding a padded brocade mat, a sheet, and a comforter, and set up my sleeping arrangements. Another teenager came with a second set of bedding. Abdumejit and his wife left me with the two young women and Elias. We played a long time, especially peekaboo behind frilly pink curtains, before settling in to sleep.

Getting up at 5 AM for breakfast, it was so cold! Elias wore his father's furry hat and then removed it to reveal a white embroidered Islamic hat. His father put a furry jacket on him, and I took photos. He looked adorable. His balance was still getting fine tuned, so he toppled over occasionally.

Back in his shop, Abdumejit spent hours grinding powders with a mortar and pestle, mixing them with honey while attending to a steady stream of clients. He was making special medicine for my water retention so I could bring it back to America and take it after his teacher's medicine wore off. Unfortunately, it was so heavy and full of pasty liquids that I was not allowed on the plane with it.

I sat with an old man, looking over pictures from my travel guide and socializing, without language, with the people who came and went. One man ordered a large amount of honey from a giant metal barrel. Abdumejit poured it into a double layer of open-mouthed plastic shopping bags. I thought, "What a mess if it spills." Abdumejit's brother brought in an electronic scale, like the ones used to weigh vegetables at the supermarket. The bag of honey was too full to close completely, but after putting the bag in a bowl, he was able to get the weight.

The bus station was a shiny building made with the familiar bathroom tile outside and shiny stone floors inside. While typing about my experiences in Hoten on my little computer, I was surrounded by a constant stream of onlookers: kids selling jade, passengers going to smaller towns, and employees looking over my shoulder. I liked how unabashed people were about their curiosity. Women examined my clothes and jewelry, trying on my purse, jacket, and accessories. I didn't mind. It was a form of communication. Enjoying novelty in exotic people is natural on both sides. Their fascination with me was like my fascination with people riding donkey carts, piling their motorbikes high with sheepskins, wearing elaborate traditional hats, and grinding herbal concoctions by hand. I was exotic in this remote corner of the world, and probably made a few people's day by giving them something to tell their friends.

From Hoten, it took another full day to get to Tashkurgan, near the Pakistani and Tajik borders. Tashkurgan is a Tajik speaking "autonomous county" within the Xinjiang Autonomous Region. I wondered "How can there be so much official autonomy when the ubiquitous bathroom tile is popping up everywhere, and the most important officials are all Chinese?" Anyway, these doubly autonomous people have a different culture and speak Tajik, a language from the Persian family.

In the wee hours of the morning, the bus from Hoten let me off in Kashgar. Kashgar is between Hoten and Tashkurgan. It's the end of the line for buses from Hoten and the place where trips to Tashkurgan begin. I queried "Tashkurgan?" The station was a dusty yard full of private cars and trucks. A man hawking rides showed me a rusty heap of an old bus and said, "It won't leave for another three hours."

Instead of waiting for the bus, I let him lead me to a shiny new jeep and sat next to a Tajik couple. The woman was wearing a colorfully embroidered hat with a silky white scarf tied on top.

We rode for five hours on the Karakoram Highway, the highest paved international road in the world. It connects the northern areas of Pakistan with the Silk Road. The weather turned dry and ice cold, making me glad I had brought a faux-sheepskin coat from Urumqi. Over the Kunjerab Pass, we rode past snowy mountains in the distance and dry brown desert mountains that were closer. We saw swampland, yaks, two-humped camels, and lots of sheep, goats, and cattle.

Although it was Ramadhan, everyone was munching on grapes and bagels. I was surprised when the driver smoked endless cigarettes. During Ramadhan, you're supposed to give up all bad habits. When traveling over a certain distance, you can hold off on fasting and make it up after Ramadhan, but smoking is not negotiable.

As we entered the Kizilu Kyrgiz Autonomous Prefecture, the language changed from Uyghur to a similar language called Kyrgiz. Locals stood by the side of the road selling trinkets. Some of the pieces looked like family-heirloom antiques, and others were Chinese-made curio-shop junk. Although we weren't crossing into another country, there was a border-patrol stop where we had to show our passports. A family of yaks crossed the wrong way (without passports?) and got kicked by a border-patrol officer.

I read a sign in several languages, including English, "You are entering the Tajik Autonomous County." The Tajik couple got off in a little mud village where dozens of women stood outside, all dressed in identical dark jackets, skirts just below the knees, and thick hose, topped off with the traditional hat and white scarf.

Soon after I arrived in Tashkurgan, a small town of about 5000, I asked to go to the Pamir Hotel. There was only one street in the town and it was only a few blocks long, so the Pamir was easy to find. A Tajik woman named Gulli, who looked South American and was the only person in town who spoke English, was called to the front desk. She said, "It's so cold in the winter and there is nothing to do, so one year I taught myself English with textbooks." I asked where I could hear Tajik music, and she said, "I have a guest from Beijing and we're going out tonight. You're welcome to join us."

Meanwhile, I had a few hours to roam around so I visited Stone City. Tashkurgan means Stone City, but on the edge of town were remains of the original, a fortress of crumbling mud and stone. Climbing to the top of the ruin, I was afforded a beautiful view of the surrounding mountains, a green valley, and white *yurts* (round tentlike dwellings).

I walked down to the yurts, expecting to find nomads, but they were party yurts, to be rented out by the evening. One had a disco ball and colored lights, frilly cushions, brightly patterned fabric walls, and a big-screen TV with VCD player.

In this region there are a collection of several small Iranian ethnic groups. Tajiks look shades of Middle Eastern, often combined with more Asian-looking eyes. Their hair ranges from red to black, but they are better distinguished by their way of dressing. Most people I saw had skin that was usually dark and roughened by sun, wind, and harsh weather. Even the children had weathered skin.

Women donned embroidered pillbox hats with scarves tied over them. A more modern version of this was the pillbox hat with pulled-back hair held by a big fake-flower barrette. An older style consisted of plaited hair with decorations, pillbox hat, and silver chain jewelry over the hat. Skirt lengths varied from below the knee to several inches above. Women always wore thick stockings: either flesh toned, which looked like therapeutic hose, or dark knitted. These often ended at the ankle with a pair of ankle-high socks worn beneath. Fashion statements ranged from totally mismatched outfits to classy versions with boots and modern denim skirts and jackets.

Gulli and I walked to a Tajik restaurant called Al-Mas, which resembled a small, dark version of the mammoth Uyghur restaurant that Aynur took us to in Kashgar. It had some flashing lights, a keyboard player, and a singer.

The only other customers were at a large table containing three nationalities: Uyghur, Tajik and Kyrgiz. Four men from the table got up to dance to a Tajik song. I was mesmerized. Their movements were like soaring eagles with graceful steps and arm movements. After only one song the music stopped, but Gulli knew the management and talked them into having it continue.

Most items on the menu were unavailable, but we got lagman noodles and some sort of lamb. The meat in both was so tough it was inedible. I'd been fasting, and now I couldn't chew the leathery meat. Oh well. It's been said that dancing is like food for the soul, so once the music kicked in, I was happy.

A Uyghur song played, and Gulli and I got up to dance. Suddenly, six attractive young men burst onto the floor flailing their arms with big, rough energy. "Where did they come from?" I asked.

"They had been hanging out downstairs drinking, heard the music, and got inspired." Gulli told me, "I don't like local Tajik guys because they drink too much." The older men who were at the table were drinking too. During Ramadhan, this was surprising. One handsome red-haired guy hovered around us. He was tall and skinny, with funky clothes, tanned skin, and a combination of Asian and Turkic features. We let him stick around.

Soon Gulli's friend, a filmmaker and photographer from Beijing, arrived and sat with us. This man was drop-dead gorgeous, tall and well built. He kept shooting masculine, seductive looks at Gulli, but she said, "You're too fat. I don't like fat men." The man was unfazed and didn't give up his attempts at conquest. He was in Tashkurgan working on the film version of *The Kite Runner*, one of my favorite books, which takes place in Afghanistan. Part of the filming was in the Stone City.

The following day, I asked Gulli where to buy Tajik music. She said, "You can buy only Uyghur and Chinese music in the store." I persisted, so she led me to an office where a young man sold Tajik music from his computer. I wondered how local musicians made any money if their music wasn't available in stores.

After a walk around town and back up the Stone City, I stopped a random SUV parked by the side of the road, and asked "Kashgar?" Luckily, this man was headed to Kashgar and waiting for passengers. He took me to the hotel to get my bag but was surprisingly rude, so I no longer wanted to go with him. Fortunately, a tourist from Hong Kong was standing by and translated. I explained, "When someone is a paying customer, you have to be polite." He changed completely and started treating me like a queen. The fact that he was chomping and slurping on a pork bone during Ramadhan wasn't helping attract additional passengers. Obviously, he wasn't Muslim.

Three women with two babies finally got in. One of the babies must have been teething because he cried and screamed uncontrollably. We headed out past snow covered mountains and green valleys. A terrible video of people dancing badly in weird futuristic outfits played over and over on a screen right in front of my face. I braced myself for a very long ride. The driver couldn't take the noise. Soon he was screaming energetically too. Suddenly the car turned around and he took the women back home.

We went to the Pakistani border on the edge of town, then drove around town a couple of times looking for passengers. At least five people got in, then out again in short order. I didn't know if it was the price or the driver's attitude, but he had some sort of repelling effect. Sticking with this guy wasn't going to get me anywhere, so after two hours I found another car and was back on the Karakoram highway once again.

Back in Kashgar, the atmosphere was more sedate than my last visit because of Ramadhan. Much of the urban liveliness had revolved around food—samsas, duq, nan, kebabs, and so forth. Now, no one was eating.

I visited Mohammed as he was making jam with walnuts and honey. He said, "It is for strength." His pot of hot syrup boiled over onto the sidewalk because we were talking instead of paying attention. Then the bees honed in. I hoped it wasn't a lost batch. He gave me another jar of rose jam and explained that they leave the roses and sugar out in a high summer temperature for forty days, adding, "for your health."

Aynur and I had dinner at our favorite polo place. It was crowded. A fight broke out between two waitresses. The staff looked like teenagers, and when the stress intensified because of the crowds coming to break the Ramadhan fast, they became ill-mannered. As always, the food was good. We had extra entertainment watching the action.

I went to the airport, which was mobbed. Instead of having different counters for each airline, in Xinjiang one can go to any counter. Queues are nonexistent in China. Everyone pushes their way in, and if you don't join the fray, you never get to the front. I got good at winding my way forward, only occasionally getting nudged out of the way. Using my dancing skills, I would slink my way to the front instead of pushing and shoving like everyone else.

Of course my Uyghur traditional medicines had to be opened. Other than that, all went smoothly. I couldn't read the Chinese characters on my ticket but identified my flight by the color-coded boarding pass. A guard only let a few people at a time into the security area, holding back the mobs shaking their boarding passes.

Back in Urumqi, Kamelia, her daughter Khaderia, and her niece Sameera took me to Pasha's mother's home. The house was inside a big complex of pink bathroom-tiled high-rises. Up a staircase of raw cement, the apartment was beautiful and spacious inside, with rugs and nice furnishings.

The younger women weren't fasting, because if you're sick or it's that time of the month you don't have to fast. (They pointed to their stomachs and made a grimacing face.) Consequently, I was greeted by a table full of fruits, nuts, sweets, and Uyghur delicacies. I figured "when in Rome . . ." or when in the Islamic world, surrounded by young women with stomachaches during Ramadhan, I might as well eat too. Time came to break fast, so Kamelia and her mother joined us. After that, Sameera, Khaderia, and I danced Uyghur and belly dance. We put on one of my Jordanian CDs. It was interesting trying to teach basic dabke steps, up and down the hallway. Dabke is totally earthbound and always leads with one foot stomp, whereas Xinjiang dance has the opposite energy, balanced and lifted toward the sky. Their difficult and detailed hand movements combined with delicate steps were hard for me, but it was even harder to teach them to stomp. How weight is used in each style of dance makes a world of difference.

I had a secret desire for my travels to end with something exciting or dramatic. But this is real life, not the movies. Everyday life, a blend of modernity and tradition, is not nearly as romantic or cinematic as such a daring feat—being a woman wandering aimlessly through little known lands that adhere to a religion we are taught to fear—might lead one to expect.

On my fortieth night, I was invited to Kamelia's apartment. This high-rise complex of weathered concrete looked dingy from the outside, but her place was beautifully decorated within. She had a large TV. We practiced with my teaching DVD, of which I gave a copy to both Khaderia and Sameera. Khaderia gave me a lesson in dancing with bowls balanced on my head.

Kamelia's husband used to be a chef, so he prepared a wonderful meal. Sameera spoke some English, but after a week and a half without verbal communication, I found it just as easy to communicate with body language, watching the context of actions, and dancing. Thus my travels ended in a flurry of music, dance and food.

I flew out the next morning. Under my baggy shirt was a leopard-print spaghetti-strap top. Once airborne, I peeled off the baggy layer, and then looked around, wondering if people would think I forgot to finish getting dressed. Everyone was Chinese, and some women were no more covered than I was. Strange how quickly reality shifts.

When asked what I remember most from each culture I visited, I reminisce about Xinjiang. Having a lust for life and steadfastly surrounding themselves by beauty and pleasure define the Uyghurs. They have been unknown to much of the world, dominated for centuries, and sold as a tourist attraction. Nonetheless, they continue honing their exquisite dance skills, listening to the music they've played for centuries, enjoying splendid varieties of food, experimenting with herbs in search of new ways to heal, and decorating in grand style. Uyghurs epitomize self-expression.

I also think of Jordan's benevolent monarchy that is universally loved. Though it may not be the most beautiful or artistic nation, peace prevails. The strongest message Jordan gave me was that people want peace and peace is not impossible.

In Zanzibar, I experienced an island of sultry, melancholic music, tender with the sounds of a forgotten era. A cycle of darkness and corruption continues to eclipse the sunshine, enveloping the land. Sorrow from slavery, revolution by mass killing, poverty, disease, and now young men's futures dimmed by heroin addiction permeate the stones of forgotten mansions that slowly crumble away. Despite the hardship, people still meet every night at sunset to sit on benches, sip coffee, and share the simple pleasure of one another's company.

Although Siwa is veiled in the illusion of innocence and natural beauty, this long-time closed society is in danger of losing its way of life unless they set some limits soon. It risks the introduction of AIDS. The environment is suffering, and salt water may drown the unique farming culture. Yet people continue their ancient methods of date and olive farming, transporting their produce in wooden donkey carts, and baking bread in palm-frond-fueled ovens in sun-baked mud homes. Women are slowly being introduced to the modern world via the internet, and their embroidery skills are being seen on high fashion runways in Europe.

Although I visited only four of Indonesia's 17,000 islands, I found the teeming metropolis of Jakarta possessing extremes of wealth and poverty, historical Javanese palaces in Cirebon, an intellectual haven in Bandung, and one of the world's last matrilineal cultures (which happens to be Muslim) in West Sumatra. Aceh, a land decimated by thirty years of war and a tsunami that is beyond anyone's capacity to imagine, is a testament to human faith and resilience. Passion and strength are reflected in their unwavering devotion to Allah.

During a total of 200 days in the Islamic world, I didn't get beheaded or abducted. I learned that Islam is not the same in every country. It adapts and accommodates cultural differences. Some cultures are more willing to share their religion and philosophies with a foreigner than others. Like in the Christian, Jewish, Hindu, or Buddhist worlds, the level of adherence varies, but militant fundamentalism is still fringe. Extremism is dangerous, whether Muslim, Christian, or any religion that manipulates people by mixing faith and politics. Most ordinary citizens haven't encountered such fanatics and don't share their interpretation of God's word.

Exploitation has existed since the dawn of history, with stronger, richer nations ruthlessly dominating those who are unable to defend their resources. We haven't outgrown that, but finding vestiges of ancient music, medicine, and art fused with the modern world makes me realize that we are living in a special moment in history. Communication face-to-face and via electronic means brings us closer than ever to understanding one another. Once we look beyond our perceptions, life has more beauty than ugliness and the world is a fascinating and wonderful place.

SINCE...

DURING MY VISIT WITH DIBA IN JORDAN, where we discussed ways to help the nomadic Dhom, the idea occurred to me to start a fund to help artists, grass roots organizations, or other deserving causes in the countries I visited. Shortly thereafter, I met Ali Abdella Buaisha in Dubai and heard stories of Ikhwani Safaa's former grandeur and how he had attended their 100th Anniversary celebration, bringing back so many memories. It was then that I decided to set aside ten percent of the earnings from the book, film, and DVDs and dedicate it to what would become the 1001 Nights Fund.

The 1001 Nights Fund started with a small donation to a breast cancer awareness program in Egypt. Soon, people began to donate, and members of the belly dance community began to raise money for the fund. It became a joy as well as an education for me to make sure that the money gave direct aid without fostering dependency or getting lost in bureaucracy or administrative costs. I believe that when people donate money, it is a sacrifice given from the heart, and they want to be confident that it will reach people who need it. I've often thought back on how Azwar Hassan started the FBA by having his friends come and stay with families to see what they needed.

I had spent time with Ikhwani Safaa and saw how their instruments were well worn. A man named Luka Dziubyna donated money to buy instruments in Egypt for the musicians, as well as to do major repairs to the group's clubhouse, so their master teacher could live upstairs and continue to pass his legacy to the musicians. I traveled to Zanzibar from Cairo's Ahlan Wasahlan dance festival to attend the 2007 Zanzibar Film Festival and carry instruments. My weight allowance was sorely exceeded. Luckily Kenya Airways bent the rules and even gave me an extra seat to strap in a delicate oud.

Ikhwani Safaa was thrilled when presented with most of the instruments on their wish list. Although I have yet to figure out how to obtain and transport a cello and a double bass, the music of Zanzibar has been enriched by violins, flutes, an oud and percussion instruments.

I tried my hand at fashion design with a new concept in evening gowns that could double as a belly dance costume, using the talents of people in countries from *40 Days & 1001 Nights*. A tailor in Zanzibar made me a black chiffon evening gown.

During a three-day sand bath in the Siwa Oasis, Malek's mother and three friends decorated that evening gown with cowrie shells, sequins, beads, shell buttons, and Berber symbols whose meanings were long forgotten. During the final touches, I sat and worked on another costume while we sewed and ate. Women came by to plop fabrics and jewelry on my lap just in case I wanted to buy. Besides embroidery and doing henna on visitors' hands and feet, selling their clothes or family heirlooms is among the few ways Siwan women can make money.

On a return trip to Indonesia, Bambang invited me to present this book and give a talk at Bandung Islamic University. I gave his daughters a dance lesson and was urged to perform (covered up) several times. People were enthusiastic on both counts.

Nearly three years after the tsunami have brought many changes to the flood-ravaged province of Aceh. Now local restaurants and food stalls are everywhere. Shiny new signs tout KFC, A&W and Pizza Hut.

Many people have bought big SUVs and new motorbikes. As I rode around town on a becak, I wondered about the criteria for obtaining a driver's license. It was scary how big ones tailgated little ones, making eight lanes out of two and dodging cows in the pouring rain.

The city of Banda Aceh is on the way to recovery, although villages haven't fared so well. I saw identical tin-roofed cement houses built by aid organizations. Some were inhabited, and others looked abandoned or had never been lived in. These villages had few survivors, so when the former residents returned, homes that had been rebuilt for a reduced number of survivors left the remaining land empty. New growths of bright green plant life covered what had once been splinters and debris.

People looked healthier than before, although I learned that not everyone who smiles and says "hello" is happy inside. Many have started their lives anew. Others only hope their prayers will soften the memories and the pain of being alone.

There have been many transitions in people's lives since the book began. Christine opened Jakarta's first belly dance school. Arief moved from Batam to Australia to work on an advanced degree. Mo found a woman to take him to live in Europe. Hamid, the second in command at the Siwa's police station, met a girl, got married and moved to the US. And the government of Tanzania banned plastic bags in an attempt to curb the litter.

Musafir of Banda Aceh married Fifi, and they recently had a daughter. Amina, my neighbor in Zanzibar, got married too. Biashura, the Kabuki leader in Zanzibar, passed away, and sadly, so did my friend Frederic, the man who was in his farming phase in Siwa.

Although Taariq's resolve to stay drug free wavered after a few days, he did decide soon after to give up drugs for good. He returned to Kenya, where he has been clean for one and a half years and is attending college.

Two years after embarking on my journeys into the Muslim world, I have begun to re-examine the proverb quoted on the back cover of this book, "To understand a people, you must live among them for 40 days." I have revisited Zanzibar, Siwa, and Indonesia. During each visit, the people I meet show increasing confidence in my intentions, and they open their lives more and more.

For updates and updated travel journals, log onto:

http://40daysand1001nights.blogspot.com

RESOURCES

Islam

Sardar, Ziaddin, *Introducing Islam* (Totem Books, 2004), www.icon-books.co.uk

en.wikipedia.org/wiki/sharia

Indonesia

Rimac, Melissa, "Matrilineal Minangkabau," *WellBeing*, March 2005, www.wellbeing.com.au/natural_health_articles?cid=7158

"Indonesia: First Ferry Since Tsunami Moors at Ulee Lheu Port," United Nations Development Programme, December 9, 2005, www.undp.org/tsunami/feature091205.shtml

Coffey, Margaret, prod., "The Tale of The Grand Mosque of Banda Aceh," *Encounter*, December 18, 2005, http://www.abc.net.au/rn/relig/enc/stories/s1530093.htm

Thaib, Lukman, Dr., ed. "Aceh after Tsunami: The Reconstruction Agenda," http://www.forumbangunaceh.org/info/thk_corner/4_Acheh%20after%20Ttsunami.pdf

en.wikipedia.org/wiki/padang_indonesia

en.wikipedia.org/wiki/minangkabau

en.wikipedia.org/wiki/aceh

Siwa Oasis, Egypt

www.siwaoasis.com

Larsen, Torben B.,"Siwa Oasis Extraordinary," *Saudi Aramco World*, September/October 1988, www.saudiaramcoworld.com/issue198805/siwa-oasis.extraordinary.htm

Fakhry, Ahmed, *Siwa Oasis* (American University in Cairo Press, 1973)

"Siwa Panorama," *Al Ahram* #526, March 22, 2001, http://weekly.ahram.org.eg/2001/526/tr2.htm

El-Kaissouni, Mahmoud, "Festival of Faith," *Al Ahram* #728, 3 February 3, 2005, http://weekly.ahram.org.eg/2005/728/tr3.htm

Zanzibar, Tanzania

"Juju: The Black Magic of Zanzibar," www.allaboutzanzibar.com/indepth/culture/1-juju.htm

www.zanzibar.net/zanzibar/music_and_culture

www.artmatters.info

Larsen, Kjersti, "Multiculturalism Through Spirit Possession," *ISIM Newsletter*, June 14, 2004, www.isim.nl/files/newsl_14/newsl_14-14.pdf

www.zanzibarmusic.org/history

www.sunrisesafaris.com/zanzibar

"Silent Drum," *Sauti Za Busara Music Festival Newsletter*, December, 2006

en.wikipedia.org/wiki/kiswahili

The Xinjiang Autonomous Region of China

www.china.org.cn/english/features/xinjiang1144543.htm

www.hrw.org/press/2000/11/xinjiang

en.wikipedia.org/wiki/tajiks

Read the ongoing news of *40 Days & 1001 Nights*, the 1001 Nights Fund, and my revisits at http://40daysand1001nights.blogspot.com.

ABOUT THE AUTHOR

One of the world's most respected exponents of the art of belly dancing, Tamalyn Dallal has taught and performed in 34 countries. She has taught thousands of dancers around the world. During 16 years of directing a nonprofit arts organization, Ms. Dallal produced numerous stage productions and dance festivals, including the famed Orientalia Festival of Ethnic Dance in Miami Beach for 14 years. She has also authored two books, *They Told Me I Couldn't*, about living and dancing in Colombia, and the instructional book *Belly Dancing for Fitness*.

40 Days & 1001 Nights is a multifold project that has grown to involve music, dance and film. All of the following items are available from Tamalyn Dallal at:

www.tamalyndallal.com
www.40daysand1001nights.com

The Film DVD

40 Days & 1001 Nights: Seeing the Islamic World through the Eyes of a Dancer
Available on DVD, $50 / 1 hour 45 min.

This subtitled documentary is a sensory feast of sights, sounds, music, and dance filmed by Tamalyn Dallal during her 40-day sojourns in Indonesia, Siwa, Zanzibar, Jordan, and Xinjiang.

The Music CD

40 Days & 1001 Nights, Belly Dance Music for Tamalyn Dallal
By the Ikhwani Safaa Musical Club of Zanzibar
$20 / 50 min.

You can read about the inspiration and story behind this CD in the Zanzibar section of this book.

The Dance Concert DVD

40 Days & 1001 Nights, Dancing Between the Lines
$45 / 1 hour 45 min.

This is the culmination of a long-distance collaboration between selected dancers in the United States and the musicians Ms. Dallal encountered on her travels. This concert was sold out and received rave reviews in Miami Beach. Later, copies of the DVD were sent to the musicians so they could see how their music was appreciated in the United States.

1001 Nights Fund

Ten percent of the proceeds from every book and DVD sold go into this fund, which directly helps worthwhile grassroots and arts projects in the countries this book covers.

Other books written by Tamalyn Dallal

Belly Dancing For Fitness (Berkeley: Ulysses Press, 2004)
They Told Me I Couldn't, A Young Woman's Multicultural Experiences in Colombia (Seattle: Talion Press, 1998)